College Counseling: Issues and Strategies for a New Millennium

Edited by

DEBORAH C. DAVIS

KEREN M. HUMPHREY

5999 Stevenson Avenue
Alexandria, VA 22304-3300

College Counseling: Issues and Strategies for a New Millennium

10 9 8 7 6 5 4 3 2

American Counseling Association
5999 Stevenson Avenue
Alexandria, VA 22304

Director of Publications
Carolyn C. Baker

Copy Editor
Sharon Doyle

Cover design by Kim DiBona

Library of Congress Cataloging-in-Publication Data
College counseling: issues and strategies for a new millennium/[edited by]
Deborah C. Davis, Keren M. Humphrey.
p.   cm.
Includes bibliographical references and index.
ISBN 1-55620-220-2 (alk. paper)
1. Counseling in higher education–United States. 2. Student counselors–United
States.
I. Davis, Deborah C. II. Humphrey, Keren M.
LB2343.C3293 2000
378.1'94 ¼ dc 21   00-021361
                                                              CIP

DEDICATION

**With respect, we dedicate this book
to:**

college counselors, who are making a positive difference
on college campuses every day;

our students, who inspire us with their struggles and
successes;

the past and present leaders of the American College
Counseling Association, for their advocacy and caring dedication to the profession;

**and,
with greatest love and appreciation,
to:**

Jim, for his steady partnership in the journey;

Dennis and Cortney, for their unfailing support and
encouragement;

P and S, our extraordinary companions.

ACKNOWLEDGEMENTS

Many friends, family members, and colleagues have provided time, effort, and encouragement to us in the preparation of *College Counseling: Issues and Strategies for a New Millennium*, and we are deeply appreciative of their contributions. We especially thank the following persons: graduate assistants Melissa Dykes Spriggs, Amy Kreider, Shannon Garrison, and Carrie Hernandez for service above and beyond the call of duty; Jim DiTulio and the staff of the University Counseling Center at Western Illinois University for their interest in and contributions to this project; Larry Kingry, Linda Berg Smith, Cyndi Spear, Michael Turner, Marge Hays, and Barbara Markley of the University of Alaska Anchorage for believing in and encouraging this project when it seemed just a fuzzy vision in a far distant future; Sam Gladding for his personal support and professional advocacy for our endeavors; and our contributors for joining us on this journey. Finally, we offer our heartfelt thanks to our American Counseling Association editor, Carolyn Baker, whose patient support helped us stay on track.

CONTENTS

FOREWORD

My first experience as a counselor was in a college counseling center. It was during the early 1970s, a time of commotion, concern, and sometimes chaos. The students whom I saw as an intern brought in problems that ranged from large social issues related to war, poverty, and politics to those dealing with more personal matters such as depression, dating, and academic success. I remember feeling almost overwhelmed at times by the nature of the material my clients presented while simultaneously thinking there was no better place to be than in a college environment as a counselor. Ironically, 20 years after that initial experience, I returned to the same university where I began and have volunteered from time to time in the same college counseling center. Although some of the issues have changed, just like the fashions and interests of each student generation, my thoughts and feelings about the importance of college counseling have remained virtually the same. It is an essential component on most campuses.

I am not alone in my assessment. Indeed, counseling is an integral part of most college environments. The reason is simple. Students of all ages and developmental stages encounter problems that they need to resolve at this time in their lives, and many of them are ready to do the hard work involved in making needed changes.

In *College Counseling: Issues and Strategies for a New Millennium*, Deborah Davis and Keren Humphrey have assembled a wealth of information that addresses the entire gamut of issues inherent in a campus setting. The contributors to this volume are among the best in college counseling; they are experienced professionals whose awareness, sensitivity, expertise, and practicality are evident. They deftly handle difficult issues such as the roles, challenges, and ethics of working with college students. They explore different aspects of providing services for those with traditional and non-traditional backgrounds. They also elucidate on handling special areas within the profession, such as life and career planning and outreach programming. In short, the authors of this text have covered virtually all of the general and specific areas that college counseling encompasses. Furthermore, they have done so in a readable and inviting style that encourages beginning counselors, and even seasoned professionals, not only to peruse but also to reflect on and digest the materials contained in each chapter.

Although I have read many counseling texts during my career, I have encountered none better than what Davis and Humphrey have produced. These two authorities have used their experience to put together what will be and should be a classic text with a long shelf life and future editions. I only wish that a book of this quality was available during my initiation into working with college students. Had such been the case, I would have been a better counselor—more informed, creative, and empowered to help students work through their transitions and traumas. Therefore, I am pleased that as the millennium begins this book has arrived.

—Samuel T. Gladding, PhD
Professor of Counselor Education
Wake Forest University

PREFACE

College counseling is a dynamic and stimulating profession with practically limitless opportunities for counselors to help others and to develop themselves personally and professionally. This book is a labor of love, created to support counseling professionals who, on a daily basis, in small and significant ways, positively affect the lives of college students across the United States.

College Counseling: Issues and Strategies for a New Millennium is a practical resource and guide for college counselors who are meeting the challenges of work in higher education. Additionally, it is a valuable resource for counselor preparation programs and for individuals investigating careers in college counseling. The book explores college counseling as a profession, examines the diverse characteristics of today's college students, and details the variety of roles and services provided by college counselors. It also discusses the relationship between college counselors and their institutions and identifies trends in the college counseling field. Case vignettes, appendixes, and examples strengthen the translation of knowledge to practice in this book. Recommendations for action, in the form of guidelines, interventions, and strategies, accompany each chapter.

Whom This Book Is for

Although *College Counseling: Issues and Strategies for a New Millennium* is intended primarily for practicing college counselors, it is also valuable as a personal resource, as a textbook for counselor preparation programs, and as a guide for higher education administrators wishing to enhance their understanding of the depth and breadth of college counseling.

Contents of the Book

Three primary themes guided our preparation of *College Counseling: Issues and Strategies for a New Millennium*. First, college counselors must prepare themselves to meet the challenges of changing roles, changing institutions, and changing students in the new millennium. Second, college counseling is developmentally based, recognizing and valuing the unique interaction of life transitions with the learning environment of higher education. Finally, college counselors work in diverse settings and fulfill a variety of roles, but they share a common philosophy and training as counseling professionals.

The book is organized into four sections, each representing a unique challenge for college counseling in the new millennium. Part I, The College Counseling Profession, offers the reader an introduction to college counseling as a profession, including its history and current status, diverse institutional settings, and professional preparation. Differences and similarities between college counseling and college student personnel work are described, and the unique contributions of college counseling to college life are outlined. An exploration of ethical issues and challenges for the college counseling profession is also included.

Part II, Counseling Today's College Students, provides an overview of the diverse characteristics of today's college students, with special attention to traditional and nontraditional learners, minority and international students' experiences, and the types of problems presented at college counseling centers. Recommendations for how college counselors can use this information to improve service delivery are provided.

Part III, Today's College Counselor and the Institution, explores the diverse roles fulfilled and the services provided by today's college counselors and makes recommendations regarding effective practices and maximization of resources. The challenges of providing developmentally based and clinically informed counseling, career and life development counseling, and outreach programming are examined. This section further explores the relationship between college counselors and their institutions, with a focus on establishing successful alliances with faculty, staff, and administration. Part III concludes with an examination of the unique challenges of small staff counseling centers.

Part IV, College Counselors and the Future, looks at stories of day-to-day life from college counselors and examines ways that college counselors can maintain mental, emotional, and physical wellness amid the demanding and fast-changing college counseling environment. Part IV concludes by identifying trends in college counseling and ways that college counselors can prepare themselves to meet the challenges of the future.

This book is designed to provide an overview of the holistic, developmentally based profession of college counseling and, intentionally, does not duplicate related publications of other authors about specific topics, such as student affairs preparation, techniques for counseling special populations (e.g., people with disabilities; multiracial individuals; and gay, lesbian, and bisexual individuals), or cybercounseling. The contributors have cited valuable resources on a multitude of topics that will assist readers in exploring their individual interests in greater detail.

We are delighted with the quality of the contributors who joined together to produce this valuable book. They are noted leaders, practitioners, teachers, and trainers from the college counseling profession. We hope that this book will significantly enhance your understanding of the nature of college counseling and that our recommendations and strategies will substantially benefit your college counseling practice and preparation.

Best wishes,
Deborah C. Davis
Professor Emeritus of Counseling, University of Alaska Anchorage

Keren M. Humphrey
Professor of Counselor Education, Western Illinois University

ABOUT THE EDITORS

Deborah C. Davis, EdD, NCC, ACS, LMFT, is Professor Emeritus of Counseling at the University of Alaska Anchorage and is currently a Visiting Professor at Cumberland University in Lebanon, Tennessee. Dr. Davis has been a professional counselor for more than 26 years. She has provided counseling services on both small and large campuses, directed a college counseling center, and served as Dean of Students. She chaired the counselor education program at the University of Alaska Anchorage and has received numerous awards for her exemplary teaching and counseling. Dr. Davis is a former president of the American College Counseling Association.

Dr. Davis's current professional interests include research and writing on the emerging field of life coaching. She is a motivational speaker, author, and personal life coach and is committed to helping others live the lives of their dreams.

Keren M. Humphrey, EdD, NCC, LPC, LCPC, is Professor of Counselor Education and Adjunct Professor, University Counseling Center at Western Illinois University in Macomb, Illinois. She has been a professional counselor for almost 20 years, including working as a family counselor for juvenile and domestic relations court, in a private psychotherapy practice, and in college counseling. Dr. Humphrey has served as national secretary of the American College Counseling Association; has been the editor of its newsletter, *Visions*; and was national media chair during the development of the *Journal of College Counseling*. Additionally, she is the recipient of the Outstanding Professional Leadership Award and the Award for Dedicated and Outstanding Service from the American College Counseling Association.

Dr. Humphrey has been a counselor educator for 13 years and is the coauthor of *ProblemSolving Technique in Counseling*, an innovative CD-ROM used by counselor preparation programs. She is a member of the editorial board of the *Journal for Technology in Counseling*. Her professional interests include grief counseling, loss transition, college counseling, sexuality counseling, and counselor preparation.

ABOUT THE CONTRIBUTORS

James M. Bensboff, PbD, LPC, ACS, is an Associate Professor and Coordinator of the Student Development in Higher Education Program in the Department of Counseling and Educational Development at the University of North Carolina at Greensboro. His professional interests include nontraditional college students, clinical supervision, group work, counselor training issues, and creative approaches to counseling.

John B. Bishop, PbD, is the Assistant Vice President for Student Life, Director of the Center for Counseling and Student Development, and Associate Professor of Individual and Family Studies at the University of Delaware. His professional interests include college counseling and student affairs administration.

Atticia P. Bundy, MS, NCC, is a counselor at Surry Community College in Dobson, North Carolina. Her professional interests include gender issues in counseling, nontraditional college student development, and college counseling.

Deborah Cohen, PbD, is a psychologist at the Center for Counseling and Student Development at the University of Delaware, Newark. Her primary professional interest is college counseling.

Deborah C. Davis, EdD, NCC, ACS, LMFT, is Professor Emeritus of Counseling at the University of Alaska Anchorage. She is currently on the faculty of Cumberland University in Lebanon, Tennessee, and provides consulting and coaching for individuals and organizations. She is a former president of the American College Counseling Association. Her professional interests include holistic adult development, counselor wellness, and life coaching.

Laura A. Dean, PhD, NCC, is the Dean of Student Development at Pfeiffer University in Misenheimer, North Carolina. She is a former president of the American College Counseling Association. Her professional interests include college counseling, small college issues, and quality assurance efforts for student services.

Dennis W. Engels, PhD, NCC, NCCC, LPC, is a Regents Professor of Counselor Education at the University of North Texas, Denton. His professional interests are in career and human resource development, institutional accreditation, ethics, interpersonal communication, decision making, and related concerns in the private and public sectors.

Perry C. Francis, EdD, NCC, LPC, is Assistant Professor of Counseling at Northwestern State University of Louisiana. He is president-elect of the American College Counseling Association. His research interests include ethical issues faced by college and school counselors, sexual misconduct in religious settings, family counseling, and suicide risk assessment and treatment.

Robert P. Gallagher, EdD, is Vice Chancellor for Student Affairs and Associate Professor in Counseling Psychology at the University of Pittsburgh. He authors the National Survey of Counseling Center Directors, which is published annually, and also writes and speaks on the changing counseling needs of college students, ethical issues in the field, and the use of humor in stress reduction.

Keren M. Humphrey, EdD, NCC, LPC, LCPC, is Professor of Counselor Education and Adjunct Professor of the University Counseling Center at Western Illinois University in Macomb, Illinois. Her professional interests include grief and loss transition, college counseling, sexuality counseling, and counselor preparation.

Bonita C. Jacobs, PhD, is Vice President for Student Development and Assistant Professor of Higher Education at the University of North Texas. Her professional interests include student development, ethics and civility, enrollment management, and new-student orientation and transitions. She is the editor of the *Journal of College Orientation and Transition.*

Carolyn W. Kern, PhD, NCC, LPC, is Associate Professor of Counselor Education in the Department of Counseling, Development, and Higher Education at the University of North Texas. Her professional interests include high school to college transitions, college counseling, counselor preparation, and counseling supervision.

Helen Kitchens, EdD, LPC, is Associate Professor of Counseling and Human Development at Troy State University in Montgomery, Alabama. Her research interests include attention deficit disorder, learning disabilities, and college counseling.

Jun-chih Gisela Lin, PhD, ABPP, is a psychologist at the Student Counseling Service, Texas A&M University, College Station. Her professional interests include multicultural counseling, couples counseling, developmental supervision, mentoring, service delivery issues, and organizational development.

Mary Finn Maples, PhD, NCC, is Professor of Counseling and Educational Psychology and Coordinator of the graduate program in College Student Development/Counseling at the University of Nevada in Reno. She is also an adjunct faculty member for the National Center for State Courts and the National Judicial College. Her professional interests include holistic adult development, spirituality, organizational development, motivation, and gracious confrontation.

Barbara L. Markley, MA, is Counselor and Student Interventions Coordinator at the University of Alaska Anchorage. Her professional interests include college counseling, crisis intervention, the development and implementation of retention programs, and the instruction of college success skills for underprepared students.

Robert Mattox, EdD, NCC, LPC, is the Director of Counseling and Advising Program Services and Adjunct Professor at Kennesaw State University. He is a former president of the American College Counseling Association. His professional interests include working with chronically ill individuals and with clients experiencing anxiety, panic, and depression.

Mark E. Meadows, EdD, is Professor Emeritus of Counseling and Counseling Psychology at Auburn University. He was the first president of the American College Counseling Association. His research interests include college counseling, vocational and career development, and group dynamics.

John Patrick, DEd, NCC, CRC, LPC, is Associate Professor of Counseling and Human Development at Troy State University in Montgomery, Alabama. His professional interests include college counseling, career counseling, multicultural counseling, and counselor training.

Susan E. Spooner, PhD, NCC, LPC, is Professor of College Student Personnel Administration at the University of Northern Colorado, Greeley. Her professional interests include student development, intimacy, counseling, and student affairs.

Joyce R. Thomas, MSEd, NCC, LPC, is a counselor at Ozarks Technical Community College in Springfield, Missouri. Her professional interests include developmental issues of college students, test anxiety, resilience building, depression, grief, healthy body image, and enhancement of adult students' satisfaction and success with their pursuit of college education.

Patty Galatas Von Steen, PhD, LPC, NCC, MAC, is the Outreach Coordinator and a Staff Counselor in the Counseling and Testing Center at the University of North Carolina at Greensboro. Her professional interests include adults who witnessed domestic violence as children, work-place stress and violence, counselor supervision, and college student family dynamics.

Doris J. Wright, PhD, is Associate Professor in the Department of Counseling and Educational Psychology at Kansas State University. Her professional interests include multicultural counseling and supervision, college student development practice, ethics, and sexual assault prevention.

PART I

THE COLLEGE COUNSELING PROFESSION

1

The College Counseling Environment

SUSAN E. SPOONER

FOCUS QUESTIONS

1. What is the nature of college counseling, and what influences counseling service delivery?

2. What is the difference between college counseling and college student personnel services?

This chapter introduces the college counseling profession and the influences that shape it. Campus climate, campus ecology, and the developmental approach are presented as foundations for understanding the profession today. An overview of the relationship between college counseling and student affairs is offered, and readers are referred to subsequent chapters in which they may explore related topics in depth.

THE NATURE OF COLLEGE COUNSELING: WHAT IS COLLEGE COUNSELING?

College counseling is an exciting profession offering varied opportunities to support the healthy personal, academic, and social development of postsecondary students. College counseling is defined as the delivery of counseling services by trained counseling professionals in a postsecondary educational setting. Counseling services may include, but are not limited to, individual, couples, and group counseling; assessment; treatment planning; consultation; outreach programming; and teaching, training, and supervision of counselor trainees and paraprofessionals. Personal issues, career planning, academic success, and crisis intervention are some of the most frequently found counseling focuses on many college campuses.

Professional preparation of college counselors typically requires a minimum of a master's degree in counseling or a related field. Doctoral preparation in counseling or counselor education is common for those seeking advanced degrees. In addition, a variety of certification and licensure paths are available for professional college counselors. Chapter 4, "Professional Preparation for College Counseling: Quality Assurance," provides a detailed examination of the preparation process and addresses the increasing level of professionalism and training expected of college counselors.

INFLUENCES ON COLLEGE COUNSELING

Institutional Type

There are 4,096 institutions of higher education in the United States **(see Box 1)**, and most of them offer some form of counseling services. Institutional type influences the models of counseling services delivery that a campus elects. Although no standard models are required, guidelines provided by the Council for the Advancement of Standards in Higher Education (CAS; 1997) and the International Association for Counseling Services Accreditation Standards for University and College Counseling Centers (Kiracofe et al., 1994, p. 38) are helpful to counselors and institutions wishing to design effective practices.

Box 1

Institutional Types in Higher Education (U.S.)

Public, four-year	615
Public, two-year	1,092
Private, four-year, nonprofit	1,536
Private, four-year, for-profit	169
Private, two-year, nonprofit	184
Private, two-year, for-profit	500

From *Chronicle of Higher Education*, 1999, 1999-2000 Almanac Issue, XLVI, 7. Copyright 1999 by *Chronicle of Higher Education*. Reprinted with permission.

Most colleges provide some form of counseling services, and many use an organized counseling center model. On 4-year campuses, in general, the larger the institution is, the more comprehensive the counseling services are. Multiple counseling centers may even be found at large, comprehensive institutions. Smaller 4- and 2-year campuses often combine the counseling center with related student services, such as financial aid, disability support services, and learning centers. Specialized institutional types, such as women's colleges and proprietary schools, tailor their counseling services to match the institutional mission and the unique needs of their students. Additionally, some counseling center models place heavy emphasis on training and preparation of professional college counselors. These centers often offer practicum and internship opportunities for counseling, social work, and psychology students in master's and doctoral programs.

Institutional type also influences what kinds of counseling services are provided and how they are administered. Career advising and academic advising occur at almost all institutions of higher education whether or not there is a designated counseling center housing them (see Chapter 11, "Life-Career Development Counseling"). Outreach programming is provided by college counselors at most institutions regardless of institutional type (see Chapter 12, "Outreach Programming From the College Counseling Center"). Many counseling centers also provide significant testing and assessment functions for their campuses. However, in some cases, it seems that these activities are being relocated outside of counseling centers into specialized career or learning assistance centers. This shift raises concern over diminished roles for counseling centers. There are continuing debates over costs and benefits to be accrued by retaining or removing these services from counseling centers (Phillips, Halstead, & Carpenter, 1996).

The inclusion of personal counseling services is also influenced by institutional type. Two-year and community colleges vary widely on whether personal counseling services are available for students. These institutions often offer one-stop counseling centers providing a wide spectrum of services, including personal counseling, academic advising, outreach programming, career counseling, and study skills assistance. On other campuses, although a designated counseling center may exist, the services that are provided frequently focus largely on academic advising and career planning. In these cases, personal counseling is usually offered under the umbrella of a developmental model supporting student success or is arranged through referral to external mental health agencies. Chapter 14, "Strategies for Small Staff College Counseling Centers," examines the unique challenges and opportunities of working at these smaller institutions.

On many 4-year campuses, especially larger public institutions, college counselors provide the services of smaller institutions (e.g., career counseling, outreach programming, study skills assistance) and also use their clinical preparation in treating a full range of personal counseling concerns, such as eating disorders, anxiety disorders, substance abuse, domestic violence, sexuality issues, and even couples and relationship counseling. College counselors at these larger institutions face the challenge of balancing "individual, problem-solving counseling with preventative and developmental services" (Archer & Cooper, 1998, p. 7).

Campus Climate

The college campus climate is changing, and professional college counselors must remain constantly aware and prepared if they aspire to effectively serve the needs of their constituents. On many campuses, the climate of higher education is one of a strong emphasis on retention, a confused effort to show outcomes through assessment measures, and shrinking budgets. This climate directly affects the nature of college counseling services. The CAS Standards and Guidelines for Counseling Programs and Services (1997, p. 65) describe counseling services as having three complementary functions: developmental, remedial, and preventative. This stance is not always valued by institutional leaders and requires vigilant education and promotion by college counselors.

Similarly, the nature of the college campus climate is fluid with regard to the changing characteristics of traditional-age college students and an increasingly diverse student population in terms of ethnicity, sexual orientation, gender, disability, and age. Effective college counselors must be diligent in ensuring that they are competent to provide quality counseling services for changing student populations. The reader is referred to Chapter 7, "Traditional-Age College Students"; Chapter 8, "Nontraditional College Students"; Chapter 9, "College Counseling and the Needs of Multicultural Students"; and Chapter 10, "College Counseling and International Students," for further discussion and recommendations regarding diverse student populations.

Campus Ecology

One of the important contributions that college counselors make to higher education is alerting the campus community to changing student problems and issues. College counselors are also in a unique position to recognize systemic problems on campus. A significant contribution of counseling in the 1970s was the realization that institutions could be "toxic" to students and staff and that not all difficulties encountered by students arose from within the students. Counselors are challenged to maintain a delicate balance between educating those in power in an effort to accomplish environmental change and staying "tolerable" to the community. Campuses are notably political, and the clues in this area are particularly subtle. Operating within a highly politicized environment requires sensitivity, risk taking, and the ability to judge what strategies will have the desired effect. College counselors who seek to effect change must be astute and consciously attuned to the change process on their campuses. Leading successful change or becoming a political victim is often a fine distinction in a political campus climate.

The idea that a campus has an ecology is properly attributed to James Banning (Banning & Kaiser, 1974), who brought theoretical ideas from the fields of architecture and behavioral and industrial psychology and applied them to college campuses. Environments shape behavior, intentionally or unintentionally, and contribute heavily to the behavior of the individuals who reside and work in them. There are always unintended results, but the idea that one can design campus environments to enhance student learning and retention is an important contribution. When able to view the student community from a reasonably unbiased perspective, the college counselor, regardless of setting, should be able to characterize student needs and concerns and articulate these to the opinion leaders and decision makers of the campus community.

Being one of the opinion leaders on campus is a highly desirable position for politically effective college counselors. As a force for change, the counselor can educate, bring forward data, and use good human relations skills to effect alterations in the campus ecology. For example, an important factor in the success of college counseling services on campus is the attitude of the administrator who oversees them. If that individual recognizes and understands the significant role such services play in the education of college students and the contributions they make to the overall campus climate, then appropriate delivery services and resources to support them are apt to exist on that campus. Chapter 13, "Building Effective Campus Relationships," provides additional discussion and recommendations regarding the counselor's role in effecting systemic change on campus.

The Developmental Approach

Today, college counseling is firmly rooted in the developmental perspective. The developmental approach means viewing students within the context of life transitions rather than from the standpoint of psychopathology. Counseling Centers, from their position in the broad base of the student affairs profession, began promoting the concept of developmental counseling as an alternative, or at least as a supplement, to traditional therapy for an already existing problem.

Understanding students from a developmental perspective led to new ways of serving them. Developmental interventions may seem commonplace today because we more fully understand the nature of human growth and development. Many innovations that we take for granted as acceptable, expected practice were developed at Colorado State University between 1964 and 1976 (Morrill & Hurst, 1990). However, in 1974, when Morrill, Oetting and Hurst published an article addressing obstacles to change in the higher education environment, their ideas were considered revolutionary and were not readily accepted. The Cube, first described by Morrill et al., delineated an exciting new way of looking at services offered by counseling centers. In the years since, it has appeared with various additions, alterations, or enhancements (Pace, Stamler, Varris, & June, 1996). There are individuals, groups, and institutions (targets) to be served; there are delivery processes to be used (methods); and there are interventions (with purposes) that include remediation, prevention, and developmental strategies. This fundamental concept has taken firm hold in the college counseling field.

A strong developmental perspective does not negate the clinical training and perspective that college counselors bring to their work. College counselors also use clinical skills (i.e., assessment, mental health diagnosis, treatment planning, and therapeutic intervention) in their work. In fact, a major challenge for today's college counselors is figuring out how to use the strengths of developmental and clinical approaches while remaining mindful of the disadvantages of both approaches. This means viewing the developmental and clinical approaches to college counseling as mutually informative rather than as mutually exclusive (K. M. Humphrey, personal communication, July 20, 1999).

Other Influences

One of the largest issues facing counselors on college campuses is the climate of shrinking budgets. Finding and retaining the funding necessary to provide an appropriate level of counseling services requires tenacity, solid data, and creativity. Some campuses have tried such strategies as charging for services, restricting services only to students, limiting the number of times an individual student can be seen for counseling, and relying on student health insurance for third-party payments. Others have combined these limitations with the use of brief therapies, followed by referral to outside agencies after the first few sessions.

Recently, a few colleges have investigated privatizing or "outsourcing" college counseling services to local community mental health agencies. However, the actual move to outsource does not seem to be a growing trend (Phillips et al., 1996). In a 1996 survey of counseling center directors, almost 20% reported that their institutions were considering such a move, but by 1998, less that 1% reported outsourcing as being under consideration (Gallagher, 1996, 1998). Institutions that turn exclusively to community agencies often find long waiting lists and already overburdened caseloads. Insurance reimbursement, on which most community mental health agencies rely, is likely to be limited or absent for many college students. The most serious disadvantage of outsourcing counseling services for college students is that institutions lose the definitive understanding of college student development and the ability to network with other student affairs professionals that professional counselors can provide. Many institutions have found that outsourcing certainly is not in the best interest of either universities or students.

College Counseling and Student Affairs

College counseling and student affairs are often overlapping professions, with some distinct differences. Many current college counselors have some professional preparation in student affairs, and some student affairs professionals may provide counseling services on their campuses. Professionals in both arenas make profound and positive impacts on college campuses. Nuss (1996) described the profession of student affairs as historically committed to the development of the whole person and supportive of the diversity of institutional and academic missions. College counselors share this commitment. For the purpose of this book, it is important to recognize the unique roles that college counselors play in higher education and the importance of ensuring that those providing counseling services are professionally prepared. Chapter 3, "College

Counseling Today: Changing Roles and Definitions," provides a detailed examination of the current core roles and primary responsibilities of college counselors.

General distinctions result from professional preparation avenues. Student affairs professionals may or may not have additional counseling training. Student affairs professionals tend to be generalists who aspire to a broader spectrum of student services settings. College counseling, however, is distinctly different from student affairs work in its emphasis on the delivery of therapeutic counseling services to college students. This involves professional training in both developmental and clinical perspectives. Additionally, ethical responsibilities can distinguish student affairs professionals from college counselors. College counselors have specific responsibilities to their clients that, at times, may not equate with their institution's viewpoints, particularly on confidentiality and dual relationship issues (see Chapter 5, "Practicing Ethically as a College Counselor," for a specific discussion of college counseling ethics). Although many current college counselors have not trained especially for college settings, a distinct speciality in college counseling, requiring course content and supervised field experience specific to college counseling, is emerging. The reader is referred to Chapter 4, "Professional Preparation for College Counseling: Quality Assurance," for further discussion of this topic.

Further indicators of distinctions between college counseling and student affairs are described in Chapter 2, "The Evolution of College Counseling." The development of the American College Counseling Association (ACCA), a division of the American Counseling Association, signifies the desire of college counselors for a professional organization focused entirely on their unique campus role. The rapid growth of the ACCA (Edwards & Davis, 1997) and subsequent listserv (ACCA-L), newsletter (*Visions*), and journal development (*Journal of College Counseling*) demonstrate the enthusiasm that college counselors hold for a professional association with an identity that is unique from other related student affairs professionals.

LOOKING AHEAD

The growth of the college counseling profession has long been fore-casted by those studying both the profession and students' needs (Magoon, 1987; Stone & Archer, 1990; Varris, as cited in Rentz & Saddlemire, 1988). The profession of college counseling has strong historical roots and evidence of dynamic growth ahead. However, as discussed in Chapter 16, "Trends in College Counseling for the 21st Century," college counseling professionals must look ahead and stay ever vigilant in preparing themselves to best serve students of the new millennium. College counselors will find their role increasingly politically influenced and the campus climate increasingly competitive as a result of limited resources. Effective college counselors must be professionally trained, multiculturally and technologically competent, and creative at solving problems. The environment for college counseling requires professionals who can advocate, network, collaborate, and provide students with outstanding developmental and clinical skills.

College counselors must also remain balanced in physical, mental, and spiritual domains if they are to successfully meet the challenges of the new millennium. Chapter 15, "College Counselors' Well Being," describes strategies that support counselors' wellness in the diverse and constantly changing higher education climate.

SUMMARY

This chapter has examined campus climate, campus ecology, and the developmental approach as foundation components of the college counseling profession. The emergence and rapid growth of the American College Counseling Association, a unique professional organization for college counselors, speaks to the strength and momentum of the college counseling movement. This chapter sets the stage for subsequent chapters in this book, which explore the diverse and dynamic environment of college counseling and offer recommendations for individuals entering the profession or seeking renewal of their skills and passions for college counseling.

REFERENCES

Archer, J., Jr., & Cooper, S. (1998). *Counseling and mental health services on campus: A handbook of contemporary practices and challenges.* San Francisco: Jossey-Bass.

Banning, J., & Kaiser, L. (1974). An ecological perspective and model for campus design. *Personnel and Guidance Journal, 52*, 370-375.

Chronicle of Higher Education. *(1999). 1999-2000 Almanac Issue, XLVI,* 7.

Council for the Advancement of Standards in Higher Education. (1997). *The CAS book of professional standards for higher education.* Washington, DC: Author.

Edwards, D. M., & Davis, D. C. (1997). *Membership trend comparisons: 1996-1997. The American Counseling Association and the American College Counseling Association.* Alexandria, VA: American Counseling Association.

Gallagher, R. F. (1996). *National survey of counseling center directors.* Alexandria, VA: International Association of Counseling Services.

Gallagher, R. F. (1998). *National survey of counseling center directors.* Alexandria, VA: International Association of Counseling Services.

Kiracofe, N. M., Donn, P. A., Grant, C. O., Podolnick, E. E., Bingham, R. P., Bolland, H. R., Carney, C. G., Clementson, J., Gallagher, R. P., Grosz, R. D., Handy, L., Hansche, J. H., Mack, J. K., Sanz, D., Walker, L. J., & Yamada, K. T. (1994). Accreditation standards for university and college counseling centers. *Journal of Counseling and Development, 73,* 38-43.

Magoon, T. (1987, October). *Future trends in counseling centers.* Paper presented at the 36th Annual Conference of University and College Counseling Center Directors, Rockport, ME.

Morrill, W. H., & Hurst, J. C. (1990). Factors in a productive environment. *Journal of Counseling and Development, 68,* 247-252.

Morrill, W. H., Oetting, E. R., & Hurst, J. C. (1974). Dimensions of counselor functioning. *Personnel and Guidance Journal, 52,* 354-359.

Nuss, E. M. (1996). The development of student affairs. In S. R. Komives, D. B. Woodard, Jr., & Associates (Eds.), *Student services: A handbook for the profession* (3rd ed., pp. 22-42). San Francisco: Jossey-Bass.

Pace, D., Stamler, V. L., Varris, E., & June, L. (1996). Rounding out the Cube: Evolution to a global model for counseling centers. *Journal of Counseling and Development, 74,* 321-325.

Phillips, L. C., Halstead, R., & Carpenter, W. (1996). The privatization of college counseling services: A preliminary investigation. *Journal of College Student Development, 37,* 52-59.

Rentz, A. L., & Saddlemire, G. L. (1988). *Student affairs functions in higher education.* Springfield, IL: Charles C Thomas.

Stone, G. L., & Archer, J. (1990). College and university counseling centers in the 1990s: Challenges and limits. *The Counseling Psychologist, 18,* 539-607.

2

The Evolution of College Counseling

MARK E. MEADOWS

FOCUS QUESTIONS

1. What can college counselors and others accountable for counseling programs gain from understanding the history of college counseling?

2. What individuals, events, and institutions have been most influential in the development of college counseling? What was the nature of these influences?

3. How did vocational counseling, student personnel counseling, and developmental counseling emerge as dominant models for college counseling?

The purpose of this chapter is to explore the history of college counseling in the United States. Historical information provides current and prospective college counselors with both a framework for understanding their profession and important normative data that are useful for comparative or advocacy purposes. The historical perspective helps college counselors to place themselves squarely within the larger context of a profession that is still developing, still changing, and still evolving. As we cast our eyes across the diverse threads of the past, perhaps we will come to understand the present more accurately and will be better prepared as college counseling enters the 21st century.

Systematic literature reviews and comprehensive historical accounts of the development of college and university counseling have not been conducted. Although several publications (Hedahl, 1978; Heppner & Neal, 1983) have included historical content as part of their more extended treatment of other counseling-related topics, none have focused exclusively on the development of college counseling. Archer and Cooper (1998), Davis (1998), and Dean and Meadows (1995) are more recent examples of publications with synopses of the development of college counseling. Publications with more in-depth historical information are largely those presenting the history of a particular counseling program; for example, Williamson (1936), Thrush (1957), Hanfmann (1978), and Morrill and Hurst (1990), respectively, described developments at four universities: the University of Minnesota, Ohio State University, Brandeis University, and Colorado State University. This chapter explores the historical literature, illustrates significant chronological periods, and highlights the persons and institutions instrumental in developing the college counseling profession. A consistent theme throughout this chapter is the evolution of three distinct paradigms of college counseling as identified by Dean and Meadows: vocational counseling, mental health counseling, and student personnel counseling. This chapter largely relies on published documents, notes, persons, and programs representative of various key transitions.

PRIOR TO 1930:
PRECURSORS AND EMERGING PARADIGMS

Fitzpatrick (1968) provided accounts of early activities of college personnel responding to nonacademic concerns of students, including social and emotional needs. Fitzpatrick stated, "If the early college was alma mater to her students, clearly the president was the pater familiae" (p. 5). Likewise, some faculty were recognized as being advocates for good mental health practice among students. As institutions of higher education developed in size and complexity, it became impossible for presidents and faculty to respond to the myriad tasks of student life. Student personnel specialists began to appear in the second half of the 19th century (Fitzpatrick, 1968). Although some leaders in higher education in the mid-19th century began to advocate a more humane and enlightened response to students' needs, a patriarchal model was clearly dominant throughout the 19th century (Dean & Meadows, 1995). Other late 19th-century higher education trends influencing the development of formal college and university counseling programs included elective subjects, pluralism in higher education, coeducation, an increase in knowledge and application of individual differences, and psychometrics (Cowdery, 1933; Lloyd-Jones, 1929).

NOTED CONTRIBUTIONS PRIOR TO 1930

Lloyd-Jones (1929) used the term *certain great personalities* when referring to the pioneering work of two activist social reformers of the first decade of the century, Frank Parsons and Clifford Beers. It is a rare introductory text in counseling and student personnel that does not refer to their influence on the profession. Parsons's (1909) classic counseling model was designed to promote growth in youth and to prevent later career problems. This model provided the framework on which later developments in interest and aptitude measurement, occupational information, and career choice theory would be built in developing a vocational counseling paradigm.

Clifford Beers's (1950) book and mental health advocacy had profound influences on the emerging disciplines of psychology and psychiatry and on collegiate response to the mental health needs of students (Bragdon,

1929; Farnsworth, 1957). Student mental hygiene clinics were established at Princeton University and the University of Wisconsin by 1910 and 1914, respectively (Farnsworth, 1957). Washburn College and the U.S. Military Academy established clinics in 1920, followed by Dartmouth College, Vassar College, and Yale University (Farnsworth, 1957). By 1925, it was possible to discern a mental health paradigm for college and university counseling. Beers's advocacy for mental health was important in the development of the college counseling profession. Williamson, in an interview with Ewing (1975), dated the inception of student counseling programs at the University of Minnesota to the initiation of a faculty advising program and the work of Donald Paterson, who structured faculty counseling around measurement and casework methods. This model was the prototype of what became the University Testing Bureau in 1932. The University Testing Bureau was the earliest separate higher education unit for educational and vocational counseling (Hedahl, 1978). A primary function of this bureau was to provide counseling services to students. The scope of the counseling function of the bureau was substantial, as evidenced by an analytical description of student counseling during the period from 1932 to 1935 (Williamson & Bordin, 1941a). The student counseling program at the University of Minnesota is recognized for contributing the "Minnesota Point of View," a model for the student personnel counseling paradigm.

Williamson, director of the Student Counseling Bureau, was author or coauthor of more than 400 publications, including 2 texts that were selected among a group of 16 "classics" in counseling (Walsh, 1975). He was among the earliest researchers to conduct counseling research using a control group (Williamson & Bordin, 1940) and to publish books (Williamson, 1934, 1939) specifically related to college counseling. He was the only leader in college counseling to serve as president of four major national organizations in counseling and student personnel work, namely, the National Association for Student Personnel Administrators, the American College Personnel Association (ACPA), the American Personnel and Guidance Association (APGA), and what is now Division 17 of the American Psychological Association (APA; Ewing, 1975). In addition to Paterson and Williamson, significant counseling leaders associated with the University of Minnesota included Albert Hood, John Darley, Ralph F.

Berdie, Edward S. Bordin, Lenore Harmon, Thomas Magoon, Leona Tyler, Barbara Kirk, and C. Gilbert Wrenn.

Caple (1992), Cowdery (1933), Gladding (1993), and Roberts (1994) described the contributions of Esther Lloyd-Jones to counseling and student personnel work. Lloyd-Jones was a Phi Beta Kappa graduate of Northwestern University. After receiving a master's degree at Columbia University, she returned to Northwestern University, where she was instrumental in developing the student personnel program. She returned to Columbia University in 1928 and received a PhD degree in student personnel administration in 1929, the first person to receive a doctoral degree in that field. Lloyd-Jones was also Professor and Chair of the Department of Guidance and Student Personnel Services at Columbia University from 1939 until her retirement in 1966. She provided leadership in defining the student personnel profession and its various components, including student guidance and counseling. Another influence of Lloyd-Jones was through the vast number of master's and doctoral students whom she taught, including Carl Rogers, Albert Ellis, Rollo May, and Nancy Schlossberg (Caple, 1992). Roberts (1994) summarized her contributions in this way: "Her gifts created student personnel work and helped transform the organization and purpose of American higher education in the 20th century" (p. 75).

1930–1944: PERSONNEL GUIDANCE TO PROFESSIONAL COUNSELING

Prior to 1930, most counseling was viewed as the responsibility of faculty members, although few efforts to prepare or train faculty for that role were in evidence before that date (Williamson & Bordin, 1941a). After 1930, student personnel work was characterized by more emphasis on counseling and professional preparation for counseling roles (Hedahl, 1978). Although the 1930s witnessed the devastating effects of the Great Depression, government-sponsored efforts to respond to conditions created by the Great Depression influenced the development of college and university counseling during that period. The National Youth Administration, for example, was specifically targeted at unemployed youth and provided resources for testing, job training, career information services, and career counseling and placement. Counseling emerged as a component of higher education that was unique from student personnel work, although that transition was not complete.

Ohio State University (Hedahl, 1978) is an example of institutions that developed units to provide counseling services prior to 1940. Francis Robinson established a remedial counseling program for students enrolled in "how to study" courses in 1938; counselors were seniors enrolled in a teacher education practicum. The practicum was formalized into a graduate course in 1940, eventually leading to the development of a graduate preparation program in student personnel work. The program, an example of the student personnel counseling paradigm, was renamed the Occupational Opportunities Service in 1940 (Thrush, 1957).

Another type of counseling service developed at Ohio State University and at the University of Missouri prior to 1940 (Embree, 1959). At Ohio State University, a mental health program for treatment of students existed in the psychology department as a parallel activity to the educational and vocational counseling available in the Occupational Opportunities Service. At the University of Missouri, the College Adjustment Clinic was created in 1938 as an outgrowth of the Student Health Service; the program existed in tandem with a central counseling facility of an educational and vocational nature. Embree identified similar dichotomous emotional and vocational/educational services at the University of Chicago and the University of Illinois. The Board of Vocational Guidance and Placement was established at the University of Chicago in 1927 and a comprehensive service, the Student Personnel Bureau, at the University of Illinois in 1938.

By the time the United States entered World War II, a substantial number of institutions had created counseling programs. Graduate programs for preparation of counselors had been established. National professional associations concerned with college counseling were active, and a growing body of literature existed. Professional associations included the National Vocational Guidance Association (NVGA), the ACPA, the Association for Applied Psychology (later to become Division 17—Counseling Psychology of the APA), and the National Association of Women Deans, Administrators and Counselors. Although the war slowed the development of college counseling (e.g., some institutions closed their counseling services; T. M. Magoon, personal communication, March 12, 1999), the profession was strongly rooted in higher education.

NOTED CONTRIBUTIONS FROM 1930 TO 1944

Several books related to college counseling were published between 1930 and 1944, including *How to Counsel Students* (Williamson, 1939), *A Student Personnel Program for Higher Education* (Lloyd-Jones & Smith, 1938), *History of Vocational Guidance* (Brewer, 1942), and *Counseling and Psychotherapy* (Rogers, 1942). It is ironic that the last two titles were published in the same year, because Rogers presented a counseling approach that was to challenge vocational and educational guidance as it was practiced at the time.

Relatively more college counseling-related journal articles can be found in the literature from this period. Articles by Williamson and Bordin (1941a, 1941b) were among the earliest efforts to apply empirical research methodology to issues related to college counseling. Such studies are of inestimable value to the counseling profession because they helped to define the nature of what was termed *clinical* counseling, introduced recurring themes in college counseling research, and stimulated later research on college counseling.

1945-1960: EXPANDING SCOPE AND PROFESSIONAL STATUS

The years immediately following World War II were marked by rapid expansion in the scope and professionalism of college counseling. Government activity responding to the educational and career needs of veterans, major developments in college counseling organizations, expansion of college counseling preparation programs, and theoretical advances marked this period as perhaps the most influential in establishing college counseling programs (Embree, 1959; Warnath, 1973). Gaudet (1949) described the Veterans Administration (VA) counseling program to assist veterans returning from service duty in selecting appropriate educational or vocational objectives as the largest guidance program ever undertaken in the world. Because the VA lacked the resources to respond to caseloads of up to 50,000 per month, a decision was made in 1944 to contract with colleges and universities that either had established counseling programs or had qualified faculty and staff to offer such services. The first center was established at the City College of New

York. Four hundred and twenty-nine centers were eventually established in all but one state (Muensch, 1970).

NOTED CONTRIBUTIONS FROM 1945 TO 1960

Paterson, Williamson, and Lloyd-Jones continued to play large roles throughout this period. Additional significant contributors in the years following World War II included Barbara Kirk, who came to the University of California, Berkeley in 1946 to establish and serve as Director of the VA Counseling Center. When the VA contract ceased in 1951, Kirk and the center's staff contributed their time without receiving payment while students, faculty, and staff appealed to the University Regents to preserve the service. In 1952, students voted to tax themselves $2 per person to support the center (A. Frank, personal communication, February 10, 1999). Kirk believed that the Student Counseling Center's central emphasis was to help students understand their interests and abilities in the context of the nature and demands of educational fields and academic majors available to them. She believed that personal and academic problems could be ameliorated if individuals could clearly understand and act on this relationship. Kirk led the Student Counseling Center to a national and international model of professional service.

Another professional whose college counseling contributions came into play after World War II was Leona E. Tyler. Tyler graduated from the University of Minnesota at age 19. When the university contracted with the VA in 1945 to provide counseling services for veterans, Tyler became the Director. Tyler served on the counseling center staff until she became Dean of the Graduate School in 1965. Her widely used and influential text, *The Work of the Counselor*, was published in 1953, with later editions in 1961 and 1969. "The three editions were perhaps the leading influence on the development of the counseling profession in their day" (Sundberg & Littman, 1994, p. 212). Tyler may be viewed as being among those who anticipated and influenced the developmental emphasis in counseling that was to mark the 1970s.

By 1950, there was an expanded body of college counseling literature. Brayfield's (1950) *Readings in Methods of Modern Guidance* is an anthology of 46 articles published in the 1930s and 1940s. Several are empirical studies, which were still somewhat rare at that time. The book is noteworthy not only for the significance of the studies reported but also for the fact that the authors included persons who were among prominent leaders in counseling from the 1930s through the 1960s. Many articles were based on doctoral dissertations, for example, those of Ralph Berdie, H. B. Pepinsky, Theodore Sarbin, V. C. Raimy, William U. Snyder, E. H. Porter, John Darley, and Julius Seeman. Most of these doctoral dissertations were completed at the University of Minnesota or Ohio State University, reflecting the dominance of these two institutions in the development of counselor preparation. A number of the earliest studies of the new nondirective approach were included, no doubt influenced by the fact that Rogers served on the Ohio State University faculty.

PROFESSIONAL ASSOCIATIONS

The decade of the 1950s was a period of extensive change in professional associations related to college counseling. Initially, the NVGA and later the ACPA and the National Association of Women Deans, Administrators and Counselors were the primary professional associations related to college counseling. In 1952, the Division of Counseling and Guidance of the APA was renamed Division 17—Counseling Psychology. In the same year, the APGA was formed, merging the NVGA, the ACPA, and the National Association of Guidance Supervisors and Counselor Trainers, renamed the Association for Counselor Education and Supervision at the time of the merger. The ACPA and Division 17 emerged as the primary homes for those identified with college counseling. Super (1955) published an influential and widely quoted article (Walsh, 1975) in which he described a transition from vocational guidance to counseling psychology. In the article, Super drew sharp distinctions between the new field of counseling psychology and the work of those in organizations under the APGA umbrella. Although Super described the APGA as a strong and important association, he concluded that the APGA was more similar to an interest group than a professional association. He envisioned vocational counseling in colleges primarily as a function of counseling psychologists and the higher education setting as the primary home for counseling psychologists.

Members of the new APGA were projected for lesser roles because that organization had not developed preparation and practice standards as had Division 17 (Nugent, 1981). In retrospect, counseling psychology did not sustain the mantle of vocational counseling as predicted by Super. A frequent criticism of counseling psychology preparation and practice has been the perceived or actual decline in its vocational emphasis (Archer & Cooper, 1998; Gelso, Birk, Utz, & Silver, 1977).

Another important college counseling-related organization was established in 1951 when 33 directors of college and university counseling centers met at the University of Minnesota. Those attending included individuals from both counseling psychology and counseling and guidance affiliations (Hedahl, 1978). An influential action of the group, later named the Association of University and College Counseling Center Directors (AUCCCD), was to institute an annual survey of counseling centers, now known as the Counseling Center Data Bank Survey. Thomas M. Magoon was responsible for the survey in the early 1960s and continued to coordinate the activity until his retirement in 1988. The survey is still conducted from the Counseling Center of the University of Maryland (T. M. Magoon, personal communication, March 12, 1999).

Congressional provision for counseling of World War II veterans was previously discussed. A second governmental stimulus to the counseling profession and indirectly to college counseling was passage of the National Defense Education Act (NDEA) of 1958. The purpose of NDEA was the identification and development of scientific and academic talent (Nugent, 1981). Title V-A of NDEA provided funds to upgrade secondary school counseling; Title V-B provided funds and stipends to train counselors through counseling and guidance institutes in institutions of higher education. Within 6 years, 480 institutes provided counselor training to 15,700 teachers and counselors (Gibson & Mitchell, 1990). Although NDEA was not focused on college counseling, it had substantial indirect effects. Counselor preparation programs contracted to conduct training institutes to prepare school counselors, thus creating a large demand for counselor educators. These programs offered stipends to doctoral students to assist in providing instruction and supervision of institute students, thus increasing the supply of counselors prepared at the doctoral level. An additional stimulus was the fact that, by 1965, more than 35,000 counselors were employed in public schools (Gladding, 1993), creating a constituency of students, parents, and teachers who were familiar with the positive role that counseling could play in educational and other decision making. Counseling had reached such a critical mass that one might reasonably question its absence at any level of education.

Virtually every author describing the development of counseling after 1945 gives strong emphasis to the profound influence of Carl Rogers and his client-centered focus. Gibson and Mitchell (1990) compared the impact of Carl Rogers on counseling to that of Henry Ford on the automobile industry. Other theoretical approaches to counseling were also being emphasized before 1960, including the behavior theory of Wolpe and the rational approaches of Berne and Ellis (Gladding, 1993). Additionally, Super (1955) and other career development theorists were presenting career choice and career development as one aspect of the larger task of human development. This enabled career counseling to be viewed as an example of personal counseling and as being amenable to models other than the clinical vocational counseling models of Williamson and his followers. College counseling was clearly characterized by a more variegated appearance by the end of the 1950s.

1960-1980: THE BEST AND WORST OF TIMES

The 20-year period from 1960 to 1980 observed the highest development of college counseling as well as serious challenges to its progression. Several factors combined in the 1960s to fuel expansion of counseling services, including rapid growth in the number of 2-year colleges (Litwack, 1977), standards of accreditation and professional associations that encouraged the provision of student counseling programs (Dean & Meadows, 1995), expansion of college counselors' role beyond traditional educational and vocational counseling (Kirk, 1978), increased emphasis on counseling needs in small colleges (Heston & Frick, 1967), and social forces and changes that increased the need and the demand for counseling on the part of college students (Hedahl, 1978; Tyler, 1969). By the late 1960s and especially after 1970, strains and stresses began to appear that would both challenge the viability of college counseling and lead to dramatic change in its nature (Hedahl, 1978).

Heppner and Neal (1983) described the period after 1970 as a period of economic decline and broadening of the mission of counseling to include more diverse clientele and to conceptualize the institutional environment as a target for intervention. Efforts to implement a broadening mission would change the way in which counselors viewed their roles and organized their functions. See Chapter 1, "The College Counseling Environment," for further discussion of the influences of institutional environment on college counseling and Chapter 3, "College Counseling Today: Changing Roles and Definitions," for examination of counselors' roles and responsibilities.

NOTED CONTRIBUTIONS FROM 1960 TO 1980

Thomas M. Magoon has been a key figure in college counseling from the 1950s to the present. Currently Emeritus Professor and Director of the Counseling Center at the University of Maryland, Magoon initiated activities during the 1960s that continue to be formative in the development of college counseling. Magoon conducted the AUCCCD Data Bank Survey from the early 1960s until his retirement. Survey data have been widely referenced in college counseling research and are used extensively by counseling center directors and those researching college counseling (Cooper, Canar, & Fulks, 1994). Magoon's extensive research and publication record includes works in such areas as advocacy of college counseling programs, expansion of college counselors' roles, the economics of college counseling, changes in college counselors' functions, trends and directions in college counseling, and nontraditional counselor training programs.

Charles F. Warnath is perhaps best known for his challenge to college counseling and his explanation of core conflicts confronting college counseling as the decade of the 1970s was underway. In *New Myths and Old Realities: College Counseling in Transition* (Warnath, 1971), *New Directions for College Counseling: A Handbook for Redefining Professional Roles* (Warnath, 1973), and a journal article entitled "College Counseling: Between the Rock and the Hard Place" (Warnath, 1972), Warnath delineated problems in college counseling that threatened its stability and viability. Warnath believed that college counselors were discovering that their freedom to decide which student needs should receive highest priority attention and which manner of offering services is most appropriate is circumscribed by institutional considerations. . . . [The] college counselor is finding that when individual needs conflict with those of the institution, one is expected to resolve the conflict in favor of the institution. (Warnath, 1971, p. 230)

Warnath's recommendations for change were as dramatic as his critique. First, he called upon counseling as a profession to encourage and lead counseling staff to pursue alternatives to traditional administrative frameworks (Warnath, 1972). Alternatives included cutting ties to institutional budgets and control by negotiating with student government for support, developing joint services with noncampus agencies, or moving off-campus altogether to offer counseling and consultation on a fee basis to the campus community and community at large. Less drastic was his call for counselors to be more active in outreach beyond the confines of their offices as they sought to create change from within the institution (Warnath, 1972).

Staff of the Colorado State University Counseling Center in the late 1960s and into the 1970s also played key roles in shaping changes in college counseling that continue to influence the field. Weston Morrill, Eugene Oetting, Allen Ivey, Ursula Delworth, and Richard Weigel developed concepts and programs and authored publications that moved college counseling beyond traditional goals, clients, and procedures. Other significant contributors during this period included Chickering (1969), King (1976), and O'Banion and Thurston (1972).

College counseling's response to the challenges created by events and conditions in the 1960s and 1970s resulted in creative and productive outcomes that continue to give direction and focus. Newer conceptualizations of counseling for the purposes of primary prevention, institutional change, and student and organizational development came to the forefront. Intervention strategies expanded from direct individual and group methods to include alternative approaches based on assessment of personal, environmental, and situational conditions that limited student and institutional potential (Conyne & Clack, 1975; Morrill, Oetting, & Hurst, 1974). Such strategies involved cooperation and collaboration with students, faculty, and administration and moved counselors' activities away from the counseling center to all areas of the campus community. Considerations around these applications provided major impetus to college counseling activities such as outreach and consultation. See Chapter 12, "Outreach Programming From the College Counseling Center," and Chapter 13, "Building Effective Campus Relationships," for further discussion of outreach and consultation, respectively.

1980–PRESENT:
TRANSITION TO COUNSELING AND MENTAL HEALTH

As the 1970s ended, both the country in general and higher education specifically were faced with daunting challenges and problems. The leveling of traditional college student enrollment and the increasing enrollment of female, older, ethnic minority, part-time, commuter, and other students were shaping higher education. Students with more severe personal-social-emotional problems and a shift in emphasis from vocational to personal counseling were observed (Robbins, May, & Corazzini, (1985). Counseling center administrators were reporting budget cuts and progressive changes in the focus and activities of counseling to the extent that the survival of some centers was at stake (Aiken, 1982). A strong emphasis on accountability (Archer & Cooper, 1998; Bishop & Trembley, 1987) continued throughout the period. Publications by Heppner and Neal (1983) and Whiteley, Mehaffey, and Geer (1987) were especially effective in presenting a picture of college counseling during the 1980s and those of Archer and Cooper (1998), Bishop (1990, 1995), and Stone and Archer (1990) during the 1990s. College counseling would undergo a major transition during these two decades.

Whiteley et al. (1987) conducted a national study of staffing patterns and services of counseling centers. The study is noteworthy for the extremely large number of responding institutions on which data were based. This and similar studies of the period (Meadows & Pipes, 1982) created extensive dialogue in the profession about the roles, responsibilities, and demographics of college counselors. However, some researchers found problems with the samples for some of the surveys. Stone and Archer (1990) observed that most college counseling research is based on a relatively small portion of the population of counseling centers, that is, those whose directors participate in AUCCCD, are accredited by the International Association of Counseling Services (IACS), or have APA-approved internships. Counseling programs in regional universities, small colleges, and 2-year institutions are often not represented when data are sought about college counseling programs; thus, less is known about these programs. For example, 87% of counseling programs in higher education are not accredited by the IACS, more than four fifths have staffs of five or less, two thirds or more are in institutions of less than 4,000 students, and most are in privately funded institutions. Most directors and staff are prepared in programs other than those in psychology departments. The highly diverse nature of college and university counseling is apparent in these findings, and caution is well given to those who wish to conduct research on college counseling.

Professional Associations and Publications

The history of the college counseling profession is evidenced in the evolution of its professional associations. Caple (1991) described the ACPA's disaffiliation from the American Association of Counseling and Development (AACD), now the American Counseling Association. In April 1991, ACPA members voted to disaffiliate and to form a separate and autonomous national professional association. In May 1991, AACD President Jane Myers appointed a committee of AACD members to serve as the Committee to Establish a New Division to Address the Needs of College Counselors (available from Mark E. Meadows). The committee immediately began its tasks by meeting in Alexandria, Virginia in June 1991 to develop its philosophy, mission, objectives, bylaws, and other documents for submission to the AACD Governing Council. In July 1991, the council approved the Task Force on Establishment of a New Organizational Affiliate of AACD (to be named the American College Counseling Association [ACCA]) and a plan of action for that purpose.

In 1992, the organization elected its first slate of officers. By March 1992, ACCA had met all requirements for Division Status within AACD, and the Governing Council approved the ACCA's petition for Division Status just 9 months after its creation. There were approximately 2,000 members by that time. Davis (1998) provided a historical view of ACCA and identified three factors that set the stage for its development: the dynamics of organizational change, changing professional identity and affiliation needs of counseling professionals, and the commitment of leaders to address those needs. Davis pointed out that no national organization existed at the time that espoused a focus on college counseling as a professional identity and student development as a foundation for college counseling.

Williams and Buboltz (1999) observed the interaction between the history of a publication and an organization. Establishment of a college counseling journal was an immediate goal of the ACCA (Mattox, 1998), and through diligent leadership, that goal was achieved in 1998 with publication of Volume 1, Number 1 of the *Journal of College Counseling*. The *Journal of College Counseling* joins the *Journal of College Student Psychotherapy* as the only journals in the United States that are expressly related to counseling in higher education and is the only journal with a singular focus on counseling from a student development perspective.

Increase in Severity of Student Problems

Chapter 6, "College Student Problems: Status, Trends, and Research," and Chapter 16, "Trends in College Counseling for the 21st Century," examine the current research on student problems and associated impacts and trends for the college counseling profession. From a historical perspective, it is important to note the research conducted during this period supporting a perception of an increasing severity of student problems (Johnson, Heikkinen, & Ellison, 1988; O'Malley, Wheeler, Murphy, O'Connell, & Waldo, 1990; Stone & Archer, 1990; Westefeld & Patillo, 1987). Sharkin (1997) reviewed research concerning psychopathology among counseling center clients and reexamined the contention that psychopathology is on the rise. Sharkin held that it may be concluded only that there is a perception among counseling center personnel that problems presented by students have become more severe and that most studies do not present empirical data but perceptions. He was especially dubious about data on the topic from national surveys and data bank sources on the basis that they report directors' perceptions, may reflect biases, and are subject to pressure to justify the need for counseling services given threats of financial cutbacks.

College and university counseling administrators and staffs have struggled to respond to increased demand for personal counseling occasioned by actual or perceived increased levels of student pathology in the face of increased administrative scrutiny related to cost-effectiveness, efficiency, and use of student services (Stone & McMichael, 1996). Response has ranged from merging student counseling and student health services, reverting to an earlier focus on vocational and educational counseling, instituting limits on numbers of sessions, focusing on brief or very brief therapy models, to privatizing personal counseling services. Federman and Emmerling (1997) concluded that the fact that fully half of all mergers of counseling centers and mental health services occurred from 1991 to 1994 evidences a press to meet demands for counseling students with more severe problems.

Managed Care and Outsourcing

Whitaker (1997) described the potential impact of managed care on mental health agencies in higher education, for example, services minimized in favor of drug treatment, referral out, and outsourcing. He concluded that preventive and developmental ideals are better served within institutions. "What a good college or university in-house service does is to provide counseling and psychotherapy in the context to considerable first-hand knowledge of the institution, its kinds of students, and the personal and developmental challenges they face" (Whitaker, 1997, p. 39).

Phillips, Halstead, and Carpenter (1996) studied 31 of 64 institutions that had addressed the issue of privatizing counseling services. Of the 31 institutions, 9 had adopted some model of outsourcing, and 3 had a long-standing history of outsourcing and never had a counseling center. Three institutions that once practiced some form of outsourcing abandoned the practice and returned to a college-operated counseling center. Nineteen colleges gave some consideration to outsourcing but did not implement the model. Some colleges reported that consideration of outsourcing was related to lack of satisfaction with existing counseling services on the basis of the use of clinical or therapy models instead of a student development model. Cost was the other motivating factor. Most saw advantages in maintaining a campus-operated center. It seems noteworthy that of the 9 colleges with privatized models, 8 were smaller institutions. All had retained career and academic counseling on campus while outsourcing personal counseling. Widseth, Webb, and John (1997) provided a critique of the concept of outsourcing counseling services in higher education. Extensive use of staff with master's degrees, a tendency to overemphasize psychopathology of students or to underestimate the factors of stress in the college environment, and entrenchment in a service point of view shaped by policies for reimbursement were cited as concerns with the practice. They believed that off-campus professionals have a limited understanding of the institutional context and culture and that experienced staff of on-campus services are knowledgeable about the developmental issues of late adolescence, college life, psychological problems inherent in such settings and age groups and are attuned to the college culture in which they work.

Current Status and Future Prospect

Stone and Archer (1990), Bishop (1990, 1995) and Pace, Stamler, Yarris, and June (1996) reviewed the status of college counseling in the 1990s. Stone and Archer provided an overview of the challenges and limitations that would face counseling centers during the 1990s. They identified challenges in areas of clinical services, outreach and consultation, training, staff development, research, and administration. The challenges were based on environmental assumptions that ethnic, social, national, and experiential backgrounds of students would change; that psychological, health, safety, and financial needs of students would increase; and that competition for higher education resources would grow. Stone and Archer recommended strategic actions for response to each challenge. Bishop (1990) identified institutional concerns that counseling centers would need to address in the 1990s. Concerns centered on increasing demands for counseling and crisis management services, career development services, services for special populations, and retention issues. Bishop described responses to these concerns. Stone and Archer and Bishop focused on consultation, career development, outreach, enlistment of aid from potential helpers other than counselors, briefer treatment approaches, evaluation and accountability activities, and strong managerial and administrative skills and strategies to respond to the challenges of the 1990s. Pace et al. proposed an adaptation of the Cube of Morrill et al. (1974) in light of the realities and demands of the 1990s and beyond (e.g., multicultural issues, sexual and racial harassment, date rape and other physical violence, alcohol and substance abuse).

Archer and Cooper (1998) provided perhaps the most comprehensive statement on college counseling near the end of the 20th century in their book entitled *Counseling and Mental Health Services on Campus*. They presented contemporary challenges confronting college counseling and suggested models, methods, and programs to meet the challenges. Three broad topics provided the foci for their presentation: meeting needs for basic counseling services, developing strategies for outreach and consultation, and continuing administrative and professional issues. Brief therapy and group counseling are models of choice for basic counseling services. Proactive outreach and consultation are advocated for prevention, student and faculty development, intervention in health issues, and promotion of campus diversity and multiculturalism. Archer and Cooper conceptualized the college counselor's role as that of an "initiator catalyst." The book title chosen by Archer and Cooper is instructive in that it signals that the long debate in the literature concerning the purpose of college counseling is closed. Knowledge of contemporary college students, environments in which they function, and experience of college counselors suggest that college counseling must address the entire range of student needs whether they be career, educational, or mental health in nature. What seems clear is that counseling remains the primary function of college counselors, but needs and demands require more if students are to be effectively served.

Several conclusions seem warranted on the basis of a review of the development of college counseling. College counseling is a 20th-century phenomenon. Having faced many challenges and responded with some success, college counseling will enter the next century as a mature and established function in the higher education environment. College counseling will no doubt continue to interact developmentally with social, economic, and political processes; draw on the knowledge base of diverse disciplines; enhance its intellectual and professional maturity; respond to critical events and conditions in higher education and the broader context; and, finally, proceed along its developmental course. If these actions represent the future of college counseling, then the profession will change in ways that support viability and growth. Review of the literature reveals no paucity of strategies to enhance college counseling. Cooperative efforts among diverse professional associations and among differing levels of higher education will enable college counseling to develop in more unified and collaborative ways and thus will strengthen its position as a profession.

SUMMARY

This chapter has explored the history of college counseling in the United States to provide current and prospective college counselors with an understanding of where they stand within the larger historical context of their profession. An extensive review of the historical literature, documentation of significant chronological periods, and highlights of individuals and institutions instrumental in the development of college counseling were examined. The status of college counseling through the 1990s and prospects for the future provide the reader with the most extensive account, to date, of the evolution of college counseling.

REFERENCES

Aiken, J. (1982). Shifting priorities: College counseling centers in the eighties. *NASPA Journal, 19,* 15–22.

Archer, J., & Cooper, S. E. (1998). *Counseling and mental health services on campus.* San Francisco: Jossey-Bass.

Beers, C. W. (1950). *A mind that found itself* (Rev. ed.). New York: Doubleday.

Bishop, J. B. (1990). The university counseling center: An agenda for the 1990s. *Journal of Counseling and Development, 68,* 408–412.

Bishop, J. B. (1995). Emerging strategies for college and university counseling centers. *Journal of Counseling and Development, 74,* 33–37.

Bishop, J. B., & Trembley, E. L. (1987). Counseling centers and accountability: Immovable objects, irresistible forces. *Journal of Counseling and Development, 65,* 491–494.

Bragdon, H. D. (1929). *Counseling the college student.* Cambridge, MA: Harvard University Press.

Brayfield, A. H. (1950). *Readings in methods of modern guidance.* New York: Appleton-Century-Crofts.

Brewer, J. E. (1942). *History of vocational guidance.* New York: Harper.

Caple, R. B. (1991). Now is the time. *Journal of College Student Development, 32,* 483.

Caple, R. B. (1992). Esther Lloyd-Jones 1901–1991. *Journal of College Student Development, 33,* 291–292.

Chickering, A. W. (1969). *Education and identity.* San Francisco: Jossey-Bass.

Conyne, R. K., & Clack, R. J. (1975). The consultation intervention model: Directions for action. *Journal of College Student Personnel, 16,* 413–417.

Cooper, S. E., Canar, W. J., & Fulks, N. J. (1994). The utilization of counseling center data banks. *Journal of College Student Development, 35,* 489–490.

Cowdery, K. M. (1933). The guidance of youth in the colleges. *Occupations, 12,* 14–20.

Davis, D. C. (1998). The American College Counseling Association: A historical view. *Journal of College Counseling, 1,* 7–9.

Dean, L. A., & Meadows, M. E. (1995). College counseling: Union and intersection. *Journal of Counseling and Development, 74,* 139–142.

Embree, R. B. (1959). Developments in counseling bureaus and clinics. *Educational and Psychological Measurement, 10,* 465–475.

Ewing, D. B. (1975). A reminiscence. *Personnel and Guidance Journal, 54,* 78–87.

Farnsworth, D. L. (1957). *Mental health in college and university.* Cambridge, MA: Harvard University Press.

Federman, R., & Emmerling, D. (1997). An outcome of mergers of university student counseling centers and student mental health services. *Journal of College Student Psychotherapy, 12,* 15–21.

Fitzpatrick, R. (1968). The history of college counseling. In M. Siegel (Ed.), *The counseling of college students* (pp. 1–14). New York: Free Press.

Gaudet, F. J. (1949). The Veterans Administration advisement and guidance program. *School & Society, 69,* 251–254.

Gelso, C. J., Birk, J. M., Utz, P. W., & Silver, A. E. (1977). A multigroup evaluation of the models and functions of university counseling centers. *Journal of Counseling Psychology, 24,* 338–348.

Gibson, R. L., & Mitchell, M. A. (1990). *Introduction to counseling and guidance* (3rd ed.). New York: Macmillan.

Gladding, S. T. (1993). *Counseling: A comprehensive profession.* Columbus, OH: Merrill.

Hanfmann, E. (1978). *Effective therapy for college students.* San Francisco: Jossey-Bass.

Hedahl, B. M. (1978). The professionalization of change agents in counseling and development. In B. M. Schoenberg (Ed.), *Handbook and guide for the college and university counseling center* (pp. 24–39). Westport, CT: Greenwood Press.

Heppner, P. P., & Neal, G. W. (1983). Holding up the mirror: Research on the roles and functions of counseling centers in higher education. *The Counseling Psychologist, 11,* 81–89.

Heston, J. C., & Frick, W. B. (1967). *Counseling for the liberal arts campus.* Yellow Springs, OH: Antioch Press.

Johnson, R. W., Heikkinen, C. A., & Ellison, R. A. (1988). Psychological symptoms of counseling center clients. *Journal of Counseling Psychology, 36,* 110–114.

King, S. D. (1976). *College student development: The identity crisis revisited.* Lecture presented at Auburn University. Available from author.

Kirk, B. A. (1978). Foreword. In B. M. Schoenberg (Ed.), *Handbook and guide for the college and university counseling center* (pp. xii–xvi). Westport, CT: Greenwood Press.

Litwack, L. (1977). Counseling services in community colleges. *Journal of College Student Personnel, 18,* 359–361.

Lloyd-Jones, E. (1929). *Student personnel work at Northwestern University.* New York: Harper.

Lloyd-Jones, E., & Smith, M. (1938). *A student personnel program for higher education.* New York: McGraw-Hill.

Mattox, B. (1998). President's message. *Journal of College Counseling, 1,* 5–6.

Meadows, M. E., & Pipes, R. B. (1982). Characteristics of position applicants: Counseling center directors' preferences. *Journal of Counseling Psychology, 29,* 95–99.

Morrill, W. H., & Hurst, J. C. (1990). Factors in a productive environment: Colorado State University, 1964–1976. *Journal of Counseling and Development, 68,* 247–253.

Morrill, W. H., Oetting, E. R., & Hurst, J. C. (1974). Dimensions of counselor functioning. *Personnel and Guidance Journal, 52,* 354–359.

Muensch, G. A. (1970). Counseling of war orphans and services veterans. In P. J. Gallagher & G. D. Demos (Eds.), *The counseling center in higher education* (pp. 353–359). Springfield, IL: Charles C Thomas.

Nugent, F. A. (1981). *Professional counseling: An overview.* Belmont, CA: Brooks-Cole.

O'Banion, T., & Thurston, A. (1972). *Student development programs in the community junior college.* Englewood Cliffs, NJ: Prentice Hall.

O'Malley, K., Wheeler, I., Murphy, J., O'Connell, J., & Waldo, M. (1990). Changes in levels of psychopathology being treated at college and university counseling centers. *Journal of College Student Development, 31,* 464–465.

Pace, D., Stamler, V. E., Yarris, E., & June, L. (1996). Rounding out the Cube: Evolution to a global model for counseling centers. *Journal of Counseling and Development, 74,* 321–325.

Parsons, F. (1909). *Choosing a vocation.* Boston: Houghton Mifflin.

Phillips, L., Halstead, R., & Carpenter, W. (1996). The privatization of college counseling services: A preliminary investigation. *Journal of College Student Development, 37,* 52–59.

Robbins, S. B., May, T. M., & Corazzini, J. G. (1985). Perceptions of client needs and counseling center staff roles and functions. *Journal of Counseling Psychology, 32,* 641–644.

Roberts, D. C. (1994). Esther McDougald Lloyd-Jones. *Journal of College Student Development, 35,* 74–75.

Rogers, C. R. (1942). *Counseling and psychotherapy.* Boston: Houghton Mifflin.

Sharkin, B. S. (1997). Increased severity of presenting problems at college counseling centers: A closer look. *Journal of Counseling and Development, 75,* 275–281.

Stone, G. L., & Archer, J. (1990). College and university counseling centers in the 1990s: Challenges and limits. *The Counseling Psychologist, 18,* 539–607.

Stone, G. L., & McMichael, J. (1996). Thinking about mental health policy in university and college counseling centers. *Journal of College Student Psychotherapy, 10,* 3–28.

Sundberg, N. D., & Littman, R. A. (1994). Leona Elizabeth Tyler (1906–1993). *American Psychologist, 49,* 211–212.

Super, D. E. (1955). Transition: From vocational guidance to counseling psychology. *Journal of Counseling Psychology, 2,* 3–9.

Thrush, R. S. (1957). An agency in transition: The case study of a counseling center. *Journal of Counseling Psychology, 4,* 184–190.

Tyler, L. E. (1969). *The work of the counselor* (2nd ed.). Englewood Cliffs, NJ: McGraw-Hill.

Walsh, W. M. (1975). Classics in guidance and counseling. *Personnel and Guidance Journal, 53,* 219–220.

Warnath, C. F. (1971). *New myths and old realities: College counseling in transition.* San Francisco: Jossey-Bass.

Warnath, C. F. (1972). College counseling: Between the rock and the hard place. *Personnel and Guidance Journal, 51,* 229–235.

Warnath, C. F. (1973). *New directions for college counseling: A handbook for redefining professional roles.* San Francisco: Jossey-Bass.

Westefeld, J. S., & Patillo, C. M. (1987). College students' suicide: The case for a national clearinghouse. *Journal of College Student Personnel, 28,* 34–38.

Whitaker, L. C. (1997). The influence of managed care. *Journal of College Student Psychotherapy, 12,* 23–40.

Whiteley, S. M., Mehaffey, P. J., & Geer, C. A. (1987). The campus counseling center: A profile of staffing patterns and services. *Journal of College Student Personnel, 28,* 71–81.

Widseth, J. C., Webb, R. E., & John, K. B. (1997). The question of outsourcing: The roles and functions of college counseling services. *Journal of College Student Psychotherapy, 11,* 3–22.

Williams, M. E., & Buboltz, W. C. (1999). Content analysis of *Journal of Counseling and Development,* Volumes 67 to 74. *Journal of Counseling and Development, 77,* 344–349.

Williamson, E. G. (1934). *Vocational counseling at the University of Minnesota.* Minneapolis: University of Minnesota Press.

Williamson, E. G. (1936). Faculty counseling at Minnesota. *Occupations, 14,* 426–433.

Williamson, E. G. (1939). *How to counsel students.* New York: McGraw-Hill.

Williamson, E. G., & Bordin, E. S. (1940). Evaluating counseling by means of a control group experiment. *School and Society, 52,* 434–440.

Williamson, E. G., & Bordin, E. S. (1941a). An analytical description of student counseling. *Educational and Psychological Measurement, 1,* 341–354.

Williamson, E. G., & Bordin, E. S. (1941b). The evaluation of vocational and educational counseling: A critique of the methodology of experiments. *Educational and Psychological Measurement, 1,* 5–24.

3

College Counseling Today: Changing Roles and Definitions

LAURA A. DEAN

FOCUS QUESTIONS

1. What are the core roles and primary responsibilities of college counselors across settings?

2. How do the roles and balance of responsibilities of college counselors vary with institutional type?

3. What are the issues that college counselors face as they fulfill multiple roles?

4. What other roles do professional counselors hold on campuses, and how does their counseling training affect the work they do?

5. How can college counselors best respond to the characteristics and needs of their institutions and their students?

The roles fulfilled by counselors on campuses throughout higher education vary widely depending on the type of institution, the mission of the service, the needs and resources of the campus, and the training and philosophy of the counselor. However, there are also commonalties in roles and responsibilities that form the core of what it is to be a college counselor.

This chapter examines the changing roles and primary responsibilities of college counselors across institutional settings. It offers recommendations for counselors seeking to clarify the vital role they play on campus as they provide developmental, remedial, and preventive services to their students and their institutions.

ISSUES

College counselors have expertise both in their professional practice and in the characteristics of the higher education setting. What sets them apart from counselors in other settings is their understanding of the context in which students exist, including the stresses present and the resources available. The college environment has distinct characteristics, and the unique advantage that college counselors have to offer is expertise related to that environment and its effects on students. Nuss (1996) noted that the profession of student affairs has historically been committed to the development of the whole person and has been supportive of the diversity of institutional and academic missions. College counseling reflects these concepts as well.

College counselors are increasingly being called on to serve not only individual students but also the campus as a whole. Stone and Archer (1990) described the historical expansion of the role of counseling centers from a focus on vocational issues to one that encompasses not only personal counseling of individuals but also the entire campus environment as the client for counseling services. As student needs have become more complex, so have the responses and services offered on campus. The changing demographics and characteristics of students and institutions include multiple factors: changing ethnic, racial, national, and experiential backgrounds; increasing psychological, health, safety, and financial needs of students; increasing competition for resources; and increasing emphasis placed on accountability across campus services (Stone & Archer, 1990). Archer and Cooper (1998) described the challenge of balancing "individual, problem-oriented counseling . . . [with] preventive and developmental services" (p. 7) as well as the need to respond to increasing levels of pathology and serious campus issues. College counselors, then, are being challenged to maintain traditional developmental services while also responding to increasingly severe issues.

Blimling and Alschuler (1996) placed college counselors in the broad category of student development educators, which they described as

> those people in student affairs engaged in promoting the growth, development, and learning of students. . . . The primary role of student development educators is to teach—through experiences inside and outside the classroom—skills that empower students with self-knowledge and enhance the quality of students' lives now and later. The classrooms of student development educators include, among other areas, the individual and group therapy rooms of the counseling center. (p. 207)

Counselors are trained to apply knowledge and skills to help people. College counselors have the advantage of working in an environment that can be seen, in itself, as an intervention; for changes that occur during college, the environment is the mediating variable (Astin, 1993). Counselors' knowledge of that environment is an important tool in working with college students. All individuals are developing, but those enrolled in college have specifically chosen to put themselves in an environment designed to effect change in them (Astin, 1993). The primary goal of the college environment is to promote learning and growth in students; such personal change requires adjustment, and the unique role of college counselors is to assist students in dealing with the developmental challenges that accompany personal growth.

Core Roles and Responsibilities

The basic responsibilities of college counselors include ones that are both internal and external to the counseling service or counseling center. The counseling service provides direct services to individuals and requires administrative management; it also serves the needs of various constituencies across campus. The Standards and Guidelines for Counseling Programs and Services by the Council for the Advancement of Standards in Higher Education (CAS; 1997) describe counseling services as having three complementary functions: developmental, remedial, and preventive.

> The developmental function is to help students . . . enhance their growth . . . [and] to help students benefit from the academic environment; . . . the remedial function recognizes that some students experience significant personal adjustment problems that require immediate professional attention; . . . the preventive function role is to anticipate environmental conditions that may negatively influence student welfare and initiate interventions that will neutralize such conditions. (CAS, 1997, p. 65)

The Accreditation Standards for University and College Counseling Centers by the International Association of Counseling Services (IACS; Kiracofe et al., 1994) also suggest three broad roles for the counseling service:

> providing counseling/therapy to students experiencing personal adjustment and/or psychological problems that require professional attention; . . . the preventive role of assisting students in identifying and learning skills which will assist them in effectively meeting their educational and life goals; . . . [and] contributing to a cam-

pus environment that facilitates the healthy growth and development of students. (p. 38)

College counselors, then, are working at several levels at once. They are assisting students with specific needs that interfere with successful functioning, providing students with opportunities for growth and development, and offering their expertise through consultation with others on campus.

The specific responsibilities of college counselors are related to these broad areas of focus, and there is general agreement in the field about what these responsibilities entail. According to Stone and Archer (1990), the functions of college counselors include clinical services, outreach and consultation, training, staff development, research, and administration. Both CAS and IACS address in their standards the range of services considered to be necessary for an effective counseling service. The CAS Counseling Program Standards (1997, p. 65) describe the specific services that must be provided for effectiveness:

- individual counseling,
- group counseling,
- testing and other assessment techniques,
- outreach efforts,
- support focused on correcting specific educational deficiencies,
- crisis intervention and emergency coverage, and
- professional development programs for staff and faculty.

Similarly, the IACS standards (Kiracofe et al., 1994, p. 39) state that accredited programs must provide
- individual and group counseling and therapy services,
- crisis intervention and emergency coverage,
- programming focused on the developmental needs of students,
- consultative services to members of the university community,
- research and evaluation of services, and
- training, professional development, and/or continuing education experiences for staff, interns, practicum students, and others in the university community.

The IACS standards further note that counselors "perform other assigned functions that contribute to the service offerings of the center and the academic mission of the institution (e.g., teaching, committee work, liaison with academic or administrative units, participation in university program development)" (Kiracofe et al., 1994, p. 42).

The campus consultant role can take several forms. Although professional standards suggest that counselors should not have a role in student judicial processes or enrollment-related decisions (CAS, 1997; Kiracofe et al., 1994), they have much to offer from their experience and expertise to other areas of campus. Crego (1996) observed that a wider range of student needs can be met when student affairs professionals expand into new arenas. Many counselors assist with training the residence hall staff in helping skills and in awareness of issues such as depression, eating disorders, and suicide. They may play a role in preparing campus crisis response plans (especially those related to sexual assault) as well as in direct crisis intervention and follow-up. They engage in consultation on campus, and their skills are particularly well-suited to mediation and conflict resolution efforts. They may provide, or assist in providing, academic advising, tutorial support, and career counseling. They serve as advisers, advocates, case managers, program presenters, and information resources. Depending on their qualifications, they may teach, particularly freshman seminar or career planning courses, and they may participate in campus-wide committees. Heppner and Johnston (1994) suggested that counselors can "take the lead in creating supportive programs for faculty on college campuses" (p. 451) by using their skills in consultation, their developmental orientation, and their knowledge of career development. The breadth of involvement across campus depends on organizational structure and culture and, to some extent, institution type (see Chapter 1, "The College Counseling Environment").

Differences in Roles by Institution Type

Institution type is probably the greatest influence on the specific functions of college counselors and on the priority of various functions for individual counselors. Organizational complexity and availability of resources, both financial and human, are important determinants of the role of the counseling service on campus. Although individual institutional models result not only from quantifiable factors but also from idiosyncratic institutional histories, there do tend to be similarities in structure and function by institution type.

Large University Counseling Services. Large university counseling centers are often organizationally more separate from other student affairs functions. Rather than being a part of the student affairs program, they are likely to be aligned with health care providers on campus. If the institution has a hospital or a medical school, the counseling center may be affiliated with it or with the institution's health service. Some institutions maintain a counseling service separate from a health center-based mental health service, with varying degrees of overlap or collaboration. At institutions with a preparation program for psychiatrists, psychologists, or counselors, the counseling service typically serves as a training site for interns.

Larger centers, by definition, have larger counseling staffs, which allow them to offer a broader range of services than smaller centers. University counseling center web pages describe varied outreach programs and support groups for a wide range of students, including adult learners, women, international students, and multicultural students, as well as programs for events such as National Collegiate Alcohol Awareness Week, Black History Month, and Gay Pride Week. Often called "counseling and psychological services," these centers offer psychological and psychiatric evaluations for which smaller institutions may have to refer students off campus.

Because of the structural separateness of such centers, linkages to other student services must be created and sustained more intentionally. The strongest linkages tend to be with those services most concerned with student functioning and well being, such as disability services.

Given larger staff size, the duties of individual counselors may be more specialized than in other institutions. For example, a counselor might coordinate testing and assessment or manage the outreach programs of the center. Counselors may focus on a more limited range of client types or presenting problems. In centers where counselors hold faculty status or are unionized, the counselors' workloads are governed by contract agreements. Crisis coverage can be shared among staff, and emergency response may be managed through the health service.

Small College Counseling Services. Small college counseling services (see Chapter 14, "Strategies for Small Staff College Counseling
Centers"), in contrast, tend to be anything but separated from other student affairs functions. Counseling is typically one of the departments
within the student affairs program, sharing in the collaborative projects
of the staff group. Because small colleges have fewer staff people to provide the various student services, counselors in these settings are more
likely to have active involvement, and often leadership, in areas such as
orientation, learning assistance, and disability services.

At small colleges, the role of the counselor within the institution can
be complicated by the expectations of faculty, staff, and students. Small
institutions often describe themselves as having a "family" atmosphere,
and campus dynamics can be as complex as family ones. The counselor
may be expected to "fix" the situation, or the student, and may need to
educate the campus community about issues of confidentiality.

Linkages to other student services happen naturally in small schools
because the staffs tend to have more interaction and to collaborate on
projects frequently. Counselors are called on for wide involvement with
campus life, including assistance with orientation, identification of and
intervention with students at risk, and residence hall staff training. In
addition to offering the full range of counseling services available on
campus, counselors at small colleges may have additional responsibilities
in career services, academic advising, or disability services.

The balance of duties for counselors at small colleges is affected primarily by the number of responsibilities that are assigned. Counselors are challenged by trying to provide, alone or with limited other staff, the full range
of counseling services. Students who choose small colleges often prefer
individual attention, and the demand for individual counseling is high.
Many counselors at small colleges struggle to meet that demand and then
to add in their other duties as time permits. However, the other factor that
particularly affects counselors at small colleges is the emergence of a crisis
situation. Whether it is the death of a student, a suicide attempt, or a student who becomes violent, the small college has limited staff to respond,
either in the moment or in follow-up. In such a situation, the usual daily
schedule must be put aside so that the immediate needs can be addressed.

Counselors at small colleges are also affected by holding multiple roles
on campus. When a counselor teaches, supervises student workers,

advises student organizations, and serves on committees with students, ethical dilemmas may arise when those students seek counseling (Dean, 1995). Although it is not always possible to avoid such situations and still serve the needs of the students, counselors must maintain a high level of awareness and seek to minimize dual relationship conflicts whenever possible (see Chapter 5, "Practicing Ethically as a College Counselor"). Kitchener (1988) identified three potential risks to the client when multiple-role relationships exist: incompatibility of expectations between roles, divergence of the obligations associated with the roles, and the power and prestige of the professional. Of particular concern are dual roles that involve counseling students who will be evaluated by the counselor, because the power differential is inherent and unavoidable. In such cases, the perception of bias can be as damaging as any real prejudice that might exist. Avoiding these situations can create a need for the small-college counselor to educate students about the roles involved and the nature of the therapeutic relationship (Dean, 1995), because students who know the counselor in other capacities may perceive such boundaries as unwillingness to be of help.

Community and Technical Colleges: Full-Service Centers. Community and technical colleges are designed to meet the needs of an extremely diverse student body. Emphasizing customer service, many such institutions offer a "one-stop shopping" model, in which a single counseling center offers personal counseling, career services, academic advising, transfer information, and learning assistance. Centers may be open extended hours to respond to students' schedules. Depending on the size of the institution, the staff may be relatively large, but services tend to be organized so that each counselor can respond adequately to the range of needs presented by each student. Such a counseling center is also likely to be well integrated into the other services of the institution, sharing responsibilities in areas such as orientation and recruitment. As Helfgot (1998) noted, "Community colleges are intimate institutions, where less division exists between functional areas than in many colleges and universities. Everyone is involved in everyone else's business" (p. 7).

The balance of duties is affected by the cycle of recruitment, matriculation, retention, and transfer or job search. Because community and technical college counseling centers offer such a broad array of services, the focus depends on the nature of the student body at the individual institution and on students' needs at various points in the academic year. Community and technical college counselors, like their colleagues at small colleges, may know their students in multiple capacities. This brings both potential complications and potential rewards to the connection. Students who know counselors through other roles may feel more comfortable approaching them when personal issues arise; in fact, they may use the other roles to initiate the contact and then present counseling needs. Although this can be effective in reducing any stigma connected to seeking counseling, it can also lead to dual relationship dilemmas and the need to clarify roles and expectations.

Distance Education

Another group of students whom counselors will increasingly need to serve are those engaged in distance education. Regardless of the medium (electronic courses, broadcast television courses, or two-way interactive televised classrooms), these students are enrolled at institutions that need to offer them services, according to both good practice and accreditation requirements. Although the means may be different, the needs are not. Schwitzer (1997) suggested that distance students are most similar to community college students in their diversity and breadth of needs and that the community college offers the most useful model for organizing counseling services.

Beyond the Counseling Center

Many college counselors spend their careers in counseling centers, perhaps moving into administrative roles, whereas others leave higher education for private practice or other opportunities (Zimpfer, 1996). Some college counselors, however, remain in higher education but move into other areas and positions. Counseling center work can be a step on a career path in student affairs, and as college counselors move into other positions, they carry with them the skills and perspective gained through their counseling training and experience. Throughout the human resources section of CAS's (1997) functional area standards, counseling is repeatedly listed as an appropriate area of preparation for other student services.

Winston (1996) used the term *allied professional counselors* to refer to student affairs professionals who are not professional counselors but who use related skills to address students' needs. He further noted that as student affairs professionals advance in the field, their principal interactions are with staff rather than students and that counseling skills remain equally important. College counselors, conversely, can find themselves in what could be termed *allied professional positions*. These roles, which can range from academic advising to student affairs administration, may not require counseling training, but the counselors' understanding of individuals and groups and how to work with them effectively provides valuable insight in these new roles. For example, many institutions now have committees focused on intervening with students at risk and thereby increasing retention. A committee member trained as a counselor brings expertise in the kinds of issues that may place students at risk as well as broad knowledge of interventions that may be successful. Similarly, a counselor working in residence life has skills in addressing roommate conflicts and hall dynamics that may make that staff member particularly effective in that role. Certainly, specialized counseling training will provide the staff member with a perspective and a set of strategies that are likely to differ from those of staff members who were trained differently.

Relatedly, the counselor's perspective on legal and ethical issues is one that can inform many other roles. Issues of confidentiality, informed consent, dual relationships, and duty to warn and duty to protect arise in many situations on college campuses. College counselors who are trained in these areas may be more aware of potential problems and can help raise such awareness among their colleagues.

Career paths for counselors within the college setting can be as varied as the individuals and institutions involved. Some may choose to teach in a counselor education or student affairs preparation program. Others will pursue student affairs administration, moving toward positions as senior student affairs officers. Still others will move into specialized student services, such as those for women; students with disabilities; international and multicultural students; and gay, lesbian, bisexual, and transgendered students.

Counselors working in other settings carry with them the advantages that their skills and experiences give them; however, they are also faced with challenges resulting from potential role conflict. Some of these are logistical. When a staff member has been on the counseling staff, especially if he or she remains at the same institution, students may continue to seek out that individual as a counselor, regardless of job position. Shifting from one kind of helping role to another can be difficult, particularly for students who have been clients. In these cases, it is important to communicate clearly and to set appropriate boundaries with students. It is also important to clarify roles. Whereas counselors have an ethical obligation to protect confidentiality, the relationship of administrator or program director to student is different. Whereas a counselor is bound to keep confidential information gained through the counseling relationship, an administrator may not be similarly obligated, legally or ethically. For individuals trained as counselors, it can be very difficult to sort out these lines of responsibility and to clarify for themselves the role relationship with individual students. Consultation with supervisors or colleagues is important in order to keep roles and obligations clear.

Other challenges are more personal. Counselors work to develop a high level of empathy with clients and to establish a trusting relationship. When an individual moves into other roles, particularly administrative ones, it may be difficult to balance the desire to understand and be empathetic with the need to address situations firmly and consistently. In the best situations, the counselor's insight contributes to his or her effectiveness. In more difficult circumstances, the counselor's inclination to provide affirmation and support may not serve the specific situation. For example, when a student in distress is acting out on campus, the counselor may want to work individually to alleviate the student's pain. However, if that counselor is working as an administrator whose primary concern must be the quality of campus life for all students, then that administrator is likely to experience conflict between wanting to assist the student and wanting to protect the environment for others. Although these two interests are not always mutually exclusive, they can be experienced as a conflict for the counselor/administrator. The counselor must learn to use his or her skills to benefit the new role and responsibilities while at the same time learning to distinguish what is appropriate for each.

RECOMMENDATIONS FOR ACTION

Institutional concerns, student demographics, available resources, and environmental pressures are all changing rapidly, and the role of the counseling center on campuses must adapt to new needs and circumstances. Additionally, Stone and Archer (1990) pointed out that for many students, developmental issues now include learning to deal with traumatic life events and serious psychological problems. Counseling centers will continue to be called on to respond to the increasing demand for clinical services while also providing for the broad spectrum of student needs.

In light of sometimes conflicting demands, it is imperative that college counselors work actively to define the mission of the counseling service, to clarify their roles, to write clear and specific job descriptions, and to clarify institutional expectations of counselors and counseling centers. The mission and role that are identified must be consistent with those of the institution and must be responsive to the particular needs of the institution, the student body, and the faculty and staff. Use of professional standards such as those disseminated by the CAS or the IACS can provide a sound basis on which to plan the basic services; institutional circumstances can then be considered as provisions are made to meet specific needs.

As institutions continue to experience pressure to provide clinical services for serious cases, it will be important for counselors to articulate a philosophy and to establish policies that preserve time for developmental and clinical work, outreach, and consultation (Stone & Archer, 1990). Counselors should consider their approaches to treatment of serious pathology, including session limits and referral options.

As careers continue to change rapidly, and individuals move through their own career development, counselors must also prepare for the possibility of change. Individuals who are trained as counselors and have counseling as their professional identity can still obtain experiences to enable them to be direct service practitioners in various settings, within higher education and outside of that setting. Skills in understanding and responding to the needs of individuals and groups are valued in many settings and at many levels.

Counseling centers can provide services to students and to the campus community that cannot be replicated by counseling services off campus.

College counselors' knowledge of higher education and of the campus environment benefits student clients. Counselors can both understand the students' context and make therapeutic use of resources available in the environment. At the same time, college counselors' knowledge of students and of psychodynamic issues benefits the institution. Counselors can share this knowledge with faculty, staff, and administrators, thereby improving the capacity of the institution to respond to students' needs. The more integral counselors are to the work of the campus, the more necessary college counseling becomes, and the less likely an institution is to consider outsourcing the counseling service. College counselors play a vital role in the lives of students and of institutions, and the more the counseling service reflects the characteristics of the institution and its students, the more effective it can be.

SUMMARY

The core roles for college counselors can be categorized as serving developmental, remedial, and preventive functions. The mission of counseling services is to address the needs of both individual students and the campus community. The basic services needed for a counseling center to operate effectively have been outlined by the CAS (1997) and the IACS (Kiracofe et al., 1994); they include individual and group counseling, testing and assessment, developmental outreach efforts, support for educational deficiencies, crisis intervention and emergency coverage, research and evaluation of services, and consultation and professional development for faculty, staff, and trainees.

Differences in the role of college counselors exist between institution types. In large university counseling centers, which are often aligned with health services, counselors may be perceived more as health care providers than are their colleagues in other institutions. In contrast, counselors in small college settings are typically more closely aligned with the array of student services, and their roles are often combined with other responsibilities. They tend to be perceived more as multipurpose resources for students and the campus. Similarly, counselors in community and technical colleges often work in settings that offer students multiple services in one location. Here, the role of counselors may involve working with students to meet a broad range of student needs. The role of counselors in distance education is emerging as that service delivery medium becomes more common; here, too, counselors will need to respond to a wide variety of students and student needs.

Career development for college counselors may involve moving up to administration in the counseling center or moving out to private practice or another setting. However, it also may involve moving over into other student services or into teaching. Individuals trained as counselors who move into other areas have a unique set of skills to use in their new roles, and students and institutions can benefit from this expertise. College counselors work in the entire range of student service areas, and their counseling background provides them with a perspective that informs their new roles. However, counselors who move into other roles must also be careful to clarify those new roles and the expectations involved, both to themselves and to the students with whom they work.

The mission, role, and scope of counseling services on any campus must be articulated and clarified. Counselors can serve in many roles, but they cannot serve all students or respond to all campus needs. It is imperative that college counselors identify and describe clearly the vital role that they play on campus as they provide developmental, remedial, and preventive services to their students and their institutions.

REFERENCES

Archer, J., Jr., & Cooper, S. (1998). *Counseling and mental health services on campus: A handbook of contemporary practices and challenges.* San Francisco: Jossey-Bass.

Astin, A. W. (1993). *What matters in college?: Four critical years revisited.* San Francisco: Jossey-Bass.

Blimling, G. S., & Alschuler, A. S. (1996). Creating a home for the spirit of learning: Contributions of student development educators. *Journal of College Student Development, 37,* 203–216.

Council for the Advancement of Standards in Higher Education. (1997). *The CAS book of professional standards for higher education.* Washington, DC: Author.

Crego, C. A. (1996). Consultation and mediation. In S. R. Komives, D. B. Woodard, Jr., & Associates (Eds.), *Student services: A handbook for the profession* (3rd ed., pp. 361–379). San Francisco: Jossey-Bass.

Dean, L. A. (1995). Counseling on the small college campus: Living ethically with dual relationships. *The College Student Affairs Journal, 15,* 54–62.

Helfgot, S. R. (1998). Introduction. In M. M. Culp & S. R. Helfgot (Eds.), *Life at the edge of the wave: Lessons from the community college* (pp. 1–9). Washington, DC: National Association of Student Personnel Administrators.

Heppner, P. P., & Johnston, J. A. (1994). New horizons in counseling: Faculty development. *Journal of Counseling and Development, 72,* 451–453.

Kiracofe, N. M., Donn, P. A., Grant, C. O., Podolnick, E. E., Bingham, R. P., Bolland, H. R., Carney, C. G., Clementson, J., Gallagher, R. P., Grosz, R. D., Handy, L., Hansche, J. H., Mack, J. K., Sanz, D., Walker, L. J., & Yamada, K. T. (1994). Accreditation standards for university and college counseling centers. *Journal of Counseling and Development, 73,* 38–43.

Kitchener, K. S. (1988). Dual role relationships: What makes them so problematic? *Journal of Counseling and Development, 67,* 217–221.

Nuss, E. M. (1996). The development of student affairs. In S. R. Komives, D. B. Woodard, Jr., & Associates (Eds.), *Student services: A handbook for the profession* (3rd ed., pp. 22–42). San Francisco: Jossey-Bass.

Schwitzer, A. M. (1997, July/August). Supporting student learning from a distance. *About Campus, 2*(3), 27–29.

Stone, G. L., & Archer, J. A., Jr. (1990). College and university counseling centers in the 1990s: Challenges and limits. *The Counseling Psychologist, 18,* 539–607.

Winston, R. B., Jr. (1996). Counseling and advising. In S. R. Komives, D. B. Woodard, Jr., & Associates (Eds.), *Student services: A handbook for the profession* (3rd ed., pp. 335–360). San Francisco: Jossey-Bass.

Zimpfer, D. G. (1996). Five-year follow-up of doctoral graduates in counseling. *Counselor Education and Supervision, 35,* 218–229.

4

Professional Preparation for College Counseling: Quality Assurance

MARY FINN MAPLES

FOCUS QUESTIONS

1. What is accreditation and who conducts it for college counseling programs?

2. What role do professional organizations play in college counseling?

3. What licenses and certifications are necessary or available for college counselors?

4. What educational degrees are required for those seeking a career in college counseling?

5. What paths are appropriate for preparation in college counseling?

ISSUES

The academic specialty of college counseling is one of the most recently recognized helping professions. As such, it is crucial that it is effectively regulated from preparation into practice. Issues related to this regulation and oversight of practice include accreditation of training and educational programs, scholastic requirements and qualifications of applicants to such programs, quality and recognition of faculty through their research and publications, professional organizations and associations that produce ethical standards to guide the practice of college counseling, and involvement of practitioners in continuing professional development. This chapter highlights a few of the aforementioned elements that contribute to assurance of quality in the preparation for and the practice of college counseling.

Accreditation

As stated by the Council for the Accreditation of Counseling and Counseling Related Educational Programs (CACREP; 1999),

> Accreditation is a process and a condition. The process entails the assessment of educational quality and the continued enhancement of educational operations through the development and validation of standards. The condition provides a credential to the public-at-large which attests that an institution and/or its programs have accepted and are fulfilling their commitment to educational quality. (p. 1)

In the United States, there are two types of accreditation in higher education: institutionalized accreditation and specialized accreditation. CACREP is specialized because only graduate study counseling programs are eligible. However, CACREP responds only to those programs that have achieved institutional accreditation.

Among the myriad reasons that support accreditation, the most prominent is the assurance of quality. Although there are many graduate programs in the country that still require 30–36 semester credits for a master's degree in counseling, there is growing concern that students emerge from these programs dramatically unprepared for the complexity of issues, concerns, and problems faced by today's college students. Stated appropriately in 1975 by Robert O. Stripling, often referred to as the "father of accreditation" (Maples, 1979), "Accreditation may not guarantee qualification, but qualification is unlikely without some form of accreditation."

Council for the Accreditation of Counseling and Counseling Related Educational Programs. CACREP was founded in 1981 as a corporate affiliate of the American Counseling Association (ACA). CACREP's mission coincides with that of ACA—to promote the advancement of quality educational program offerings. In less than 20 years, more than 340 programs in more than 130 institutions have achieved CACREP accreditation status. In addition to college-counseling curricular experiences, CACREP evaluates programs in school counseling, community counseling, student affairs practice in higher education, marriage and family counseling and therapy, career counseling, and doctoral preparation in counselor education and supervision.

The CACREP accreditation process involves the assessment of a counseling program's compliance with standards established by the profession and adapted by the decision-making group, the board of directors. The process includes the following:

1. **A comprehensive self-study** completed by the applicant program that addresses, in addition to college counseling standards, the curriculum core of human growth and development, social and cultural foundations, helping relationships, group work, career and lifestyle development, appraisal, research and program evaluation, and professional orientation. The self-study represents the program as it exists at a specific time.

2. **Documentation by CACREP initial reviewers of the self-study** that the program complies with the standards; that is, all applicant programs must present a minimum of 48 semester credits, or an equivalent in quarter credits.

3. **Validation of the self-study** documented by an on-site visiting team, usually a group of three professionally trained CACREP team members selected by the program faculty from a list pro-

vided by CACREP staff. These professionals are peers in counselor education or practitioners.

4. **On receipt of the visiting team's report, the board of directors renders its decision,** resulting in (a) full accreditation for 7 years, (b) 2-year accreditation with one or more conditions to be met in that period of time, or (c) denial of accreditation.

5. **Interim reports by the program** to CACREP (by those with full accreditation) and mid-cycle reports by those with conditions arising from the earlier team visit. On satisfaction of these conditions, the program is accorded the remaining 5 years for full accreditation.

American Psychological Association. In the early years of college counseling, practitioners came primarily from the American Psychological Association (APA), which recognized counselors with preparation in counseling psychology who were members of then Division 17. As the profession matured, doctoral students and program faculty (APA does not accredit master's programs in counseling psychology) were confronted with two choices: APA or CACREP. For a while, after 1981, programs often sought accreditation through both bodies. Now, however, the majority of programs in counseling psychology seek APA accreditation, whereas the majority of counselor education programs apply to CACREP.

Council for the Advancement of Standards. The Council for the Advancement of Standards (CAS) was established in 1979 and represents a consortium of higher education professional associations. CAS has established standards and guidelines for several programs and services in higher education. These include, but are not limited to, academic advising, admissions, college unions, financial aid, counseling services, religious programs, student orientation, and master's-level student affairs practice preparation programs (CAS, 1998).

Professional Organizations

As reviewed by Hanna and Bemack (1997), counseling meets most of the criteria necessary to be considered a profession: a national professional organization, published ethical standards, viable divisions, and an array of state associations. In addition, professionals are assumed to have advanced academic degrees and to follow standards that guide both their training and professional behavior. There are several professional organizations that are especially helpful to college counselors and those preparing for college counseling careers.

American Counseling Association. In 1952, the National Vocational Guidance Association and the American College Personnel Association combined to form what would eventually become known as ACA. Today, ACA is the umbrella professional counseling organization, with more than 50,000 members, 17 separate divisions, and one organizational affiliate, each with its own counseling speciality and mission. The professional association that is ascribed to by members of the college counseling profession is the American College Counseling Association (ACCA).

American College Counseling Association. Chartered in 1991, ACCA is the latest organization to become affiliated with ACA. ACCA was established in response to the withdrawal of one of ACA's founding groups, the American College Personnel Association (ACPA). As the American Personnel and Guidance Association evolved into the American Association of Counseling and Development and then into ACA, it became clear to ACPA that it was time to form an independent organization because their primary professional activities were not in "counseling." However, because some of the original members of ACPA were counselors, the need arose and was recognized by ACA to invite several committed higher education professionals to form ACCA. It is noteworthy that many of those 1991 founders remain involved in the activities of ACCA. They include Laura Dean, Bob Mattox, Mark "Gene" Meadows, Jane Myers, Deb Davis, Sue Spooner, and Allen Segrist, to name only a few. For college counselors, ACCA membership provides opportunities to forge professional relationships with colleagues dedicated to providing quality counseling services for all college students. Additionally, ACCA serves as a powerful advocate for the college counseling field and provides college counselors with relevant information and continuing education opportunities.

Association for Multicultural Counseling and Development.
Affiliated with ACA, the Association for Multicultural Counseling and Development represents counselors, educators, and supervisors whose personal or professional orientation, interests, and practice occur within an international, transcultural, or multicultural context. College counselors can contribute to and benefit from involvement with this organization.

Association for Specialists in Group Work. There is considerable research to support the position that the use of group counseling will continue to increase in the next millennium. Colleges, universities, agencies, and organizations are recognizing the impact of increased costs relating to individual counseling experiences. This ACA division provides unique and effective opportunities for college counselors to promote and conduct group activities for students with similar concerns, issues, or problems.

Association for Spiritual, Ethical, and Religious Values in Counseling. One of the most prominent concerns that college students bring to the table is their belief system (or lack of one). The Association for Spiritual, Ethical, and Religious Values in Counseling, also affiliated with ACA, not only is a resource for information on issues that are of concern to today's students but also provides college counselors with a variety of methods, activities, and programs to use to reach students who are struggling with their own identity.

Association for Gay, Lesbian, and Bisexual Issues in Counseling. The mission of the Association for Gay, Lesbian, and Bisexual Issues in Counseling (AGLBIC), a division of ACA, is to educate counseling professionals about issues of sexual orientation through advocacy, resource development, consultation, and training. College counselors will find AGLBIC a wealth of information and support as they expand their knowledge and understanding of the unique needs of gay, lesbian, bisexual, and transgender individuals on campus.

Licensure and Certification

Because licensure and certification may have a variety of meanings in an equal number of contextual dimensions, the *Tenth Webster's Collegiate Dictionary* (Misk & Gilman, 1996) definitions apply: *Licensure* is "permission to act or permission granted by competent authority to engage in a business or in an activity that may otherwise be deemed unlawful" (p. 688). *Certification* is "documentation that one has fulfilled the requirements of and may practice in a field" (p. 233).

There is no specific and global certification or licensure in college counseling. However, in the next millennium, either licensure or certification, or both, will regulate the practice of college counseling. Because the National Board of Certified Counselors (NBCC) already provides a nationally recognized credential, namely, national certified counselor, college counselors are encouraged to sit for the written standardized examination that results in this credential. This certification substantiates a high level of quality preparation and holds counselors accountable to a set of ethical standards. Another pathway for college counselors is state licensure. In effect, in all but six states, licensure grants permission for counselors to perform their duties and holds counselors to legal and ethical standards set by state legislatures. Licensure titles include various forms of licensed professional counselor, licensed clinical professional counselor, or mental health practitioner. It should be noted that many states use NBCC guidelines, examinations, or both as a basis for licensure.

In the cases of both licensure and certification, professionals must qualify to "sit for the exams." In most states, a minimum of a master's degree, with significant internship preparation, is a prerequisite. The NBCC generally requires that the applicant possess at least 2 years of paid professional counseling experience. The exception to this requirement is students in their final semester at a CACREP-accredited institution. They are allowed to pursue the exam in the semester before graduating.

Additionally, through the NBCC's research arm, the Research and Assessment Corporation for Counseling, NBCC offers the Counselor Preparation Comprehensive Examination to a number of counselor education programs. This is a master's-level exit examination, which reflects the eight core curriculum areas approved by CACREP. There are two advantages to the use of this instrument. First is the benefit of standardization of the often criticized and subjectively graded final written exam, provided by the department faculty. Second, the exam provides students with an introduction to the NBCC exam process, hopefully reducing some of the natural anxiety that accompanies evaluation experiences.

Education

Master's Degree. In general, the master's degree is considered entry-level preparation for college counselors. They are varied: master of arts (MA); master of science (MS); master of education (MEd); and, in some instances, master of social work (MSW). The serious problem related to master's-level preparation is that some programs continue to confer degrees on persons with totally inadequate course work and practical experiences. Consider the following contrasting examples of preparation in college counseling.

Program A: Graduate, MA Degree
30 semester credits (nonaccredited) in
Introduction to Counseling—3
Counseling Theories—3
Counseling Practicum—6 (90 clock hours)
Career Counseling—3
Group Dynamics—3
Introduction to the College Student—3
Introduction to Research—3
Introduction to Group Testing—3
The Role of the Counselor—3

Program B: Graduate, MA Degree
60 semester credits (fully accredited by CACREP) in
Introduction to Counseling—3
Counseling Theories—3
Counseling Practicum—6 (100 clock hours)
Career Counseling—3
Group Dynamics—3
Group Counseling (emphasis on higher education)—3

Multicultural Counseling—3
Substance Abuse Counseling—3
Law and Ethics in Counseling—3
College Student Development—3
Seminar in College Student Leadership—3
Colloquium in College Counseling—3
Counseling in Higher Education—3
Appraisal (higher education emphasis)—3
Internship in Higher Education—3 (300 clock hours)
Introduction to Graduate Research—3
Administration in Higher Education—3
Curriculum in Higher Education—3
Internship in College Counseling—6 (300 clock hours)

Again, it must be noted that accreditation does not guarantee competence; however, competence is unlikely without it.

Education Specialist (Certificate or Degree). The education specialist (EdS) degree, as it is known in the western United States, or the certificate of advanced graduate study (CAGS), as it is known in the eastern United States, is evidence of preparation beyond the master's level but less than the doctorate. Ordinarily, it consists of 30–36 credits and requires a professional project (worth 6 credits) instead of a thesis or dissertation. This preparation is often offered in school psychology and social work.

Doctoral Degree. As is the case in most educational professions, there are two opportunities for the doctoral degree: the doctor of philosophy (PhD) and the doctor of education (EdD). An examination of institutional catalogs reveals that the PhD usually requires additional research and statistics courses as well as a greater number of dissertation credits. Holders of a PhD often enter the counselor education field to prepare college counselors. The EdD mandates more academic course work and practical experiences because individuals with this degree tend to enter administrative positions in higher education.

Specialty Areas

A strong argument for accredited program preparation in college counseling is the increase in litigation in higher education. It is crucial that
college students "get what they pay for"—a quality education, part of
which includes the service of counseling. Qualified and certificated counselors should be expected to provide skillful, knowledgeable, and quality counseling, thereby avoiding challenges to their credentials and
embarrassment to the institution.

When one considers the examples of curricular experiences listed earlier, it would seem that the cost–benefit ratio balance would be for institutions to employ accredited program graduates. However, although the
"practice" of college counseling has been around since the beginning of
higher education, college counseling as a specific "body of knowledge"
is relatively new. It should follow that graduates from accredited programs warrant higher salaries. Because counseling college students is not
always viewed by the power brokers (whether institutional administrators, regents, or legislators) as crucial to the collegiate experience, persons with other degrees who are willing to accept lower salaries are
hired. One of these specialties is marriage and family counseling, which
is helpful in light of the current trend toward more part-time, older students with families. Graduates from another specialty, clinical psychology, continue to be hired by college counseling centers that follow the old
"medical model" of counseling college students. Finally, it would seem
that the most appropriate and cost-effective specialty area for the college
counselor is just that—a degree in college counseling, college student
development, counseling in higher education, or some other specifically
descriptive preparation program.

RECOMMENDATIONS FOR ACTION:
PATHS FOR PROFESSIONAL PREPARATION

For the Undergraduate

Although there are no accredited baccalaureate degrees in college
counseling, there are many experts in the field of college counseling who

advocate hands-on experiences at the undergraduate level as appropriate background for pursuing a career in the area. Such experiences may include residence hall adviser, student activities, volunteer work, student government leadership, peer counseling, and community involvement.

Academic majors at the baccalaureate level that seem to provide a beneficial foundation for graduate study in the field include psychology, education, sociology, philosophy, creative arts, or other areas that tend to be people-focused. The key, though, is a passion for college students of all ages. This criterion often transcends academic background.

For the Prospective Master's Student

Above all, the most important consideration in selecting the appropriate program is the potential match between the student and the program (i.e., faculty, course work, field experience sites, specialties). Advanced education is expensive. If one is going to make a sacrifice financially, as the majority of graduate students do, it is important to achieve value benefit for value invested. In this case, accreditation again enters the picture. Increasingly, the *Chronicle of Higher Education* and *Counseling Today*, as well as the various listservs, are advertising position vacancy requirements as "graduate of CACREP-accredited institution," among others.

Most programs require, on average, Graduate Record Examination scores (or Miller Analogies Test scores) as well as the appropriate undergraduate grade point average, usually 3.0 or higher (with 3.0 representing a *B*). Letters of recommendation from persons qualified to address the applicant's potential for advanced work and a writing sample are also usually required. A screening interview indicates a program that takes seriously the issue of a good match between applicant and program.

Finally, if the applicant is fortunate to be able to relocate, it is important to seek institutions that have professionally recognized faculty and specific course work in the specialty area. The necessary course content examples are listed in an earlier section.

For the Prospective Doctoral Student

Many of the same issues discussed for master's degree students also apply to potential doctoral students, however, at an increased depth and intensity. For example, because there is greater emphasis on scholarly productivity (i.e., the dissertation), the letters of recommendation should more specifically attend to the applicant's potential for scholarly pursuits. Also, the grade point average expected of doctoral students is usually 3.5 or higher, compared with the master's level of 3.0. Attending professional conferences, conventions, and workshops, promoted by professional organizations, can help candidates to network and search for employment. Reading professional literature, textbooks, journal articles, and newsletters can put potential doctoral students in touch with professional organizations and can help them to become cognizant of both the topics and the structure of doctoral-level professional research and writing.

Of particular note is the opportunity to select (or, in some cases, to be selected by) an adviser who is a leader in the field. Acquiring a doctoral mentor of substantial character and professional accomplishment is an invaluable commodity. Above all, though, the personality match between adviser and advisee (a true mentor relationship) is highly contributory to the success of the doctoral venture.

Postgraduation: Adjustment to Career

One of the most common difficulties faced by the beginning college counselor is the separation anxiety that sets in after the relative comfort and security of academia is left behind. If the graduate has had a positive experience with a mentor, it is important that the connection be maintained, even for a short while. With the surge in availability of E-mail in college and university settings, a listserv for alumni is easy to create and is helpful in maintaining connections between faculty and graduates.

The counselor, in considering whether to accept a position offer, should examine all of the opportunities and perks that encourage professional development from the hiring college or university. Travel funds, continuing or advanced educational opportunities, and time away from work for advanced training are increasingly included in hiring packages in lieu of a higher salary. Of similar importance, particularly at the doctoral level, is the negotiation that takes place in the hiring process. Increasingly, the tendency (for counselor educators who teach college counselors) is to remain with the same institution throughout one's career (Maples & Testa, 1993).

If the networking process is important at the graduate level, it is critical once one enters the field. Often, particularly at small institutions, the counselor works alone. Connecting on regional, state, and national levels to enhance knowledge and skill development is extremely valuable. The college counselor must seek out opportunities for professional development. A variety of conferences, workshops, and networking opportunities are available from the ACCA web site (www.collegecounseling.org).

The majority of college counselors are entering the field with a master's degree. It is incumbent on their mentors and supervisors to encourage these professionals to consider continuing their education. Encouraging practitioners to bring their experience and expertise to a higher professional level can move the college counseling profession to a greater knowledge and skill base. Ultimately, the college students themselves are the beneficiaries. The more educationally and psychologically sound that counseling services and practice are, the more effective the living–learning experience will be for college students.

SUMMARY

In this chapter, the credentialing and preparation aspects relating to college counseling have been addressed. Because of accrediting organizations like CACREP, academic program quality is becoming increasingly sophisticated. Professional organizations are taking on increased challenges. As they proliferate, their goals and objectives must address the needs of better-qualified and more demanding members. ACA and its partner in counseling professionalism, ACCA, are providing meaningful professional development opportunities for counselors and must continue to do so into the next century.

Although there is as yet no specific license for college counselors, those entering the field are encouraged to demonstrate their knowledge base in counselor preparation through the NBCC as well as to become licensed counselors (if available) in their state. Academic preparation is becoming increasingly intensive and extensive. Where once a bachelor's degree in almost any field was acceptable to work with college students, institutions now recognize the value in hiring professionals who are well trained in the discipline of college counseling.

Finally, college counselors are encouraged to continue networking with colleagues and peers from throughout the country to maintain and enhance their skills and knowledge. Above all, this networking helps college counselors to maintain that elusive yet critical component that no one can teach a passion for the profession and all those that it serves.

REFERENCES

Council for the Accreditation of Counseling and Counseling Related Educational Programs. (1999, September). *A student's guide to accreditation*. Alexandria, VA: Author. Retrieved September 1, 1999 from the World Wide Web: http://www.counseling.org/CACREP/student.html

Council for the Advancement of Standards. (1998). *What is CAS?* [Brochure]. Washington, DC: Author.

Hanna, F., & Bemack, F. (1997). The quest for identity in the counseling profession. *Counselor Education and Supervision, 36,* 33–40.

Maples, M. F. (1979, April). *Reflections on the father of accreditation.* Speech delivered at the Robert O. Stripling Retirement Celebration, University of Florida, Gainesville.

Maples, M., & Testa, A. (1993). The counselor educator crunch: Extinction or distinction? *Counselor Education and Supervision, 29,* 135–141.

Misk, F., & Gilman, E. (1996). *Webster's tenth new collegiate dictionary* (10th ed.). Springfield, MA: Merriam-Webster.

Stripling, R. O. (1975, April). *The purpose and value of quality in counselor education.* Paper presented at the American Personnel and Guidance Association, New York.

5

Practicing Ethically as a College Counselor

PERRY C. FRANCIS

FOCUS QUESTIONS

1. What are the primary issues faced by college counselors today, and how do ethics affect the practice of college counseling?

2. How can college counselors balance their ethical obligations to students with the goals and procedures of their institutions?

3. How can college counselors ensure that they are practicing ethically?

ISSUES

The practice of college counseling, at all levels of higher education, is becoming increasingly complicated (Archer & Cooper, 1998). Some research suggests that students are coming into counseling with increasingly severe problems (Gilbert, 1992; Hersh, 1985; Murphy & Archer, 1996; O'Malley, Wheeler, Murphey, O'Connell, & Waldo, 1990). Institutions of higher learning are demanding more information and cooperation from counselors when dealing with problem students (Archer & Cooper, 1998; Gilbert, 1989; Hayman & Covert, 1986; Hersh, 1985), and counseling centers are being asked to do more throughout institutions with fewer resources (Stone & Archer, 1990). The ethical issues related to these and other similar problems have become increasingly complex. This chapter examines some of the primary ethical issues faced by college counselors today and how these issues affect counseling services. These issues include confidentiality, dual relationships, session limitations and referrals, mandatory counseling, and harm to others–duty to warn. It is assumed that readers have professional preparation in foundation issues of ethics; therefore, this chapter focuses on the practical application of ethics to the working lives of professional college counselors.

Confidentiality

The obligation to maintain confidentiality in a counseling relationship, although not absolute, is one of the major ethical and legal tenets of the counseling profession (Grayson, 1986; Welfel, 1998). The American Counseling Association's (ACA; 1995) *ACA Code of Ethics and Standards of Practice* state that "counselors respect their client's right to privacy and avoid illegal and unwarranted disclosure of confidential information" (Section B.1.a., p. 3). Without reasonable assurances that what is discussed in a counseling session will remain confidential, trust cannot be built, the relationship between client and counselor will suffer, and therapeutic progress is hampered. Yet, the ability to maintain confidentiality is being challenged in several ways on college campuses. Kaplan and Rothrock (1991) pointed out,

Difficulties keeping confidentiality on a college campus are often complicated by three factors: institutional enmeshment, organizational issues, and professional identity issues. Smaller schools may have administrators who want to know everything about everybody while larger school administrators do not seem to have time for this. Some administrators take pride in keeping in touch with any difficulties a student may have and see themselves acting, as Steve Mullinix points out, "in loco parentis. Therefore, the administrator may not respect professional boundaries between his/her office and the Counseling Center." (p. 17)

Confidentiality is challenged at all levels of college counseling and by many different people. College counselors need guidelines that help them manage and maintain confidentiality (Archer & Cooper, 1998; Harding, Gray, & Neal, 1993; Stone & Lucas, 1990). The following discussion will assist college counselors wishing to maintain ethical practice.

Informed Consent. During the initial session, all college counseling clients should receive a clearly written informed-consent statement describing the limits of counseling and confidentiality. Clients must understand how and when confidentiality may be broken and, in the case of mandatory counseling, who has access to what kind of information concerning counseling sessions. Additionally, counseling centers must provide a clear explanation of confidentiality in all public relations materials, including brochures, handouts, and web pages. College counselors specifically can use counseling centers' web sites to explain the nature and limitations of confidentiality. **Box 2** illustrates a sample college counseling center's web-site reference to confidentiality.

Records Maintenance and Information Release. Counseling centers must establish clear guidelines for the storage and release of counseling records. Paper files must be kept in locked cabinets, and access

---

Box 2

Sample College Counseling Confidentiality Statement

The Counseling Center carefully adheres to professional standards of ethics and confidentiality. If students want information concerning contact with their staff counselor released, they must sign a specific written authorization.

In order to provide effective and up-to-date services, we sometimes consult with colleagues at the counseling center about our work with students. Otherwise, information revealed in counseling, even the information that you have made appointments, is not disclosed to others unless you provide written authorization for information to be released. The following are exceptions to this practice:

- If a counselor believes you present an imminent danger to yourself or others;
- When the life or safety of a readily identifiable third person is endangered;
- When a counselor believes that a child or vulnerable adult is being subjected to abuse, neglect, or exploitation;
- When disclosure is made necessary by legal proceedings.

In all other cases, what you discuss in counseling will remain confidential. A full explanation of confidentiality will be provided during your initial session of counseling.

---

should be limited to the counselor who is directly involved with the client (and his or her supervisor if the counselor is under supervision). Special attention must be given to records that are stored on computers. Computers must be maintained in a secure location to avoid unauthorized access. Passwords, encryption, and backups of all computer files are necessary when computer storage is used. If the computer is on a network, additional security must be provided. Best practice dictates that student records and other confidential information should never be transmitted through voice mail, E-mail, or other electronic means. Special attention must be given to faxed documents to ensure that confidentiality is not breached.

Educating the Campus Community About Confidentiality.
Educating relevant campus entities about confidentiality and the policies
and procedures necessary for college counselors to protect clients' confidentiality is essential. These campus entities should include, but are
not limited to, provosts and presidents, various deans and vice presidents, health center staff, housing directors, judicial–disciplinary committees, and residence hall staff. Chapters 3, 13, and 14 of this book discuss particular strategies for communicating ethics concerns in various
campus environments.

Some institutional officials may request information about some students' progress in counseling as a way of deciding the students' future
at the institution (Gilbert, 1989; Knight, 1995; Stone & Lucas, 1994). This
request creates an ethical dilemma for college counselors because they
must maintain a balance between meeting the needs of the college (and
employer) and maintaining the client's right to privacy. Legal and ethical practices support the client's right to keep his or her records confidential. Prudent ethical practice dictates that any information that is
requested by institutional officials or an outside source (including parents) should not be honored without the expressed written permission
of the client. When counselors do have permission to release information, a case summary should be provided, rather than unedited counselor notes.

Dual Relationships

Herlihy and Corey (1992) identified five ways in which counselors may
become involved in dual or multiple relationships. They include conflicts
in the counselor's role, conflicts in the instructor's role, conflicts in the
supervisory role, conflicts in the administrative role, and private practice
and referral issues. Common examples include the following:

- A student worker who forms a good working relationship with a
  member of the counseling staff and seeks counseling from that same
  staff member.
- A counseling center staff member is involved with teaching a class
  on campus. A current student seeks counseling with that staff member because "he is so nice in class, I just know he will understand."

- A former client has now entered graduate school in the counselor education department and seeks to do his or her practicum or internship in the counseling center.
- A client has reached the limit for the number of counseling sessions allowed for a student at a rural college and is being referred out for continuing counseling services. The only referral in her area is the private practice of the counselor from the college counseling center.

Ethical guidelines call for counselors to avoid dual relationships whenever possible, recognizing the power imbalance implicit in such relationships (ACA, 1995, Section A.6.a.). Yet, some dual relationships are inevitable (Herlihy & Corey, 1997). The primary guideline for managing dual relationship issues is to minimize potential harm to the student client (Kitchener & Harding, 1990). In some cases, the dual relationship issue is easily addressed by referral. However, in the case of a small staff counseling center, for example, this situation cannot be easily avoided. A frank discussion of the nature of counseling, the limits of confidentiality, the effects of multiple roles on the counseling relationship, and possible future conflicts should occur with potential clients so that they can make informed decisions regarding counseling services at the institution (Corey, Corey, & Callanan, 1998).

Another practical issue regarding dual relationships arises when college counselors maintain their own private practices. Students may be referred for counseling outside of the college setting for various reasons. Typically, they may require services that are beyond the expertise or scope of the college counseling center. Sometimes, however, there are so few mental health resources available that the only viable referral source may be a college counselor's private practice. If this is the case, the counselor must ensure that all other avenues for treatment have been investigated before continuing the relationship in his or her private practice. The institution must also be made aware that students are exhausting their resources so that it can assess the situation to determine if additional staff is needed.

Session Limitations and Referrals

Research has shown that college counselors are seeing an increasing number of students with severe problems and psychopathology (Gilbert, 1992; Murphy & Archer, 1996; Pledge, Lapan, Heppner, Kivlighan, & Roehlke, 1998). See Chapter 6, "College Student Problems: Status, Trends, and Research," for a detailed discussion of this research. These types of problems require greater expertise on the part of counselors, lengthier treatment protocols, and more resources. Yet, many counseling centers are reducing staff, budgets, and resources. Some college counseling centers are also limiting the number of sessions a student may have in a semester and promoting the use of short-term and goal-directed therapy (Archer & Cooper, 1998). Two significant ethical issues arise from these actions: appropriate referral practices and professional competence. College counselors must know the limits of practice, both with the number of sessions they can offer a student and the expertise they can provide. It is legally and ethically unsound to offer services to a student whose problems clearly demand more than the number of sessions allowed by the college counseling center (O'Malley et al., 1990). Additionally, in those circumstances in which students have used up their allotted number of counseling sessions, termination of services without appropriate referral can be considered client abandonment and is prohibited by law in many states. It is also legally and ethically unsound to provide counseling services to a student whose problems are outside of the expertise or training of the college counselor or when effective supervision is unavailable (Gilbert, 1992). The following strategies are offered on the topic of session limitations and referrals.

1. Use effective intake assessment procedures to identify students whose problems are beyond the expertise of staff or beyond the time limitations set by the counseling center. Clear policies based on this assessment information must be developed and articulated to the counseling center staff and to students and administration (Archer & Cooper, 1998).
2. Establish off-campus referral systems. It is important to identify area mental health providers, including those who use a sliding fee or who provide pro bono services.

3. Educate administrators about legal and ethical considerations of practicing outside of their area of expertise and the necessity of proper mental health referrals.

4. Explore a policy of not serving students with problems outside of the counseling center's expertise or limits. Gilbert (1992) pointed out that as long as a student is not at risk of harming self or others, it is better and more ethical not to offer services when the problems are outside of the expertise or ability of the college counselor or college counseling center. If the student's behavior is problematic to the institution's administration (e.g., resident life, grade policies), then the student will be exposed to the natural consequences of reality, which can be a learning experience of more value than inadequate or ineffective counseling.

The issues of professional competence and appropriate referral become especially problematic at small staff counseling centers, in areas that are underserved by mental health professionals, or when the presenting issue masks a more severe problem for the student. One effective solution for these problems is to contract with outside service providers (e.g., local hospitals, psychiatric hospitals, recovery centers) to work with specific issues, such as eating disorders and substance abuse. Such action requires that the college counseling center staff and administrators work closely to identify problematic areas, target appropriate resources, and effectively manage service contracts.

Mandatory Counseling

College counselors bear a responsibility to the institutions that support their services and provide for their employment. They also have a duty to maintain the educational environment of the institutions so students can learn in a safe and secure environment (Archer & Cooper, 1998). Many colleges and universities include mandatory counseling as part of a disciplinary action or as a requirement to continue in or return to school or the residence halls (Archer & Cooper, 1998; Gilbert & Sheiman, 1995; Stone & Lucas, 1994). Clear guidelines and policies must be negotiated between the counseling center and the administration of the institution regarding mandatory counseling. These guidelines and policies should be reviewed annually to ensure that they are meeting the needs of the institution, the college counseling center, and the students.

College counselors are often ambivalent about using counseling as a part of disciplinary actions (Gilbert & Sheiman, 1995; Stone & Lucas, 1994), with some counselors even suggesting that mandatory counseling does not work and borders on unethical practice (Gilbert & Sheiman, 1995). Most ethical guidelines support the client's right to choose how counseling will proceed and with whom it should proceed. There is a legitimate fear that the counseling center may become an unofficial enforcer of the institution's administration or lose its reputation as a fair and impartial agency within the university.

Mandatory counseling has existed for decades in many different settings, including prisons, schools, and court systems. In some cases, what actually occurs is "disciplinary education" that is tailored to the specific violation (Stone & Lucas, 1994). In these cases, students are given information and suggestions that may not require disclosure of personal information. When presented effectively by college counseling center staff, this form of education can be beneficial and, in most cases, not harmful to the reputation of the counseling center.

Alternatively, mandatory counseling may require the "client" to participate in a determined or undetermined number of sessions that may or may not be productive and whose content may or may not be disclosed to another source. This places the college counselor in the awkward and contradictory position of being both therapist and reporter. Ethical considerations regarding confidentiality, potential harm to the client, and potential harm to the student body must be weighed by college counselors. College counselors who adopt a hands-off policy of neutrality may miss the opportunity of fulfilling their role in providing a safe, secure, and disciplined campus environment (Stone & Lucas, 1994). In contrast, college counselors who too freely share information with administration in mandatory counseling cases do breach confidentiality and may harm clients. Ethical guidelines inform counselors that no information can be shared with the administration of a college or university without prior permission of the student involved. If the student is required to obtain counseling and have the counselor report on his or her progress, it must be the student's decision about what is reported. This empowers the student to take ownership of the counseling process and removes the counselor from the role of reporter.

Harm to Others and Duty to Warn

Some research suggests that the level of stress has been rising on college and university campuses across the United States, and there is also evidence of a corresponding rise in suicidal ideation and behavior (Dixon, Rumford, Heppner, & Lips, 1992; Pledge et al., 1998). Related to these issues is the duty to warn others when a client has the potential to act violently or to infect others with a communicable disease (e.g., HIV/AIDS). In each of these situations, the counselor can intervene to protect clients or an identified third party (Anfang & Appelbaum, 1996; Fulero, 1988; Harding et al., 1993; McGuire, Nieri, Abbott, Sheridan, & Fisher, 1995; Welfel, 1998). This may mean hospitalization for the client, notification of campus police or local law enforcement, or notification of a third party identified by the client. All of these responses center on issues of confidentiality and least restrictive interventions.

Again, many college counselors had significant training on this important topic during their professional preparation, and it is not the intent of this chapter to replace critical foundations. Rather, I remind college counselors of their important role in these situations.

Counselors must act to protect suicidal clients from themselves or to protect identified persons from clients who may do them harm. The question is not if, but how, that action will take place. College counselors should provide the least restrictive intervention possible and, at the same time, make every effort to protect the client's right to privacy. It is important that college counseling centers have protocols in place that clearly delineate the steps that counselors will follow when seeking a client's hospitalization, when notifying any intended victims or third parties, or both. If centers do not have such protocols, counselors must advocate to establish them. Consultation among counseling center staff and other appropriate mental health professionals should take place in developing protocols, and the institution's administration and legal counsel should review any related policies and procedures. Finally, it is essential to good practice that college counselors receive continuing professional training in suicide and violence assessment, ethical concerns, and legal issues.

RECOMMENDATIONS FOR ACTION

Recommendations for action concerning specific issues and dilemmas have been made throughout this chapter. This section provides additional recommendations to college counselors regarding the balancing act of conflicting obligations associated with maintaining an effective and ethical college counseling practice.

College counselors participate in a constant balancing act, weighing their ethical obligations to students–clients against their responsibility to support the mission of the educational institution that employs them. At times, it may seem as if they are in a no-win situation. If college counselors inflexibly support the ethical guidelines of the counseling profession, they may be in constant conflict with their institution. If college counselors inflexibly support the mission of the institution, they may eventually violate the ethical codes of the counseling profession. As Gilbert (1989) noted, "A psychological service agency in higher education has responsibilities to individuals, institution, and profession and all too often finds itself caught between the rock and the hard place of these conflicting loyalties" (p. 477).

Gilbert (1989) suggested the following guidelines for college counselors when attempting to balance their professional ethical responsibilities and their obligations to the institution:

1. Client confidentiality takes precedence over the needs of the institution, except in situations that involve harm to self or others. The limits and necessity of confidentiality are defined by ethical guidelines and by state laws. The policies of the institution must not run contrary to the laws of the state in which it is located.

2. College counseling centers should be considered administratively neutral. In this way, the center's staff can most effectively assist both students and the institution. It is an appropriate role of the counseling center to evaluate students for possible hospitalization or for more extensive outpatient treatment. It is the role of the

university administration to determine a student's fitness for academic study on the basis of outward actions and behaviors. The counseling center should not make decisions on a student's suspension from a residence hall or removal from school; these are administrative roles.

3. A client's diagnoses or psychotherapeutic treatment should not affect that client's status at the institution. A student's academic status should be dependent on his or her academic abilities, behavior, and attendance. For example, a female student struggling with anorexia should not be dismissed from the institution because of the diagnosis. This same student may be withdrawn from the university (after reasonable accommodations have been made for her psychological diagnosis) because she cannot complete class assignments and has poor grades due to her inability to make it to class. It is in the best developmental interest of students to understand that there are clear boundaries for their behavior and academic performance that will be enforced by the university as a whole. In this way, stability is offered; ego development is supported; and students can take responsibility for their choices, actions, and behaviors on both interpersonal and intrapersonal dimensions. Institutions of higher education also should have clear policies concerning students with disabilities, so as to comply with the Adults With Disabilities Act (Schepp & Snodgrass, 1995).

4. An important role for college counselors within their institutions is that of consultant. College counselors provide universities with expertise that helps instructors, administrators, and support staff more effectively relate to the student population. Counselors help the university staff to better understand their role in student development and encourage their active participation in developmental work. For example, rather than providing a mandatory workshop on anger management that is required for students who are referred by the dean of students, the counseling center could consult with the dean's office regarding workshop contents, which could be presented by the dean's administrative staff.

5. All policies and procedures of the college counseling center and those of the institution regarding the college counseling center

should be reviewed and revised in light of effective ethical practice. The ethical codes for each profession represented at the counseling center (e.g., professional counselors, psychologists, social workers) should be included in that review.

6. College counselors must clearly understand the administrative structure of their institution, how college counselors' role is viewed by administration, and how individual college counselors perceive their role or roles within that institution. Additionally, college counselors must advocate for their professional identity and job within the institution in order to minimize ethical conflicts. Chapter 13, "Building Effective Campus Relationships," provides further discussion about college counselors' relationships with institutional constituents.

7. College counselors must actively seek consultation and connection with other college counselors regarding evolving ethical dilemmas, current trends in the field, and professional renewal. Interaction with other college counselors occurs on local, regional, and national levels through membership in relevant professional organizations (e.g., American College Counseling Association, American College Personnel Association, state college counseling organizations) and attendance at conferences and workshops (e.g., Southern College Counseling Center Personnel Conference). Another excellent resource for college counselors is the E-mail listserv of the American College Counseling Association, ACCA-L (contact information is available from http://www.collegecounseling.org). Here, college counselors around the world exchange information, discuss relevant topics, and provide and obtain support for the ethical practice of college counseling. Finally, college counselors must stay abreast of developing trends in ethical issues by reviewing relevant professional journals (e.g., *Journal of College Counseling, Journal of College Student Psychotherapy*) and taking advantage of continuing education opportunities.

SUMMARY

This chapter has outlined the many ethical decisions that a college counselor faces. They include issues of confidentiality, dual relationships, and mandatory counseling. Each issue has a twist that requires the college counselor to consider carefully the welfare of the student client, the needs of the institution, and the role of the counselor in a college or university setting. Counseling on a college campus has grown more complex. Therefore, it is increasingly important to have in-depth knowledge of the legal and ethical issues that surround the work of college counselors. It is equally important that college counseling centers clearly communicate these issues to the institution's administration. Yet, even armed with that knowledge and supported with clear policy, the issues raised in this chapter do not always have simple or explicit answers.

College counselors must diligently maintain high standards of practice and ethics to ensure that students receive high-quality counseling services. This work not only ensures appropriate and effective counseling but also provides the counselor with a clear identity in the higher education environment and enhanced protection from liability.

REFERENCES

American Counseling Association. (1995). *ACA code of ethics and standards of practice*. Alexandria, VA: Author.

Anfang, S. A., & Appelbaum, P. S. (1996). Twenty years after Tarasoff: Reviewing the duty to protect. *Harvard Review of Psychiatry, 4,* 67–76.

Archer, J., & Cooper, S. (1998). *Counseling and mental health services on campus: A handbook of contemporary practices and challenges*. San Francisco: Jossey-Bass.

Corey, G., Corey, M. S., & Callanan, P. (1998). *Issues and ethics in the helping professions* (5th ed.). Pacific Grove, CA: Brooks/Cole.

Dixon, W. A., Rumford, K. G., Heppner, P. P., & Lips, B. J. (1992). Use of different sources of stress to predict hopelessness and suicide ideation in a college population. *Journal of Counseling Psychology, 39,* 342–349.

Fulero, S. M. (1988). Tarasoff: 10 years later. *Professional Psychology: Research and Practice, 19,* 184–190.

Gilbert, S. P. (1989). The juggling act of the college counseling center: A point of view. *Counseling Psychologist, 17,* 477–489.

Gilbert, S. P. (1992). Ethical issues in the treatment of severe psychopathology in university and college counseling centers. *Journal of Counseling and Development, 70,* 695–699.

Gilbert, S. P., & Sheiman, J. A. (1995). Mandatory counseling of university students: An oxymoron? *Journal of College Student Psychotherapy, 9*(4), 3–21.

Grayson, P. A. (1986). Mental health confidentiality on the small campus. *Journal of American College Health, 34,* 187–191.

Harding, A. K., Gray, L. A., & Neal, M. (1993). Confidentiality limits with clients who have HIV: A review of ethical and legal guidelines and professional policies. *Journal of Counseling and Development, 71,* 297–305.

Hayman, P. M., & Covert, J. A. (1986). Ethical dilemmas in college counseling centers. *Journal of Counseling and Development, 64,* 318–320.

Herlihy, B., & Corey, G. (1992). *Dual relationships in counseling.* Alexandria, VA: American Counseling Association.

Herlihy, B., & Corey, G. (1997). *Boundary issues in counseling: Multiple roles and responsibilities.* Alexandria, VA: American Counseling Association.

Hersh, J. B. (1985). Interviewing college students in crisis. *Journal of Counseling and Development, 63,* 286–289.

Kaplan, D. M., & Rothrock, D. R. (1991). Ethical dilemmas in college counseling: The doctor is in! *Journal of College Student Psychotherapy, 6,* 15–36.

Kitchener, K. S., & Harding, S. S. (1990). Dual role relationships. In B. Herlihy & L. G. Golden (Eds.), *AACD ethical standards casebook* (4th ed., pp. 146–154). Alexandria, VA: American Association for Counseling and Development.

Knight, J. (1995, November 17). The misuse of mandatory counseling. *The Chronicle of Higher Education,* pp. B1–B2.

McGuire, J., Nieri, D., Abbott, D., Sheridan, K., & Fisher, R. (1995). Do Tarasoff principles apply in AIDS-related psychotherapy? Ethical decision making and the role of therapist homophobia and perceived client dangerousness. *Professional Psychology: Research and Practice, 26,* 608–611.

Murphy, M. C., & Archer, J. (1996). Stressors on the college campus: A comparison of 1985 and 1993. *Journal of College Student Development, 37,* 20–28.

O'Malley, K. O., Wheeler, I., Murphey, J., O'Connell, J., & Waldo, M. (1990). Changes in levels of psychopathology being treated at college and university counseling centers. *Journal of College Student Development, 31,* 464–465.

Pledge, D. S., Lapan, R. T., Heppner, P. P., Kivlighan, D., & Roehlke, H. J. (1998). Stability and severity of presenting problems at a university counseling center: A 6-year analysis. *Professional Psychology: Research and Practice, 29,* 386–389.

Schepp, K. F., & Snodgrass, G. (1995, October). *Psychological disability: A dialogue on counseling center involvement.* Paper presented at the annual convention of the Association of College Counseling Center Directors, Newport, RI.

Stone, G. L., & Archer, J. (1990). College and university counseling centers in the 1990s: Challenges and limits. *Counseling Psychologist, 18,* 539–607.

Stone, G. L., & Lucas, J. (1990). Knowledge and beliefs about confidentiality on a university campus. *Journal of College Student Development, 31,* 437–444.

Stone, G. L., & Lucas, J. (1994). Disciplinary counseling in higher education: A neglected challenge. *Journal of Counseling and Development, 72,* 234–238.

Welfel, E. R. (1998). *Ethics in counseling and psychotherapy: Standards, research, and emerging issues.* Pacific Grove, CA: Brooks/Cole.

PART II

COUNSELING TODAY'S COLLEGE STUDENTS

6

College Students' Problems: Status, Trends, and Research

JOHN B. BISHOP, ROBERT P. GALLAGHER, AND DEBORAH COHEN

FOCUS QUESTIONS

1. What are the sources of information about the problems of college students?

2. What are the identifiable trends in the current type and severity of college students' problems?

3. How can college counselors use the research about college students' problems to enhance their services?

4. How can research on the problems of college students be improved?

This chapter examines current research, status, and trends in college students' problems. Suggestions for using this information to enhance college counseling services are offered along with recommendations for improving the overall research on the problems of college students. A "Taxonomy of Client Problems Seen in College Counseling Centers" is provided.

ISSUES

College counselors use a variety of approaches to identify the kinds of problems experienced by their clientele. Beyond the obvious need for counselors to identify a student's problem before developing a treatment plan, the broader interest in documenting the types of problems that confront college students is twofold: (a) to affirm that students do have identifiable problems that interfere with their ability to succeed academically and (b) to demonstrate the need for institutions to provide counseling and related services for students.

It can be assumed that college counseling centers were initially established in response to observable student problems and needs. It is also quite likely that the changing nature of these problems and needs over the years and the growing capability of educators to understand how these issues affect college achievement and personal growth have helped to shape and structure the modern counseling center.

SOURCES OF INFORMATION ABOUT COLLEGE STUDENTS' PROBLEMS

Diagnostic Systems

Historically, the first efforts to develop systems for identifying the problems of college counseling center clients were global in nature (Williamson & Darley, 1937), were intended to assist counselors in developing treatment plans (Bordin, 1946; Pepinsky, 1948), and were dependent on the judgments of clients made by counselors. For example, the Missouri Diagnostic Classification System was developed to classify students' problems according to both type and cause (Callis, 1965) and subsequently has been used in numerous research studies about counseling center clients. Nonetheless, there are continuing efforts to develop and use more sophisticated classification systems because of the complexity of clients' problems (Heppner et al., 1994), a wish to use more behavioral descriptions of clients' problems (Chandler & Gallagher, 1996), or adaptation to changes in service delivery systems that may require specific diagnostic information. The 4th edition of the *Diagnostic and Statistical Manual of Mental Disorders*, published by the American Psychiatric Association (1994), is one such standard that is used for describing psychiatric conditions and making diagnoses.

The use of diagnostic systems by college counselors has proved to be a viable source of information about the problems that are presented by students. Most often, such information is made available when it is reported in a professional journal as a part of a research effort or, more locally, in an annual report describing the clientele served by a particular counseling agency. The primary advantage offered by such data is that they are often simple to collect and easy to understand; the most obvious limitations are that the data may not adequately convey the complexities of the problems presented by clients (Heppner et al., 1994) and that there is little consistency among counseling centers about which systems are used. For example, the 4th edition of the *Diagnostic and Statistical Manual of Mental Disorders* (American Psychiatric Association, 1994) is reported to be used by less than 30% of centers (Gallagher, Gill, & Goldstrohm, 1998), perhaps because its relevance for use outside of psychiatric treatment programs has been questioned.

Problem Checklists

Another form of information about the types of problems presented by students is more empirical in nature and is dependent on clients' self-reports. The Mooney Problem Checklist (Mooney & Gordon, 1950), the Inventory of Interpersonal Problems (Horowitz, Rosenberg, Baer, Ureno, & Villasenor, 1988), the Inventory of Common Problems (Hoffman & Weiss, 1986), the Symptom Check List-90—Revised (Johnson, Ellison, & Heikkinen, 1989), and the College Adjustment Scales (Anton & Reed, 1991) are examples of some of the problem checklists that are often used to describe clients' concerns at many college counseling centers. Such instruments are easy to self-administer and are conducive to estimating the progress made in counseling, thereby offering counseling centers an attractive alternative for assessing clients' problems.

The data derived from various forms of problem checklists have proved to be useful, mainly as a way of describing the types and severity of problems presented at a specific counseling center. Beyond that, there again seems to be little standardization among counseling centers in the use of such instruments, perhaps because of the absence of any links to specific diagnostic criteria (Zalaquett & McManus, 1996) and the scarcity of psychometric information about their validity and reliability (Miller & Rice, 1993). These limitations have worked against checklist information being used to construct a broader understanding of the problems presented at college counseling centers.

Data Banks and Surveys

There are some notable efforts to combine information from a broad representation of college counseling centers to provide a more comprehensive database about the work done in these settings. Included in these efforts are various descriptors of client problems and issues, and the data are easily reported in a form that permits comparisons among institutions as well as counseling centers themselves.

The College and University Counseling Center Data Bank is supported by the University of Maryland and the Association of College and University Counseling Center Directors and has collected annual data from college and university counseling centers since 1962. Although descriptions of clients are typically divided into global categories (career-education indecision, emotional–social issues, or educational skill development), data are also often gathered about the prevalence of a few specific kinds of problems, such as eating disorders, substance abuse, and suicide (Magoon, 1998).

The National Survey of Counseling Center Directors has been conducted by the University of Pittsburgh and has paid particular attention to trends that are occurring with respect to certain kinds of client problems and the ways in which counseling centers adapt their practices and policies in response to emerging issues in the field (Gallagher et al., 1998). Although this annual survey began in 1981 as a project of the Association of College and University Counseling Center Directors and continues to be partially funded by that association, it now summarizes data received from more than 325 counseling centers per year and is published annually as a monograph by the International Association of Counseling Services, Inc.

Needs Assessments

It is obvious that a relatively small percentage of the total college student population avails itself of the services offered by campus counseling centers. It is therefore important to consider the problems that are experienced by the populations of students who do not make their needs known by approaching a counseling service. One method of collecting such information is to use a needs assessment inventory to survey a sample of the total student population. Gallagher (1992) noted the value in using such survey results to help set clinical priorities and outreach activities as well as sensitizing the campus community to the many stresses that college students experience and increasing the community's knowledge about available resources.

The results of such efforts have been reported infrequently (Baker, 1993; Bishop, Bauer, & Becker, 1998, Carney & Bark, 1976; Gallagher, Golin, & Kelleher, 1992; Gallagher & Scheuring, 1980) and often are not generalizable from campus to campus because of the use of different survey instruments. Nonetheless, any attempt to describe the problems of college students would be incomplete if uncommon, underreported, or population-specific issues were not identified (Bishop, 1995). For this reason alone, more efforts to conduct such studies would be of great value to those who counsel college students.

Trends in the Type and Severity of College Students' Problems

Any discussion of the common developmental and psychological problems experienced by college students must provide some description of types of issues to be included. Chandler and Gallagher (1996) developed a taxonomy based on information provided by counselors about student clients (**see Appendix A**). This empirically derived system attempts to categorize, in an understandable fashion, the types of problems presented at college and university counseling centers and provides a framework for helping others understand such information. It also has the potential to facilitate the systematic study of the problems of college students. In reviewing the current research about the trends in the problems of college students, it is helpful to distinguish between studies of counseling center clients and those involving the general college population.

Counseling Center Clients. One approach to identifying the problems of college students has been to survey counseling center personnel, with the goal of determining if clients' needs have changed over time. It is common to find studies that report at least the *perception* that clients are presenting increasingly more complex and severe problems to college counselors (Gallagher et al., 1998; O'Malley, Wheeler, Murphey, O'Connell, & Waldo, 1990; Robbins, May, & Corazzini, 1985).

The 1998 National Survey of Counseling Center Directors (Gallagher et al., 1998) reported that more than 75% of universities and colleges noticed an increase in the number of clients presenting with severe psychological problems and learning disabilities, with significant numbers of institutions also mentioning increases in problems relating to earlier sexual abuse (48%) and alcohol (45%). What is often unclear is whether such perceptions are based on some identifiable data that are being used by the respondent or are more impressionistic in nature. It is fair to guess that national surveys of this type may include both types of information.

Sharf (1989) noted that a few difficult cases may bias the perceptions of counseling center staff in creating a sense that the problems clients present are more severe than objective data would support. Most counseling centers do deal with such cases. For example, Gallagher et al. (1998) found that 86% of counseling centers had to hospitalize a student for psychological reasons and that 27% of surveyed institutions reported a student suicide during the preceding year. Sharkin (1997) called for counseling centers to make efforts to provide more empirical evidence about the changes that may be occurring in the college student population to determine if the perceptions of counseling center personnel can be substantiated. Toward this end, the major annual surveys of counseling centers do include some validating information about the frequencies of specific client problems, suicide attempts, hospitalizations, and other indicators of psychological distress (Gallagher et al., 1998; Magoon, 1998).

Even if Sharkin's (1997) advice is heeded, Archer and Cooper (1998) pointed out that cultural norms may be shifting with regard to how psychological problems are regarded. Some of the negative feelings about seeking counseling or admitting that a problem exists have changed. Certainly, it is now more culturally acceptable to admit to past physical or sexual abuse, depression, anxiety, or panic attack than was true for previous generations. In addition, O'Malley et al. (1990) pointed out that there are greater levels of untreated mental illnesses in society at large and that student populations in higher education include increased diversity of all kinds, including individuals with diagnosable disorders. Such a shift in norms may also have an effect on how relatively severe a problem is judged to be by a professional counselor.

Few large-scale studies have attempted to document the type and severity of psychological problems of counseling center clients. Johnson et al. (1989) evaluated 1,589 clients by using the Symptom Check List-90—Revised and found that at least 25% of all clients and 33% of all those seeking help for personal problems had psychiatrically diagnosable disorders when compared with adolescent norms. Women reported more severe symptomatology than did men at the time of initial contact.

Chandler and Gallagher (1996) asked a sample of 474 college counselors to behaviorally describe the problems of 8,462 clients. The frequency distributions of problem areas among students included relationship difficulties (69%), self-esteem issues (59%), depression (45%), anxiety (35%), and stress (29%). Academic and career concerns were less frequently represented in the population.

General Student Population. Efforts to assess changes in the prevalence or severity of problems in the general college student population seem to be limited. There are few examples in the professional literature of longitudinal studies of trends in college students' problems. In addition, needs assessment efforts have mostly been limited to a particular institution and seldom use the same surveys or assessment devices. Still, there are some notable exceptions.

A student needs survey was administered in 1980 by Gallagher and Scheuring and in 1992 by Gallagher et al. to a 10% random sample of students at an urban university. The findings revealed that students in the 1992 survey expressed a greater need for assistance in most problem categories than did students in the earlier survey. The differences between the two samples were more dramatic in problem areas such as loneliness, anxiety, fear of failure, and suicidal feelings.

Mayes and McConatha (1982) used the Mooney Problem Checklist to illustrate how the problems of incoming students changed from 1969 to 1980 and reported an increase in concern about personal issues. Koplik and DeVito (1986) used the same instrument to compare the 1st-year classes of 1976 and 1986 at Fordham University and found that students in the latter group reported more distress in every aspect of their lives. Another longitudinal effort by Murphy and Archer (1996) used a survey instrument to compare the most frequently identified student needs in 1985 with those in 1993 and found a great deal of stability over that period of time. Still, academic stressors relating to grades, competition, professors, class environment, studying, papers, and essay exams were found to increase. Personal stress also increased in relation to finances and current jobs.

One of the first attempts to assess the potential counseling needs of college students (Weissberg, Berentsen, Cote, Cravey, & Heath, 1982) reported that academic, educational, and career issues, as opposed to personal concerns, were viewed as more frequently requiring counseling. In fact, students in this study expressed extremely strong needs in the career development area; however, the need for assistance with normal developmental concerns of a personal nature was also notable in more than 40% of the surveyed population.

In 1992, Gallagher et al. surveyed 608 university students and again found that career concerns were ranked higher than personal or academic concerns. Specific career problem areas included the need to determine career interests and abilities, make career choices, and develop effective job search strategies. The most common personal concerns focused on procrastination, public speaking anxiety, and self-confidence, but more serious problems were also evident in the sample. For example, depression (26%), finding purpose in life (26%), loneliness (20%), anger management (14%), and suicidal feelings (7%) were reported by students in the study. The most common academic need was the improvement of study skills.

Six years after Gallagher et al.'s (1992) study was reported, the same needs assessment instrument was used by Bishop et al. (1998) at a different university to survey 803 students. Although many similarities to Gallagher et al.'s results were noted with regard to career and academic concerns, more than 35% of students reported negative feelings related to a fear of failure, depression, anxiety or panic, weight control, romantic relationships, or public speaking. Bishop et al. noted the considerable potential such issues may have to negatively affect the academic success of students.

There are also other kinds of large-scale national surveys of college students that produce data of interest to college counselors. For example, the Harvard School of Public Health (Wechsler, Dowdall, Maenner, Gledhill-Hoyt, & Lee, 1998) has focused on the binge drinking of alcohol among college students and has noted the alcohol-related problems that are created. Another form of national data comes from the annual survey of college freshmen that is conducted by the Higher Education Research Institute (1998). In 1998, in a sample of more than 275,000 students, 9.3% reported that they had felt depressed in the past year, with 65.9% taking prescribed antidepressants. Finally, surveys of college men and women generally show a high incidence of rape and other forms of sexual aggression (Koss, Gidycz, & Wisnewski, 1987). College counselors certainly ought to be aware of such data and help communicate those data to others on campus to confirm that students do experience problems and are in need of counseling services.

USING RESEARCH TO ENHANCE COUNSELING SERVICES

As we pointed out earlier in this chapter, research on the nature of the problems of counseling center clients or the general college student population has been carried out for more than half a century, and yet the published reports continue to be relatively sparse. This may have to do with the fact that college counselors tend to be more practice-oriented rather than research-oriented, are not generally in tenure-track positions, and tend to work in settings where research is not highly regarded.

In a national survey of counseling center directors, only 15.6% of the respondents viewed research for publication as an essential activity, and only 10% of the chief student affairs officers (CSAOs) to whom these directors reported thought that such research was an essential function (Gallagher, Gill, & Goldstrohm, 1997). In addition, Stone and Archer (1990) described a survey that reported that only 2% of counseling center staff's time was devoted to research activities. Steenbarger and Manchester (1990) even suggested that, although time constraints and lack of interest are factors in this low research productivity, practitioners may be somewhat phobic about research.

Stone and Archer (1990), however, argued that the reluctance of college counselors to carry out research may have to do with their tendency to equate research with the carefully designed and controlled studies that appear in professional journals. They suggested that a more useful definition of research is provided by the International Association of Counseling Services, which encourages centers to conduct studies to assess the effectiveness of their services, to help them improve the quality of their programs, or both.

Counseling center directors do seem to place greater importance on research when it is defined in this broader manner. Although, as mentioned earlier, only 15.6% of counseling center directors reported that research for publication is an essential center activity, 39.8% rated research that helps to educate the campus community about student characteristics to be essential. An even higher percentage (52%) of the CSAOs to whom they reported rated this type of research as an essential activity (Gallagher et al., 1997).

This latter finding is particularly important to college counselors. If CSAOs are viewing this type of activity as more valuable than counseling center directors, this is a difference that deserves attention. Other data are available to suggest that counseling center administrators are not particularly well-attuned to the perceptions of their bosses. In the previously mentioned survey of both counseling center directors and CSAOs (Gallagher et al., 1997), directors were also asked to predict how their own CSAO would respond and underestimated the value their superior placed on a number of activities, including group therapy, crisis intervention, the training of others on campus who work with students, the need for psychiatric backup, skills training, specialized sexual assault programs, and treatment of whatever length is necessary for sexual assault survivors. It was encouraging to learn that these senior administrators were so supportive of the services that directors also viewed as important but surprising to find that directors so clearly underestimated the extent to which the CSAOs considered these services to be essential.

We also reported earlier in this chapter that counseling center personnel have been noting an increase in the severity of students' psychological problems for at least the past decade. These data have not been lost on CSAOs. Levine and Cureton (1998), drawing from a 1997 survey of 270 CSAOs conducted by the Harvard School of Education, reported that the majority of these senior administrators believe that students are coming to college more psychologically damaged than in previous years and are greatly concerned about what they are observing. It is possible that they would be very receptive to recommendations from college counseling centers on how to better address these problems if such beliefs could be documented through research efforts. For example, in recent years, there has been some evidence of a positive change in the hiring of college counselors in that counseling centers have reported gaining more new professional positions than were lost (Gallagher et al., 1997, 1998). This has reversed a trend that had been noted in previous years. If this change in hiring practices is indeed a result of the increased sensitivity of higher education administrators, it can reasonably be assumed that these individuals have been affected by the national and local research on students' problems.

The potential usefulness of national survey data can be seen in the responses of the 325 counseling center directors who responded to the 1998 National Survey of Counseling Center Directors (Gallagher et al., 1998). The directors were asked how they had used the results of the previous year's survey. It is noteworthy that 73% shared the data with their CSAO, 64% shared it with staff, 52% quoted data for in-house or institutional reports, 43% shared data with others on campus, 42% used the data to support a request for new resources, and 14% used the data in their professional writing.

Locally developed student needs surveys also can have unexpected benefits for a college counseling center. In one published report on such benefits (Gallagher, 1992), the results of a student needs survey not only provided useful data for setting clinical priorities and focusing outreach activities for counseling center programs but also helped to sensitize the campus community to the many stresses its students were experiencing and increased the community's knowledge of available services. As a consequence, the student newspaper published several lengthy articles on the findings and then established a regular counseling center column focusing on student concerns. The campus radio station ran several programs based on the findings of the survey. The vice president for student affairs used the data in presentations on and off campus. A brief report on the survey was sent to all department chairs, which resulted in a number of invitations for counseling center staff to speak at departmental faculty meetings. Similar presentations were made to student affairs directors, resident assistants, academic advisers, student health center staff, and various student organizations. The school of business also built a seminar for faculty around the survey and titled it "How to Make the School of Business a Healthier Environment for Students."

One result of all this activity was a dramatic increase in the number of referrals to the center, which in turn was used to successfully justify the funding of a new counselor's position. Other benefits included some spin-off research ideas that served as the basis for five different master's theses by graduate students.

In thinking further about the importance of research to the work of college counselors, it is obvious that such data often illustrate the problems that counselors encounter in their work and emphasize the need for counseling staff to continue to expand their knowledge base about new approaches to addressing these kinds of problems in settings that often are committed to short-term counseling models. For example, an increase in the severity of psychological problems in the student population might suggest that college counselors should become more informed about pharmaceutical treatments and work in partnership with medical personnel and external agencies to meet the longer term therapy needs of some students.

In contrast, there is ample evidence from student needs surveys that the most dominant concerns do not fall into categories of severe psychological problems. For instance, in the Chandler and Gallagher (1996) study mentioned earlier, the analysis of 8,462 clients of college counseling centers revealed that the most frequently reported problems were relationship difficulties (69.9%) and self-esteem problems (59.6%). Other primary concerns of students frequently involved issues such as career uncertainty, time management problems, public speaking anxiety, test anxiety, and fear of academic failure, as well as the more commonly discussed problems of depression and generalized anxiety. Such research evidence strongly suggests that today's well-rounded counselor must not lose sight of the fact that the majority of students on college campuses continue to need help in moving through the normal developmental crises of this age group.

IMPROVING RESEARCH ON THE PROBLEMS OF COLLEGE STUDENTS

The need for quality research on the changing problems of college students will, quite likely, continue to grow as the demands for accountability and effective use of available resources increase. There is also a need for studies that would establish baseline incidence and prevalence data on a variety of personal problems that are brought to college counseling centers, preferably using some form of standardized classification and measurement systems. It is our belief that there is an expanding need in higher education for information of this kind, and consequently, it will be important for data to be quickly accessible and broadly distributed. Furthermore, it is anticipated that national surveys that track emerging trends will continue, but pressure will increase for these surveys to be conducted electronically and made available on the Internet.

A series of studies in this regard were carried out and are continuing to be developed by the Association of College and University Counseling Center Directors Research Consortium, which is based at the University of Texas (Barón, 1993; Drum & Barón, 1996). The further standardization of the instrument developed by Chandler and Gallagher (1996) and described earlier would also provide a mechanism for gathering more consistent data about client problem trends in college counseling centers nationwide. Such developments would allow comparisons to be made among different centers as well as improve the ability to track changes over time.

In regard to on-campus research, it will be important for counseling centers to track not only the nature of the problems that students bring to their counseling centers but also the problems of the student body at large, many of whom are in need of psychological assistance. In fact, there is some evidence (Gallagher et al., 1992) that for every student who seeks help at a college counseling center, there are six to eight students with similar needs for assistance who do not seek it.

Although legitimate criticisms of needs surveys of this type have been made because of the limitations of self-report surveys (Barrow, Cox, Sepich, & Spivak, 1989), they continue, nevertheless, to be one of the most efficient means of identifying college students' concerns, and the use of a common needs assessment format will help overcome the difficulty in generalizing from the results of single-campus studies. For example, following the publication of two articles on student needs that used the same survey instrument (Bishop et al., 1998; Gallagher et al., 1992), permission was given by the authors to more than 100 requesting institutions that wished to use the instrument (or a modified version of it) on their own campuses. No attempt was made to determine if the instrument was actually used by these campuses, but there does seem to be an interest in finding a standard instrument that could be used across a large number of institutions to conduct needs assessment research.

One important observation about student needs surveys is that they do provide evidence that large numbers of students on college campuses experience psychological distress of one sort or another without seeking counseling services. In fact, the numbers are so significant that if all such students were inclined to seek psychological assistance, counseling centers would be overwhelmed and unable to provide the level of assistance that is currently available on most campuses. Consequently, counselors need to give some thought to creative ways of helping these students in less traditional ways. These methods could include writing articles on psychoeducational topics in campus newspapers; developing a counseling center web page that provides assistance, information, and links to Internet resources; working to create healthier campus environments; and training faculty and other people who have significant contact with students to respond in more supportive and helpful ways to students who exhibit signs of psychological distress.

There is also a need to have a better understanding of how students would prefer to receive information on assistance with their personal concerns. A 1992 needs survey by Gallagher et al. asked students about such preferences, and although the majority of the respondents (64.1%) preferred to receive individual counseling, almost as many (62.8%) also favored receiving printed material that related to their concerns. This was a marked change from the results of a survey conducted 12 years earlier that found only 34% of students preferred printed materials (Gallagher & Scheuring, 1980). Another shift in preferences from the previous survey was "discussion in academic courses," which was favored by 38% of the 1992 sample as compared with only 4% of the 1980 respondents. The latter two findings may reflect the increased accessibility of self-help literature and, perhaps, the more recent willingness of college instructors to engage in dialogue about these issues in their classrooms. Again, this is an issue that deserves more research attention because we must know more about the kind of supplemental reading material that could be used to facilitate the work of students who do seek formal counseling.

The available studies on college needs also raise other questions about the needs of specific populations. For example, Bishop et al. (1998) found that women had significantly more needs than men for assistance with test anxiety, feelings of depression, lack of assertiveness, public speaking anxiety, feelings of inadequacy, feelings of emotional instability, and somatic complaints. Female students also had many more fears about the future than did male students. Some of these differences may be related to the willingness of women to admit that they have such problems, or they may speak to pressures that women on college campuses experience that are different from the pressures that male college students experience. There is clearly a need for more data to determine whether these female–male differences are common on college campuses and how to best explain them if these differences do exist. In a similar vein, more studies are needed to understand the apparent differences in counseling center needs that exist between various groups: younger and older students, resident and nonresident students, and, in particular, among underrepresented populations. The survey utilized by Gallagher et al. (1992) has been used in comparative studies between self-identified procrastinating and nonprocrastinating students, between heterosexual and gay or lesbian students, between Caucasian and African American students, and between students who experienced sexual assault and those who did not.

SUMMARY

As college counselors, we need to know more about the current and the emerging needs of students who come to our centers and those who do not but are nevertheless in our charge. Through our increased knowledge of the problems that students experience, we hopefully will be in a better position to develop more effective services and provide greater assistance to our colleagues in higher education who often look to us for help in improving the overall quality of life on campus for all students.

REFERENCES

American Psychiatric Association. (1994). *Diagnostic and statistical manual of mental disorders* (4th ed.). Washington, DC: Author.

Anton, W. D., & Reed, J. R. (1991). *College Adjustment Scales professional manual.* Odessa, FL: Psychological Assessment Resources.

Archer, J., Jr., & Cooper, S. (1998). *Counseling and mental health services on campus.* San Francisco: Jossey-Bass.

Baker, H. K. (1993). Counseling needs and graduate student characteristics. *Journal of College Student Development, 34,* 74–75.

Barón, A., Jr. (1993). *Report of the Research Consortium of Counseling and Psychological Services in Higher Education.* Unpublished manuscript, University of Texas Counseling Center, Austin.

Barrow, J., Cox, P., Sepich, R., & Spivak, R. (1989). Student needs assessment surveys: Do they predict student use of services? *Journal of College Student Development, 30,* 77–82.

Bishop, J. B. (1995). Emerging administrative strategies for college and university counseling centers. *Journal of Counseling and Development, 74,* 33–38.

Bishop, J. B., Bauer, K. W., & Becker, E. T. (1998). A survey of counseling needs of male and female college students. *Journal of College Student Development, 39,* 205–210.

Bordin, E. S. (1946). Diagnosis in counseling and psychotherapy. *Educational and Psychological Measurement, 6*, 169–184.

Callis, R. (1965). Diagnostic classification as a research tool. *Journal of Counseling Psychology, 12*, 238–247.

Carney, C. G., & Bark, A. (1976). A survey of student needs and student personnel services. *Journal of College Student Personnel, 17*, 280–284.

Chandler, L. A., & Gallagher, R. P. (1996). Developing a taxonomy for problems seen at a university counseling center. *Measurement and Evaluation in Counseling and Development, 29*, 4–12.

Drum, D. J., & Barón, A., Jr. (1996). *Prepared protocol: Research consortium*. Unpublished manuscript, University of Texas Counseling Center, Austin.

Gallagher, R. P. (1992). Student needs surveys have multiple benefits. *Journal of College Student Development, 33*, 281–282.

Gallagher, R. P., Gill, A. M., & Goldstrohm, S. L. (1997). *National Survey of Counseling Center Directors*. Alexandria, VA: International Association of Counseling Services.

Gallagher, R. P., Gill, A. M., & Goldstrohm, S. L. (1998). *National Survey of Counseling Center Directors*. Alexandria, VA: International Association of Counseling Services.

Gallagher, R. P., Golin, A., & Kelleher, K. (1992). The personal, career, and learning skills needs of college students. *Journal of College Student Development, 33*, 301–309.

Gallagher, R. P., & Scheuring, S. B. (1980). The personal concerns troubling students at today's urban university. *Pennsylvania Personnel and Guidance Journal, 7*, 61–70.

Heppner, P. P., Kivlighan, D. M., Good, G. E., Roehlke, H. J., Hills, H. I., & Ashby, J. S. (1994). Presenting problems of university counseling center clients: A snapshot and multivariate classification scheme. *Journal of Counseling Psychology, 41*, 315–324.

Higher Education Research Institute. (1998). *The American freshman: National norms for Fall 1998*. Los Angeles: UCLA Graduate School of Education and Information Studies.

Hoffman, J. A., & Weiss, B. (1986). A new system for conceptualizing college students' problems: Types of crises and the Inventory of Common Problems. *Journal of American College Health, 34*, 259–266.

Horowitz, L. M., Rosenberg, S. E., Baer, B. A., Ureno, G., & Villasenor, V. S. (1988). Inventory of Interpersonal Problems: Psychometric properties and clinical applications. *Journal of Consulting and Clinical Psychology, 56*, 885–892.

Johnson, R. W., Ellison, R. A., & Heikkinen, C. A. (1989). Psychological symptoms of counseling center clients. *Journal of Counseling Psychology, 36*, 110–114.

Koplik, E. K., & DeVito, A. J. (1986). Problems of freshmen: Comparison of classes of 1976 and 1986. *Journal of College Student Personnel, 27*, 124–130.

Koss, M. P., Gidycz, C. A., & Wisnewski, N. (1987). The scope of rape: Incidence and prevalence of sexual aggression and victimization in a national sample of higher education students. *Journal of Consulting and Clinical Psychology, 55*, 162–170.

Levine, A., & Cureton, J. (1998). *When hope and fear collide*. San Francisco: Jossey-Bass.

Magoon, T. M. (1998). *College and university counseling centers data bank*. College Park: University of Maryland Counseling Center.

Mayes, A. N., & McConatha, J. (1982). Surveying student needs: A means of evaluating student services. *Journal of College Student Personnel, 23*, 473–476.

Miller, G. A., & Rice, K. G. (1993). A factor analysis of a university counseling center problem checklist. *Journal of College Student Development, 34*, 98–102.

Mooney, R. L., & Gordon, L. V. (1950). *Manual: The Mooney Problem Checklist*. New York: Psychological Corporation.

Murphy, M. C., & Archer, J., Jr. (1996). Stressors on the college campus: A comparison of 1985 and 1993. *Journal of College Student Development, 37*, 20–28.

O'Malley, K., Wheeler, I., Murphey, J., O'Connell, J., & Waldo, M. (1990). Changes in levels of psychopathology being treated at college and university counseling centers. *Journal of College Student Development, 31*, 464–465.

Pepinsky, H. P. (1948). *The selection and use of diagnostic categories in clinical counseling*. Stanford, CA: Stanford University Press.

Robbins, S. B., May, T. M., & Corazzini, J. G. (1985). Perceptions of client needs and counseling center staff roles and functions. *Journal of Counseling Psychology, 32*, 641–644.

Sharf, R. S. (1989). Have the presenting problems of clients at university counseling centers increased in severity? *NASPA Journal, 27*, 141–146.

Sharkin, B. S. (1997). Increasing severity of presenting problems in college counseling centers: A closer look. *Journal of Counseling and Development, 75*, 275–281.

Steenbarger, B. V., & Manchester, R. A. (1990). Research in college health: An introduction to the research process. *Journal of American College Health, 39*, 119–124.

Stone, G. L. & Archer, J., Jr. (1990). College and university counseling centers in the 1990s: Challenges and limits. *Counseling Psychologist, 19*, 539–607.

Wechsler, H., Dowdall, G. W., Maenner, G., Gledhill-Hoyt, J., & Lee, H. (1998). Changes in binge drinking and related problems among American college students between 1993 and 1997. *Journal of American College Health, 47*, 57–68.

Weissberg, M., Berentsen, M., Cote, A., Cravey, B., & Heath, K. (1982). An assessment of the personal, career, and academic needs of undergraduate students. *Journal of College Student Personnel, 23,* 115–122.

Williamson, E. G., & Darley, J. G. (1937). *Student personnel work.* New York: McGraw-Hill.

Zalaquett, C. P., & McManus, P. W. (1996). A university counseling center problem checklist: A factor analysis. *Journal of College Student Development, 37,* 692–697.

APPENDIX A

A Taxonomy of Client Problems Seen in College and University Counseling Centers

Personal and Social Adjustment
Relationship Difficulties
- Anger/irritability/impulse control
- Breakup of a relationship
- Dating concerns
- Death of a significant other
- Problems making friends/loneliness
- Family/parents/siblings
- Romantic partner/spouse

Self-Esteem
- Self-image
- Shyness
- Self-confidence/assertiveness
- Fear of failure

Existential Concerns
- Meaning of life
- Role of religion
- Value conflicts

Depression
- Suicidal feelings or thoughts
- Feelings of hopelessness
- Grief over loss

Sexual Abuse and Harassment
- Abuse
- Harassment

Academic and Career Concerns
Academic Concerns
- School performance
- Procrastination
- Poor study skills
- Grades

Career Concerns
- Career uncertainty
- Career path unclear
- Lack of knowledge about interests/abilities

Stress and Psychosomatic Symptoms

Stress
- Headaches/stomachaches
- Insomnia
- Posttraumatic stress disorder

Anxiety
- Problems concentrating
- Performance anxiety
- Nervousness
- Irrational fears/phobias
- Panic attacks

Distressing Symptoms
- Substance abuse
- Drugs/alcohol

Sexual Dysfunction
- Arousal problems
- Impotency

Eating Disorders
- Anorexia
- Bulimia
- Body image problems

Unusual Behavior
- Confused thinking
- Hallucinations
- Social isolate
- Paranoid ideation
- Borderline personality

7

Traditional-Age College Students

PATTY GALATAS VON STEEN

FOCUS QUESTIONS

1. What are the characteristics of today's traditional-age college student population? How are they different from yesterday's college students?

2. What developmental issues and transitions do traditional-age college students experience?

3. How can college counselors effectively address the needs of traditional-age college students?

ISSUES

The current generation of 18–24-year-olds, often labeled *Generation Xers, twenty somethings, posties,* or *neXters,* constitutes a group identified as "traditional-age students" who are attending college as the new millennium begins. Although the number of traditional-age students has declined in recent years, giving way to a dramatic increase in the number of nontraditional-age college students, 18–24-year-olds are still a major constituency on today's college campuses (TIAA–CREF, 1998), and enrollment growth through 2005 projects an increase in the number of traditional-age students on campus (Frances, Pumerantz, & Caplan, 1999). They bring to college unique viewpoints and experiences that make them different, in some ways, from the traditional-age students of earlier years. It is important that college counselors understand the viewpoints and experiences of traditional-age college students if they are to provide competent and useful counseling services to them. Indeed, college counselors must also prepare themselves for the challenges of the next generation of traditional-age students, the teenagers of the 1990s (Generation Yers) who will emerge very shortly on American college campuses.

This chapter explores some of the ways in which traditional-age college students (Generation Xers and Generation Yers) differ from yesterday's college students and examines their unique developmental experiences. The chapter concludes with recommendations to assist college counselors in working effectively with traditional-age college students.

Characteristics of Today's Traditional-Age College Students

There are some interesting differences between today's traditional-age college students and their predecessors. Many of today's traditional-age students work while attending college, and some rely heavily on that employment to pay for their college education. A study by the National Center for Education Statistics (1998) indicated that four out of five undergraduates reported working while enrolled in postsecondary education, and 50% of students were employed more than 20 hours per week. As Levine and Cureton (1998) noted, "Students [working full-time] don't work their way through college; rather, they work college into their lives" (p. 118).

Traditional-age college students often have some very clear ideas about achieving a certain quality of life, as opposed to simply achieving career success. They seek careers that allow them to balance their social and professional lives while also providing them with financial security (Burke, 1994; Cannon, 1991; Levine & Cureton, 1998). They are a generation that, in contrast to previous generations, has become increasingly disengaged from the political system and has resolved to rely on themselves for financial security.

The commitment to financial security does not negate the spirit of social activism for traditional-age college students. Activism on college campuses is still alive. However, today, student activists focus less on national-scale social and political issues and more on specific needs or injustices encountered on their campuses (e.g., gender equity, gay rights, civil rights, students' rights) and in their communities (e.g., literacy, homelessness, racial inequality; Coles, 1993; Kopp, 1992; Loeb & Magee, 1992). Students today believe they can make a difference but on a smaller scale than their predecessors. In fact, many colleges and universities have responded to the community commitment of traditional-age college students by creating campus-based service learning programs that creatively weave voluntary service into the academic curriculum (Hirsch, 1993; Levine & Cureton, 1998).

Traditional-age college students are reporting record levels of stress (Sax, Astin, Korn, & Mahoney, 1998) and coping with some serious issues, including substance use and abuse, sexually transmitted diseases, unwanted sexual experiences, and eating disorders. Binge drinking, consuming large amounts of alcohol at one time, is an especially serious problem on college campuses today. In one study of 14,521 students at 116 four-year institutions, researchers found that 2 out of 5 students (43%) were considered binge drinkers (Wechsler, Dowdall, Maenner, Gledhill-Hoyt, & Lee, 1998). The high rate of alcohol use on campus brings with it numerous associated problems, including sexual assault, injury, academic-related difficulties, and the risk of sexually transmitted diseases because of unsafe sexual practices (Pendergast, 1994; Ullman, Karabatsos, & Koss, 1999; Wechsler, 1996).

Sexually transmitted diseases and unintended pregnancies continue to be problems among traditional-age college students. Although today's traditional-age college students do report using contraceptives, limiting their number of sexual partners, and questioning their partners about their past sexual history (Simon, 1993), many students are still not using these safeguards. They continue to put themselves and others at risk by using unsafe sexual practices (Pendergast, 1994). Another important health risk, both physically and emotionally, for traditional-age college students is forced sexual intercourse. According to the U.S. Department of Justice National Crime Victim Survey, the highest incidence of sexual assault and rape in 1997 occurred to victims of two age groups: 16–19-year-olds and 20–24-year-olds (Rennison, 1999).

Students on today's college campuses are increasingly diverse with regard to age, gender, ethnicity, religion, disability, and sexual orientation. It is projected that minorities will represent 21% of the 18–24-year-old student population by the year 2000 (American Council on Education, 1998). Women may increase their share of the total college population to 57% by the year 2008 (National Center for Education Statistics, 1997). Many students embrace this diversity; some reject it. How traditional-age college students respond to this diversity is a unique challenge to their college experience. In fact, Levine and Cureton (1998) stated that multiculturalism "remains the most unresolved issue on campus today" (p. 91).

Critics of today's traditional-age students exclaim that Xers seem to be disengaged from learning. They claim that these students cannot read, do not engage in classroom discussion, and are not involved in campus activities. They increasingly live in single rooms, even in residence halls. Social contact through E-mail or chat rooms seems to encourage social disengagement. Even dating practices reflect a trend toward disengagement: Today's students are more likely to group date than spend significant time in one-on-one interactions.

The boom in technology has shaped how many of today's college students prepare for classes, communicate with their families, and make friends. They own fax machines, CDs, portable phones, and digital televisions. They rely on the World Wide Web to do research, Internet chat rooms to engage in discussions and to make virtual friends and companions, E-mail for rapid and frequent conversations, and individual web pages that serve as personal and professional testimonies. Some students are required by their institutions of higher education to purchase computers as they embark on their college journey. Others are being exposed to distance learning through on-line courses (Brown & Duguid, 1996; Pascarella & Terenzini, 1998).

Computers provide access to on-line learning, relationships for lonely or socially inhibited individuals, communication with distant family members, and stress release from academic rigors. However, they also have turned many traditional-age college students into computer addicts. There are concerns about the consequences of a "virtual" social life. One concern is that the identities of those on computers may have no relationship to who they are in reality. Brooks (1997) stated, "It is one thing to share information; it is quite another to connect on a personal level" (p. 9). Astin's (1996) research has shown that involvement in college is paramount to learning and personal development. If the primary level of interpersonal interaction occurs electronically, then it is likely that students are missing tremendous opportunities for personal growth.

As college campuses become increasingly diverse, it is obvious that "one-size-fits-all counseling" is ineffective. College counselors must recognize that traditional-age college students differ not only from the non-traditional students of today but also from 18–24-year-olds of a decade ago. Today's traditional-age students are increasingly diverse, frequently work, report high levels of stress, and arrive on campus with clear ideas about achieving a certain quality of life. They have been powerfully influenced by changing definitions of family and by technological innovation. Effective college counseling requires the ability to appropriately use both developmental and clinical perspectives within highly diverse student populations. The following section explores developmental issues and tasks common to traditional-age students.

Understanding Traditional-Age Students From a Developmental Perspective

A particularly unique facet of college counseling is the challenge of using diverse perspectives to conceptualize student problems and client issues. Effective college counselors are knowledgeable about developmental issues and transitions that commonly occur for traditional-age college students and also are knowledgeable about the signs and symptoms of mental disorders in this population. Thus, "good practice" in college counseling uses both perspectives, developmental and clinical, in providing effective treatment for students' problems. For example, a female freshman who has gained weight since beginning college comes to the counseling center describing homesickness and body image concerns. A counselor who assesses this client solely from a developmental perspective may see the weight gain as the result of environmental changes or as a struggle for independence and autonomy, therefore viewing the initial weight gain in the freshman year as normative. Counseling then might focus primarily on normalization of the weight gain, adjustment to college, and independence and autonomy issues. In contrast, a counselor who assesses this student from a purely clinical perspective may view this client's weight gain as being linked to disordered eating patterns and poor body image. Treatment would involve further assessment for the presence of a mental disorder, possibly a referral for psychotropic medication screening, and a primary focus on the eating and body image issues. An exclusive clinical perspective pathologizes the problem and may miss contributing developmental factors; an exclusive developmental perspective may not sufficiently address the long-term consequences of an undiagnosed eating disorder. College counselors must recognize that both developmental and clinical perspectives provide critical information for assessing and conceptualizing an appropriate treatment response.

The Journey From Freshman to Graduation. This section identifies key developmental issues and tasks that traditional-age college students frequently experience on their journey from freshman year through senior year. Categorization according to class designation is used here to simplify the discussion. The reader is reminded that college students, even traditional-age students, do not always fit into neatly defined groupings. Students drop out or stop out of school for indeterminate amounts of time or arrive at college with differing amounts of college credit that affect classification. Additionally, other factors, such as race, ethnicity, gender, sexual orientation, social and economic status, and disability, also influence development. For example, the developmental transitions of a traditional-age college student who is multiracial should be viewed in light of racial identity development (Wehrly, Kenney, & Kenney, 1999). The developmental experiences of a traditional-age college student who is gay, lesbian, or bisexual should be viewed in light of homosexual identity development (Evans & Wall, 1991; Wall & Evans, in press). Therefore, a flexible viewpoint regarding characteristics of various categories should be maintained.

Freshmen: "I'm free. Where do I go?" The first year of college is typically a period in which adolescents begin to differentiate from their families of origin and to achieve a greater degree of self-definition (Rice, 1992). This "separation–individuation" involves moving away from the predictable, known factors of their lives and into the less predictable world. Freshmen are stepping out of an environment that largely defined who they were intellectually, socially, physically, sexually, and spiritually and into a new phase of their life that potentially can challenge everything about their being. Some master the process without much disruption, whereas others struggle with separation–individuation. Factors that contribute to mastery or struggle include the nature of family relationships and levels of attachment (Imbimbo, 1995; Kenny & Donaldson, 1991; Lopez, 1991; McCurdy & Scherman, 1996; Rice, Fitzgerald, Whaley, & Gibbs, 1995), gender (Holmbeck & Wandrei, 1993; Rice, 1992), personality variables (Holmbeck & Wandrei, 1993), and whether they are the first generation to go to college (Terenzini et al. 1994).

Freshmen often expect college counselors to serve as their parentis in loci. That is, they look to their counselors, much as they looked in childhood to their parents and caregivers, for direction, affirmation, and answers. They want to know that what they are feeling is normal, and they seek guidance about coping with the sometimes painful transition toward autonomy. For example, how do I choose good friends? How do I become more independent of my parents? Should my loyalties lie with family and old friends or with new acquaintances at school? How do I cope with loneliness? What am I like in relationships that are not attached to my family or home? What does it mean to be accountable only to myself for where I am, when I go somewhere, and who I am with? Understandably, social life is very important to college freshmen, and it often takes precedence over their academic pursuits. Figuring out how to balance their social and academic worlds is an important challenge for traditional-age freshmen. Sometimes their attempts to answer the aforementioned questions and to balance their social and academic worlds may be problematic. Freshmen may engage in unhealthy behaviors, feel depressed, or become anxious. They may drink or use drugs to excess, withdraw, become attached to peers who encourage risky behaviors, have suicidal thoughts, or spend more time with family to avoid forming new attachments. College counselors will recognize most of these complaints as common to their freshmen clients.

Sophomores: "Do I stay or do I go?" Lemons and Richmond (1987) outlined the developmental struggles of sophomores by applying Chickering's model of college student development (Chickering & Reisser, 1993). They concluded that the slump that often characterizes students' sophomore year is marked by struggles with achieving competence, desiring autonomy, establishing identity, and developing purpose. In the first year of college, many similarities were shared with their fellow freshmen. Now, as sophomores, those similarities give way to differences. This differentiation often comes at a time when they move from the insulated, segregated freshmen residence halls into less segregated living arrangements with roommates of choice. Sophomores begin to reorder their priorities away from the freshman emphasis on their social life and toward the adult tasks required by academia, including the process of declaring a major. The choice of a major and the realization of the academic years stretching ahead of them tend to force sophomores to examine the meaning of their academic pursuits, where those pursuits will take them, and, most important, who they will be when they graduate.

Just as freshmen work on defining themselves as separate from their families, sophomores work on defining themselves as separate from their peers. This task has the potential to create internal conflict, doubt, frustration, and fear. Sophomores become particularly aware of alternative views expressed by individuals from different racial, ethnic, and cultural backgrounds (Loeb & Magee, 1992). Sometimes pursuit of this self-definition brings sophomores to counseling with complaints of depression, confusion about relationships, existential struggles, or a desire to escape by dropping out or transferring to another institution (Lemons & Richmond, 1987).

Juniors: "I'm here and I'm confident!" As traditional-age college students embark on their junior year, there is great anticipation about what lies ahead of them as seniors and as graduates, coupled with an aware-ness of what they are leaving behind. Generally, juniors become increas-ingly more committed to their personal and academic lives. This increased commitment reflects their having settled on a major and taking classes specific to that major, rather than the more general curriculum of previ-ous years. The junior year is marked by an increased focus on career, enhancement of job opportunities, or preparation for graduate school.

Another significant developmental task of traditional-age juniors is an increased commitment to intimate relationships, including friendships. The quality of relationships becomes more important than the number of rela-tionships for many juniors. College counselors often see juniors caught in the "dependence–independence" battle: They want to make commitments, but they fear that that means a loss of independence. They may feel that it is time to make serious personal commitments to others, but they also want to explore themselves as nonattached graduates. Earlier in their col-lege years, they could easily put off decisions about relational commit-ments, but as they see a graduation date approaching and the next life transition presenting itself, these commitments become more essential and more important to their future life course. Ambivalence about personal commitments and career may bring juniors to counseling with concerns about career paths, relationships, anxiety, decision-making difficulties, the impact of family history on current functioning, unhealthy or nonproduc-tive coping behaviors, confusion, and sadness.

Seniors: "What's next?" The greatest task of being a senior is facing graduation and the realization that the real world is just over the horizon. Traditional-age college students nearing the end of their undergraduate years often experience ambivalence. As they reflect on their accomplish-ments and, occasionally, their regrets, they are challenged to make peace with their college experience. This task is exacerbated by the struggle to stay motivated to complete their studies and seek jobs or attend gradu-ate school. Difficulties in marketing themselves, problems in locating a suitable job, or problems in the graduate application process can affect self-esteem and lead to discouragement, anxiety, and, sometimes, even panic that will bring seniors to counseling.

Equally as challenging for seniors is the task of examining their current relationships in light of graduation. The self-definition and self-exploration begun as juniors, about themselves in relationships, come to a head for seniors. As a result, long-term relationships with friends and partners often change or end. This self-exploration frequently causes confusion, anxiety, grief, and pain, which may cause college seniors to seek counseling.

Using Developmental Theories and Models in College Counseling. College counselors typically draw from a variety of theories, models, and techniques in their counseling practices. Life span and career development theories and models are especially helpful when counselors are working with traditional-age college students because these theories and models help counselors recognize needs, predict transitions, target critical developmental tasks, discern normative versus nonnormative experiences, and promote healthy adjustment. Although college counselors use these approaches primarily to inform their therapeutic practice, the various developmental theories and models suggest topics for outreach programming (see Chapter 12, "Outreach Programming From the College Counseling Center"). Some examples of developmental theories and models that are often used in counseling include moral development (Gilligan, 1982/1993, 1991; Kohlberg & Hersh, 1977), homosexual identity (Cass, 1979, 1984; D'Augelli, 1994), ego development (Loevinger, 1976), ethnic identity (Cross, 1995; Helms, 1993; Phinney, 1989), women's development (Belenky, Clinchy, Goldberger, & Tarule, 1986), and career development (Holland, 1985/1992; Super, 1985).

Although most college counselors use the aforementioned developmental approaches, interestingly, many college counselors are unfamiliar with theories specific to college students (possibly because student development theories are so strongly identified with the student affairs field). Student development theories include psychosocial, cognitive–structural, and typology approaches that focus on the processes of change and growth in college students. These theories emphasize stages of development that are presumed to emerge in an orderly and hierarchical manner (Evans, Forney, & Guido-DiBrito, 1998; Kuh, 1993; Pascarella & Terenzini, 1991). College counselors can use student development theories to aid their understanding of the elements and processes commonly experienced by the college students they see as clients.

These theories and models supplement the life span development perspectives frequently used by mental health professionals. Examples of helpful student developmental theories and models include identity development (Chickering & Reisser, 1993), women's identity development (Josselson, 1987, 1996), transition theory (Schlossberg, Waters, & Goodman, 1995), intellectual and ethical development (Perry, 1981), and experiential learning (Kolb, 1984).

The value of using developmental theories and models in counseling traditional-age college students is illustrated by the following examples.

Caroline. Caroline, an African American junior, is majoring in communication disorders and seems to be on track to enroll in a graduate program in speech pathology at a university in another state. Her career choice grew out of a childhood experience with speech therapy that created in her a strong desire to give back the gift that she received as a child. Caroline is excited about this next transition in her life, especially the fact that her career goals are now within reach.

Caroline and her boyfriend of 4 years have recently become engaged. She has worked hard at this relationship, making a lot of sacrifices to keep him happy, including commuting to her hometown most weekends so that they can be together. This type of behavior is nothing new for Caroline, who generally puts others, especially her family, before herself, even at great cost and inconvenience. However, a conflict that has occurred between Caroline and her fiancé has caused her to question her attitudes and beliefs. He opposes her continuing her education beyond an undergraduate degree because it would mean they would be physically separated for 4 more years. Caroline is torn: She wants to be married, but she also wants to pursue her graduate degree. She is conscious of a growing resentment of his demands and confusion about what is the "responsible" thing to do. Caroline is having problems focusing on her studies, is experiencing insomnia, and is not eating properly. She has come to the counseling center in hopes of understanding herself better so that she can make decisions about her fiancé and her career.

Theory applied to Caroline. Gilligan's (1982/1993, 1991) theory of women's moral development postulates that women's moral decision making is centered on maintaining relationships, minimizing harm or violence, and caring for self and others. Women's moral developmental typically moves through three levels and two transitions: Level I, Orientation to Individual Survival; Transition I, From Selfishness to Responsibility; Level II, Goodness as Self-Sacrifice; Transition II, From Goodness to Truth; and Level III, The Morality of Nonviolence. The levels and transitions mark a woman's progress from self-centeredness, in which survival is primal, toward an emphasis on the primacy of maintaining relationships at the cost of self, and further toward an attempt to balance care for self with care for others that minimizes harm or violence. Caroline's college counselor, using Gilligan's theory to inform her approach to working with Caroline, recognizes that Caroline, in questioning her habit of always putting the needs of others before her own needs, is moving out of Level II: Goodness as Self-Sacrifice and through Transition II: From Goodness to Truth. She is beginning to consider that her needs and desires are just as important as those of others, including those of her fiancé. At times, she feels selfish as she considers pursuing her own needs; at other times, she resents the expectations of her family and fiancé that she will abandon her career hopes in order to make them happy. Knowledge of Gilligan's theory helped the counselor to recognize Caroline's primary issues and focus counseling on Caroline's self-definition within relationships, especially recognizing the legitimacy of her own needs and how to balance care for self with care for others.

James. James is an 18-year-old, Euro-American, male freshman and is the first person in his family to go to college. He was raised in a rural community where he had been rather isolated, interacting almost exclusively with family members. In fact, he had not been allowed to participate in the routine activities offered in high school, such as athletic events, dances, or organizations. Understandably, after arriving at the university, he soon felt overwhelmed by the social and academic pressures. The most challenging task for him was making friends. He presented to the counseling center with concerns about the personal sacrifices he was making in order to obtain friends, his fear of failing at college, and loneliness. James had been binge drinking several evenings a week and had been charged with an infraction in his residence hall for a drinking-related incident. Parties had taken priority over his studies. James had begun to realize that although he was establishing friendships, he was not feeling very good about himself. He spoke about the level of teasing directed at him in his peer group when he was intoxicated and his frustration at feeling he must put up with the teasing if he was to have friends at all.

Theory applied to James. James's college counselor could use Chickering and Reisser's (1993) theory of identity development to understand her client's problems and to focus counseling on critical areas. This theory, postulating that identity development is the crucial issue for traditional-age college students, suggests seven vectors of development: Vector 1, developing competence; Vector 2, managing emotions; Vector 3, moving through autonomy toward interdependence; Vector 4, developing mature interpersonal relationships; Vector 5, establishing identity; Vector 6, developing purpose; and Vector 7, developing integrity. Although not viewed as rigidly sequential, each vector does tend to build on the previous vector's experiences. James's counselor notes that his current problems occur primarily in the first 3 vectors. His questioning regarding "Who are my friends?" "Am I capable of making it away from home?" and "What if I can't cope?" reveal his struggles with Vector 1 (developing competence). James's binge drinking and subsequent residential hall infraction highlight problems in Vector 2, managing emotions. James's frustration with himself for being so dependent on maintaining friendships even at a cost to himself highlights Vector 3, moving through autonomy toward interdependence. Thus, the counselor could use Chickering and Reisser's theory to design individual and group counseling interventions that will target the first 3 vectors.

Counseling traditional-age students requires a developmental viewpoint. Using various developmental models can help college counselors to understand the problems of student clients, formulate appropriate intervention plans, plan outreach programs, and provide effective counseling services.

RECOMMENDATIONS FOR ACTION

The following recommendations will assist college counselors in working with traditional-age college students.

1. Understand and use developmental theories and models appropriate for traditional-age college students. The theories and models aid conceptualization of clients' problems, identify needs, target critical issues, predict transitions, suggest intervention points and strategies, and inform outreach programming. Theories about life span development, moral decision making, careers, ethnic–racial identity, sexual orientation, ego development, or gender issues are most appropriate and have been cited earlier in this chapter. College counselors should also be familiar with student development theories because they are targeted especially at college students. Several of these have been cited earlier in this chapter as well. Effective college counselors add developmental knowledge to their clinical skills to bring competent counseling services to their student clients. Active participation in continuing education is one way to expand understanding of the developmental perspective.

2. Recognize the developmental transitions typical of traditional-age college students and plan interventions accordingly. Freshmen have different experiences and viewpoints from juniors, and juniors are still different from seniors. Use this information in counseling and in outreach programming. For example, a typical traditional-age sophomore begins to reorder priorities away from the emphasis on social life that is characteristic of freshmen and more toward an emphasis on academics and the choice of a major. College counselors can use this information to target decision-making skills for individual and group counseling as well as for outreach programming.

3. Recognize the advantages and disadvantages of traditional-age students' comfort and familiarity with technology and cyberspace. Offer various counseling services (when appropriate) on-line or through the counseling center's web site. Outreach programming can be offered simultaneously to both on-campus and off-campus sites by using technology. Counselors must also be attuned to the problems associated with technology: "computer or Internet addiction," disengagement, false identity, and misleading information. Awareness means picking up on these problems in counseling more quickly. Outreach programming can also address the problems associated with using technology.

4. Work with other campus departments to develop programs that address the specific needs of traditional-age students. College counselors' training and expertise are invaluable to other programs and departments on campus. One example is close collaboration between medical (health services) and counseling services on campus, affording professionals in both fields the opportunity to best meet the needs of students. Another example of collaboration is the involvement of college counselors in first-year experience programs, in which college counselors can provide insight into the mental health needs of students, especially freshmen students, through consultation, teaching, and guest lectures. A good example of a program that demonstrates college counselors' involvement in the larger campus is that of the Counseling Center at the University of Maryland, College Park. College counselors there, through careful research, identified sophomore students at risk of stopping or dropping out of the university. They then created specific interventions to help these students remain in school (V. Boyd, personal communication, May 16, 1999). Additional recommendations for networking with various campus constituencies are found in Chapter 13, "Building Effective Campus Relationships."

5. Pursue continuing education and professional preparation to address issues and problems frequently presented by traditional-age college students. General counseling preparation, although essential for the novice college counselor, must be supplemented by clinical training specific to the issues and problems frequently experienced by a traditional-age college population. College counselors must be well-informed about the nature and treatment of problems associated with sexual assault, date rape, eating disorders, substance use and abuse, depression, and anxiety. It is imperative that college counselors have a working knowledge of the latest (4th) edition of the *Diagnostic and Statistical Manual of Mental Disorders* (American Psychiatric Association, 1994). Membership in professional organizations, especially those specific to college counseling, enhances knowledge, offers networking opportunities, and promotes exchanges of ideas. For example, the American College Counseling Association (ACCA) publishes a monthly newsletter (*Visions*) and a journal (*Journal of College Counseling*), sponsors an Internet listserv

(ACCA-L), and develops college counseling-specific programming at the annual convention of the American Counseling Association.

SUMMARY

This chapter examines some characteristics of today's traditional-age college students, especially ways in which these students differ from those of previous generations. The chapter describes key developmental issues and tasks of the undergraduate experience and explores the application of developmental theories and models in college counseling. Recommendations for using this information to enhance college counselors' work with traditional-age college students are also provided.

Effective college counselors of the 21st century will competently blend a developmental perspective with clinical training to address the unique difficulties of traditional-age college students (e.g., substance use or abuse, relationship difficulties, stress-related problems). College counselors understand the substantial influences of technology and diversity on these students and are, therefore, flexible in adapting their counseling approaches to meet student and client needs. Another generation of traditional-age college students (Generation Y) will soon emerge on American campuses. College counselors can draw on their knowledge and expertise with the current generation to understand the next, but they must remain open to the unique differences that these new students will bring to campuses and to the counseling experience. What an exciting time to be a college counselor!

REFERENCES

American Council on Education. (1998). *Fact book on higher education, 1997.* Phoenix, AZ: Oryx Press.

American Psychiatric Association. (1994). *Diagnostic and statistical manual of mental disorders* (4th ed.). Washington, DC: Author.

Astin, A. W. (1996). Involvement in learning revisited: Lessons we have learned. *Journal of College Student Development, 37,* 123–134.

Belenky, M. F., Clinchy, B. M., Goldberger, N. R., & Tarule, J. M. (1986). *Women's way of knowing: The development of self, voice, and mind.* New York: Basic Books.

Brooks, J. M. (1997). Beyond teaching and learning paradigms: Trekking into the virtual university. *Teaching Sociology, 27,* 1–14.

Brown, J. S., & Duguid, P. (1996). Universities in the digital age. *Change, 28*(4), 10–19.

Burke, R. J. (1994). Generation X: Measures, sex and age differences. *Psychological Reports, 74,* 555–562.

Cannon, D. (1991). Generation X: The way they do the things they do. *Journal of Career Planning and Employment, 51,* 34–38.

Cass, V. C. (1979). Homosexual identity formation: A theoretical model. *Journal of Homosexuality, 4,* 219–235.

Cass, V. C. (1984). Homosexual identity formation: Testing a theoretical model. *Journal of Sex Research, 20,* 143–167.

Chickering, A. W., & Reisser, L. (1993). *Education and identity* (2nd ed.). San Francisco: Jossey-Bass.

Coles, R. (1993). Idealism in today's students. *Change, 25*(5), 16–20.

Cross, W. E., Jr. (1995). The psychology of nigrescence: Revising the Cross model. In J. G. Ponterotto, J. M. Casas, L. A. Suzuki, & C. M. Alexander (Eds.), *Handbook of multicultural counseling* (pp. 93–122). Thousand Oaks, CA: Sage.

D'Augelli, A. R. (1994). Identity development and sexual orientation: Toward a model of lesbian, gay, and bisexual development. In E. J. Trickett, R. J. Watts, & D. Birman (Eds.), *Human diversity: Perspectives on people in context* (pp. 312–333). San Francisco: Jossey-Bass.

Evans, N. J., Forney, D. S., & Guido-DiBrito, F. (1998). *Student development in college.* San Francisco: Jossey-Bass.

Evans, N., & Wall, V. (1991). *Beyond tolerance: Gays, lesbians, and bisexuals on campus.* Alexandria, VA: American College Personnel Association.

Frances, C., Pumerantz, E., & Caplan, J. (1999). Planning for instructional technology. *Change, 31*(4), 25–33.

Gilligan, C. (1991). Women's psychological development: Implications for psychotherapy. *Women and Therapy, 11*(3–4), 5–31.

Gilligan, C. (1993). *In a different voice: Psychological theory and women's development.* Cambridge, MA: Harvard University Press. (Original work published 1982)

Helms, J. E. (Ed.). (1993). *Black and White racial identity: Theory, research, and practice.* Westport, CT: Praeger.

Hirsch, D. J. (1993). Politics through action: Student service and activism in the '90s. *Change, 25*(5), 32–36.

Holland, J. L. (1992). *Making vocational choices: A theory of vocational personalities and work environments* (2nd ed.). Odessa, FL: Psychological Assessment Resources. (Original work published 1985)

Holmbeck, G. N., & Wandrei, M. L. (1993). Individual and relational predictors of adjustment in first-year college students. *Journal of Counseling Psychology, 40,* 73–78.

Imbimbo, P. V. (1995). Sex differences in the identity formation of college students from divorced families. *Journal of Youth and Adolescence, 24,* 745–761.

Josselson, R. (1987). *Finding herself: Pathways to identity development in women.* San Francisco: Jossey-Bass.

Josselson, R. (1996). *Revising herself: The story of women's identity from college to midlife.* New York: Oxford University Press.

Kenny, M. E., & Donaldson, G. A. (1991). Contributions of parental attachment and family structure to the social and psychological functioning of first-year college students. *Journal of Counseling Psychology, 38,* 479–486.

Kohlberg, L., & Hersh, R. H. (1977). Moral development: A review of the theory. *Theory into Practice, 16,* 53–59.

Kolb, D. A. (1984). *Experiential learning: Experiences as the source of learning and development.* Englewood Cliffs, NJ: Prentice Hall.

Kopp, W. (1992). The driven—yet undirected—generation . . . and the difference we can make. *NACADA Journal, 12,* 56–58.

Kuh, G. D. (1993). In their own words: What students learn outside the classroom. *American Educational Research Journal, 30,* 277–304.

Lemons, L. J., & Richmond, D. R. (1987). A developmental perspective of sophomore slump. *NASPA Journal, 4,* 15–19.

Levine, A., & Cureton, J. S. (1998). *When hope and fear collide: A portrait of today's college student.* San Francisco: Jossey-Bass.

Loeb, R. C., & Magee, P. M. (1992). Changes in attitudes and self-perceptions during the first two years of college. *Journal of College Student Development, 33,* 348–355.

Loevinger, J. (1976). *Ego development: Conceptions and theories.* San Francisco: Jossey-Bass.

Lopez, F. G. (1991). The impact of parental divorce on college students. *New Directions of Student Services, 54,* 19–33.

McCurdy, S. J., & Scherman, A. (1996). The effects of family structure on the adolescent separation–individuation process. *Adolescence, 31,* 307–319.

National Center for Education Statistics. (1997). *Projections of education statistics to 2008* (NCES Publication No. 98-016). Washington, DC: U.S. Department of Education.

National Center for Education Statistics. (1998). *The condition of education, 1998.* (NCES Publication No. 98-013). Washington, DC: U.S. Department of Education, Office of Educational Research and Improvement.

Pascarella, E. T., & Terenzini, P. T. (1991). *How college affects students.* San Francisco: Jossey-Bass.

Pascarella, E. T., & Terenzini, P. T. (1998). Studying college students in the 21st century: Meeting new challenges. *The Review of Higher Education, 21,* 151–165.

Pendergast, M. L. (1994). Substance use and abuse among college students: A review of recent literature. *Journal of American College Health, 43,* 99–112.

Perry, W. G., Jr. (1981). Cognitive and ethical growth: The making of meaning. In A. W. Chickering & Associates (Eds.), *The modern American college: Responding to the new realities of diverse students and a changing society* (pp. 76–116). San Francisco: Jossey-Bass.

Phinney, J. S. (1989). Stages of ethnic identity development in minority group adolescents. *Journal of Early Adolescence, 9,* 34–49.

Rennison, C. M. (1999). *National Crime Victim Survey 1998: Changes 1997–1998 with trends 1993–1998* (NCG Publication No. 176353). Washington, DC: U.S. Department of Justice.

Rice, K. G. (1992). Separation–individuation and adjustment to college: A longitudinal study. *Journal of Counseling Psychology, 39,* 203–213.

Rice, K. G., Fitzgerald, D. P., Whaley, T. J., & Gibbs, C. L. (1995). Cross-sectional and longitudinal examination of attachment, separation–individuation, and college student adjustment. *Journal of Counseling and Development, 73,* 463–474.

Sax, L. J., Astin, A. W., Korn, W. S., & Mahoney, K. M. (1998). *The American freshman: National norms for Fall 1998.* Los Angeles: University of California, Higher Education Research Institute.

Schlossberg, N. K., Waters, E. B., & Goodman, J. (1995). *Counseling adults in transition: Linking practice with theory* (2nd ed.). New York: Springer.

Simon, T. (1993). Sexuality on campus–'90s style. *Change, 25*(5), 50–56.

Super, D. E. (1985). Validating a model and a method. *Contemporary Psychology, 30,* 771.

Terenzini, P. T., Rendon, L. I., Upcraft, M. L., Millar, S. B., Allison, K. W., Gregg, P. L., & Jalomo, R. (1994). The transition to college: Diverse students, diverse stories. *Research in Higher Education, 35,* 57–73.

TIAA–CREF. (1998, March). Higher education: Enrollment trends and staffing needs. *Research Dialogues* [On-line serial], *55.* http://www.tiaa-cref.org/rds/rd55/rd55.htm (September 10, 1999)

Ullman, S. E., Karabatsos, G., & Koss, M. P. (1999). Alcohol and sexual assault in a national sample of college women. *Journal of Interpersonal Violence, 14,* 603–605.

Wall, V. A., & Evans, N. J. (Eds.). (in press). *Toward acceptance: Sexual orientation issues on campus.* Washington, DC: American College Personnel Association.

Wechsler, H. (1996). Alcohol and the American college campus: A report from the Harvard School of Public Health. *Change, 28*(4), 20–25.

Wechsler, H., Dowdall, G. W., Maenner, G., Gledhill-Hoyt, J., & Lee, H. (1998). Changes in binge drinking and related problems among American college students between 1993 and 1997. *Journal of the American College Health Association, 47,* 57–68.

Wehrly, B., Kenney, K., & Kenney, M. (1999). *Counseling multiracial families.* Thousand Oaks, CA: Sage.

8

Nontraditional College Students

JAMES M. BENSHOFF
AND ATTICIA P. BUNDY

FOCUS QUESTIONS

1. What makes nontraditional college students different from traditional-age college students?

2. What kinds of issues do older students face in their college experience?

3. What kinds of services do older students want from college counselors?

4. How do college counselors reach nontraditional students with services appropriate to their needs?

ISSUES

This chapter addresses the answers to the Focus Questions presented above. After reading this chapter, you should have a better understanding of adult college students and how to work more effectively with them in higher education settings. As you read this chapter, use the Focus Questions to think about the issues and challenges that older students might face in college and how college counselors could help them have successful college experiences.

Changes in Student Populations on Campus

The history of higher education in the United States began with church-affiliated schools for young White men in which students and faculty lived and studied together on campus. Since the first U.S. college was established more than 300 years ago, student populations have changed considerably to embrace women, minorities, commuter students, international students, and students from all socioeconomic and academic backgrounds. One of the most significant influences on U.S. higher education was the influx of veterans (mostly male) who returned from World War II with tuition benefits courtesy of the G.I. Bill and a desire to prepare for postmilitary careers by attending college. Most of these veterans were older and entered college with significantly different life experiences and, frequently, with families and other complicating factors in their lives. This postwar period might be viewed as the beginning of the influx of older, nontraditional students into college.

An overall decrease in the number of high school graduates over the past two decades has had a significant impact on higher education. By 1997, the population of traditional-age college students "had declined by 18 percent, or 5.5 million, and bottomed out at 24.7 million" (TIAA–CREF, 1998, p. 7). The percentage of nontraditional students enrolling in institutions of higher learning, however, has steadily increased (Hu, 1985), with students older than age 25 playing a critical role in sustaining enrollment growth (TIAA–CREF, 1998). Between 1970 and 1990, adults were "the fastest-growing segment of all the population groups in higher education" (Brazziel, 1989, p. 116; TIAA–CREF, 1998) and constituted between one third and one half of college enrollments (Aslanian &

Brickell, 1980). For 2000–2010, it is projected that more than 11% of Americans between the ages of 25 and 64 will be enrolled in some form of higher education and these students will make up almost 50% of those enrolled in college (TIAA–CREF, 1998).

Characteristics of Nontraditional Students

Cross (1980) defined the *nontraditional student* as an adult (typically older than age 25) who returns to school full- or part-time while maintaining other responsibilities such as employment, family, and other "adult responsibilities" (p. 627). Other terms used to describe this category of student include *adult student, reentry student, returning student,* and *adult learner.* Although these older students share educational experiences and classroom space with traditional-age students (ages 18–24), their developmental needs, issues, and stressors differ considerably from those of their younger student-peers.

A number of factors characteristically distinguish nontraditional from traditional-age college students. Adult students are more likely to have families of their own and to have the attendant financial responsibilities as well as time constraints and other interpersonal commitments. In addition, the financial impact of returning to college may be greater for adults who must pay for their education themselves while maintaining other monetary commitments (e.g., mortgage payments, family support). Many nontraditional students return to college as older students after delay or interruption of their initial higher education experience (Aslanian, 1990; Morris, 1988; Streeter, 1980).

Adults who return to school overwhelmingly are commuters who live, work, and play away from the college campus, in many cases commuting considerable distances to attend college part-time without further disrupting their lives by uprooting themselves and their families. Richter-Antion (1986) identified six factors that distinguish nontraditional students from traditional students, including greater sense of purpose and motivation, view of education as an investment, increased commitments and responsibilities outside of school, greater life experiences, lack of an age cohort at school, and limited social acceptability and support. Adult learners tend to be achievement-oriented and relatively independent with spe-

cial needs for flexible and alternative schedules and instruction appropriate for their developmental level (Cross, 1980; Marino, 1997). They generally prefer more active approaches to learning (e.g., internships, cooperative education, experiential activities in class) and value opportunities
to integrate academic learning with their life and work experiences.

Although nontraditional students typically have multiple responsibilities and complex lives, several studies have found that compared with
traditional students, nontraditional students showed less stress (Jacobi,
1987), had better time management and study skills (Devlin, 1996;
Trueman & Hartley, 1996), performed better academically, and were as
positive or more so about their college experience (Sagaria, 1989). Morris
(1988) found that nontraditional students were more likely to attend part-
time and that more of them had grade point averages higher than 3.50.

Reasons Why Adults Return to School

A number of factors contribute to nontraditional students' decisions to
return to school. Rising costs of higher education often affect students'
ability to complete their education the first time around; students may
need or choose to "stop out" to work and accumulate resources before
returning to complete their education (Aslanian, 1990). In addition, some
younger students lack the maturity and the motivation that are necessary
to complete their education and drop out; they may then return as older,
more motivated, and more mature students to finish what they began as
adolescents (Aslanian, 1990). Changes in job requirements or career
paths also may force adults to seek additional education (Aslanian &
Brickell, 1980; Rawlins, 1979).

Brazziel (1989) stated that career considerations may be the single most
important reason why adults return to college. Other reasons why adult
students return to college include family-life transitions (marriage,
divorce, death), changes in leisure patterns, and self-fulfillment (Aslanian
& Brickell, 1980; Rawlins, 1979). For some adults, the desire for social
contact can be a major factor in their returning to school (Rogers,
Gilleland, & Dixon, 1987).

To explain why adults return to higher education, Aslanian and
Brickell (1980) developed a "triggers and transitions" model that consid-

ers adults' decision to return to school within the context of developmental issues and crises faced during midlife. According to this model, most adult learners are motivated to return to school by a desire (or a need) to move from one status or role to another. Examples of transitions during midlife include changes related to career, marital status or family situation, leisure, or other life roles. Moving from one status to another requires new knowledge, skills, or credentials that often lead people back to college.

"Triggers" are events or nonevents that precipitate an adult's decision to return to school. Examples of triggers during midlife can include career events (loss of job, new job opportunities, failure to be promoted), family events (separation, divorce, remarriage, parenting), and, less frequently, avocational or health-related changes. Transitions explain the need for learning to cope with new roles, whereas triggers determine the timing of an adult's return to school. Adults have been found to return to school primarily because of career (56%) and family (16%) transitions that were precipitated by career-related (56%) and family-related (36%) triggering events (Aslanian, 1990).

Developmental Issues of Older Students

In Levinson's (1978) model of adult development, returning to school would be most likely to occur during a transition period when major tasks are to reexamine the past, make adjustments in the life structure, and continue the individuation process (Kahnweiler & Johnson, 1980). McIlroy (1984) cited several distinct themes of the midlife transition, including reviewing life accomplishments and determining new goals and directions; coping with economic issues; becoming involved in mentoring and community activities; and coping with work, relationship, parental, and family-of-origin issues and responsibilities.

Wortley and Amatea (1982) identified four primary areas of adult development (career, family, intimacy, and inner life), with each area characterized by challenges of balancing multiple roles and responsibilities and reconciling values and ideals with reality. Mezirow (as cited in Redding & Dowling, 1992) suggested that nontraditional students deal with additional issues, including examining their internalized roles and assumptions about life, coping with a sense of alienation from traditional social expectations, recognizing that others share their discontent and desire for making changes in their lives, building a sense of competence and self-confidence in new roles, and acquiring knowledge and skills needed to implement plans. Not unlike culture shock, there seems to be a period of adjustment or transformation that occurs for nontraditional students both before and after they enter higher education.

In a psychosocial model of college student development, A. W. Chickering and Reisser (1993) noted that nontraditional students often can be expected to recycle through the same vectors or developmental stages that are experienced by traditional students. For example, Butler and Markley (1993) found that nontraditional students were functioning at higher levels than traditional students on purpose, relationships, autonomy, and intimacy and at about similar levels on career planning and lifestyle, concluding that all students are confronted with some of the same issues simply by being in the college environment.

Needs of Nontraditional Students

Although male and female nontraditional students seem to confront many of the same issues or themes as traditional students, these issues also seem to take shape somewhat differently depending on gender. To date, most research on nontraditional students has focused on middle-class White women who return to school, perhaps due to the fact that there have been more of them (Brazziel, 1989; Padula, 1994). The following sections summarize some of the available research relating to the specific needs of male and female returning students.

Lamb-Porterfield, Jones, and McDaniel (1987) found that nontraditional female students needed help in developing better academic, study, and library skills. In addition, they wanted more classes offered at different times and in different formats, and they expressed a desire for staff development programs to educate faculty about the needs of adult students. To this list, Wheaton and Robinson (1983) added separate orientation for adult female students, low-cost child care available on campus, and support groups for reentry women. Other needs identified by nontraditional female students include evening hours for advising and counseling services, more available degree programs for part-time students (Wilson & Christian, 1986), and academic advising and job placement assistance (Henry, 1985). Identification of career goals and career-oriented services also is necessary (McCormick, 1995) during times when women can use them (Creange, 1980). Research on nontraditional male students has been very limited to date. Linder, Londoner, and Bauer (1988) found that nontraditional male students had a higher internal locus of control than nontraditional female students. Hayes (1990), however, found overall perceptions of differences between male and female nontraditional students (as perceived by instructors and by adult students themselves) to be small. In another study (Lauzon, 1989), full-time married male students reported that developmental transitions had precipitated their return to school and that returning to school had resulted in numerous changes for them and their families. Rogers et al. (1987) suggested that men who return to school may be less likely than women to seek out support from other students.

A comparative study of the psychosocial needs of adult male and female students (Muench, 1987) found that fear of failure and self-doubts seem to be common in both men and women, that both have difficulties balancing multiple roles and responsibilities, that both need help with building their self-confidence, and that men and women need to be actively involved in the educational process. In another study, Bauer and Mott (1990) found that men were changing careers whereas women were looking to advance within the same career field, most women were frustrated by having to cope with pressures of child care and financial and school responsibilities, and men tended to be frustrated about the loss of time and money involved in returning to school. A study by Rawlins (1979) revealed that both male and female nontraditional students were most concerned about their age and their ability to relate to younger colleagues and that more than 75% perceived themselves as having different needs than younger students.

Special Needs of Nontraditional Minority Students

Given the space limitations of this chapter, we focus on two minority populations: African American students and gay, lesbian, and bisexual students. This section is further limited because there is very little research available on nontraditional minority students as a whole. The following paragraphs introduce each group and offer suggestions that are primarily focused on personal and career counseling. Colleges and universities should tailor their services to fit the needs of nontraditional minority students.

Nontraditional African American Students. Since the 1970s, the percentage of nontraditional minority undergraduates has risen substantially (Renzetti, 1992). When thinking about the needs of nontraditional African American students, one must consider the importance of family and community. Although nontraditional students typically are not on campus for special activities, having clubs and services for African American students may offer a critical sense of belonging and community. Because church plays a very important role in African American culture, providing student activities that address and incorporate faith and religion is important (Vacc, DeVaney, & Wittmer, 1995). In addition, providing social groups specific to adult students from different minority groups (e.g., African American) can offer important opportunities for meeting other adult students, socializing, networking, and developing support.

In career counseling, African American students should be provided with information about nontraditional careers, including models, mentors, and examples of African Americans from a wide variety of occupations and professions (Vacc et al., 1995). This information could be presented to nontraditional African American students by inviting guest speakers (e.g., African American alumni who are successful in their careers) or by developing and acquiring culturally sensitive career materials for career centers (Vacc et al., 1995). Having career information and knowledgeable staff available is key in providing quality career counseling to African American and other minority students. In addition, it is important that colleges and universities make concerted efforts to hire college counselors of color to provide services to minority students, many of whom may be more comfortable with (and more likely to seek help from) counselors of color. In addition, minority counselors can serve important functions as role models, mentors, and informal advisers to these students. The reader is referred to Chapter 9, "College Counseling and the Needs of Multicultural Students," for more in-depth discussion.

Nontraditional Gay, Lesbian, and Bisexual Students. Another part of the nontraditional student population consists of gay, lesbian, and bisexual students. Research on age of "coming out" (i.e., disclosing to oneself and later others about one's sexual orientation) indicates that nontraditional students are more likely to be aware of their sexual orientation. Counseling needs may include dealing with career concerns and perhaps coming out with family and friends and in the higher education setting (Evans & Wall, 1991; Vacc et al., 1995; Wall & Evans, in press). Cass's (1979) model of homosexual identity formation can be helpful in determining where a student is in his or her sexual identity development. Cass outlined six stages of sexual identity formation: (a) identity confusion, (b) identity comparison, (c) identity tolerance, (d) identity acceptance, (e) identity pride, and (f) identity synthesis.

Gay, lesbian, and bisexual students may not feel that they can trust faculty, staff, administrators, or other students at their college. In addition, bisexual students may experience more frustration and isolation because they may not be accepted by lesbians and gays either (in addition to their families and society at large; Vacc et al., 1995). College counselors can indicate that they are safe persons with whom persons of diverse orientations can talk by having gay, lesbian, and bisexual materials, such as books, magazines, and community references, displayed in their offices and in the common areas of counseling centers.

Physical, psychological, and social safety is a significant issue for gay, lesbian, and bisexual nontraditional students, who often must be concerned with how open they can be about their sexual orientation. Many will need to test the college environment to ascertain the level of acceptance by the institution, faculty and staff, and fellow students of all ages. College counselors can provide guidance and support while these students adjust to the campus. In career counseling, it is important for college counselors to be aware of the attitudes of employers in their clients' area and to help their gay, lesbian, and bisexual clients determine how to best negotiate employment issues related to sexual orientation in ways that are most beneficial and least prejudicial to them. Strategies may include identifying ongoing sources of support and networking, such as support or business professional groups, for gay, lesbian, and bisexual individuals on campus and in the community.

Barriers

Numerous barriers and obstacles can stand in the way of nontraditional students reaching their educational goals. Redding and Dowling (1992) described three types of barriers that can affect nontraditional students: institutional, situational, and dispositional. Institutional barriers can include such challenges as course scheduling (fewer nighttime offerings and short summer terms); time restrictions on completing programs of study; availability of financial aid; lack of support services (including career, child-care, and counseling services) for nontraditional students during convenient hours; faculty, staff, and other traditional students' biases and attitudes toward nontraditional students; and costs and types of services that are made available to nontraditional students (Hagedorn, 1993; Redding & Dowling, 1992; Robertson, 1991). Situational barriers can include lack of support for returning to school from friends, family, or employers as well as from faculty, staff, or students on campuses oriented toward traditional students. One of the most common situational barriers for nontraditional students can be a lack of knowledge about how to determine an area of interest in college and the steps necessary to reach educational goals (Redding & Dowling, 1992). Dispositional barriers are those aspects of nontraditional students' personalities that influence their performance in college, including students' own attitudes about college (Redding & Dowling, 1992), feelings of inferiority and low self-esteem, and sense of academic and social competence in the college environment. Wheaton and Robinson (1983) cited a number of external and internal barriers to success for returning female students. Internal barriers included guilt and anxiety about placing their own desires or needs above those of their families, lack of self-confidence, and a general lack of decision-making skills. External barriers included standardized tests required for admissions, lack of financial aid for part-time students and requirements to consider spousal income as part of the financial-aid application process, lack of child care, and increased family demands on time.

RECOMMENDATIONS FOR ACTION

Reaching Nontraditional Students

The wide diversity of characteristics and needs among adult students makes them difficult to reach with information and services (Streeter, 1980). The fact that nontraditional students are overwhelmingly commuters means that they typically come on campus primarily to attend classes and to use library and research facilities. Their involvement in campus life and activities tends to be restricted to their academic course work, they are less likely to become involved in extracurricular activities on campus, and they are highly selective in their use of services. It has been suggested that nontraditional students are more involved psychologically rather than physically in college life (Copland-Wood, 1985).

There are a number of approaches to determining the needs of nontraditional students on college campuses. One approach is to conduct surveys of these students through mailings, distribution in classes or through advisers, or under the auspices of specific offices (e.g., counseling or career counseling centers). Surveys can help college counselors better understand the specific aspects of their programs and services that may need to be modified or enhanced to make them more accessible and appropriate for adult students.

Another approach to needs assessment is the use of focus groups. Focus groups use both structured interviews and group process with selected representative groups to obtain information about needs, attitudes, problems, and recommendations or solutions. Focus groups can offer important information to college staff and administrators, as well as serve as an instructional tool for participants (McCormick, 1995) and help them to feel understood and supported. Both survey and focus-group approaches should encourage nontraditional students to identify not only what is lacking but also what aspects of college are working well for them.

Gianakos (1996), writing specifically about career services, cited the need for "a constructive, developmental approach in which adult learners' career-pursuit activities are given meaning in the context of multiple work and family responsibilities" (p. 222). Champagne and Pettipas (1989) discussed three types of developmental interventions for adults, each with its own set of goals: (a) enhancement (self-exploration and awareness, education, skills training, career and life planning, preparation for academic life, and an understanding of adult transitions), (b) support (development of support networks and groups, mentoring and role modeling, advocacy, and information), and (c) counseling (remediation, stress reduction, assessment and action planning, individual and group counseling, peer counseling, and referral). They further suggested eight roles for college counselors when working with nontraditional students: specialized services, advocacy, referral, education, clearinghouse (information and linking to resources), program planning, networking and mentoring, and counseling.

Strategies for College Counselors

To be effective in reaching nontraditional students, college counselors first should have a broad understanding of their basic needs, developmental issues, and ways in which they differ from traditional students. In addition, it is critical to find out about the specific needs of adult students on a particular campus, as well as the needs of individual students with whom the college counselor is working. The question of "How do you feel about yourself?" can be an important one for adults returning to school (Fisher, 1997). Fisher also stressed the fears experienced by many returning adult students—fear of the unfamiliar, fear of failure, and fear of change and new experiences—and suggested that these fears are issues for exploration in counseling. College counselors can assist nontraditional students by addressing their specific needs, helping them incorporate their life experiences into the learning process, validating the multiple perspectives they bring to counseling and to education, and encouraging use of multiple sources of support.

Padula (1994) noted the critical importance for college counselors of knowing "what the important predictor variables are that differentiate reentry women from traditional students and that differentiate women developmentally" (p. 16) and of using this knowledge to design services and programs for this population on campus. College counselors should ask, "Why aren't nontraditional students using our counseling and advising services?" (Padula, 1994) as well as "What services *are* adult students using and why?"

College counselors also should take into consideration that although nontraditional students are highly motivated to succeed in college, they often lack confidence in their ability to be successful as students (Nordstrom, 1989; Padula, 1994). College counselors can play a vital role in offering support through providing individual contacts as well as through setting up support systems on campus. For example, Warmline was developed at Memphis State University as a peer counseling and support program for adult students that involved reaching out to adult students, helping to inform them about resources and services at the university and in the community, and helping adult students share their problems in being students (J. N. Chickering, 1987). Durnovo and McCrohan (1987) reported on a women's support services program that offered support and specific programs and services to adult female students, including counseling services, weekly support groups, special activities, and career-related workshops and seminars. Porter (1989) recommended offering specially designed activities for adult students to help them integrate into the campus environment, build self-esteem, develop camaraderie among adults, and deal with the unique demands and constraints faced by attending college. He also recommended forming nontraditional student organizations on campus to provide activities, support, and advocacy for adult students. Peer support groups also can be important for nontraditional students, who often need help connecting with other adult students, networking on campus, and finding a sense of belonging (Fisher, 1997; MacKinnon-Slaney, 1994).

Reaching Faculty and Administrators

As advocates for nontraditional students, college counselors can play a critical role in educating faculty and administrators and advocating for needed changes in services, programs, and other aspects of the college environment. College counselors should continually make administrators aware of changes in student populations on campus and the need to make corresponding changes in attitudes and services. Reliable methods for educating faculty and administrators include providing in-service workshops, developing training materials, and raising specific concerns with faculty and administrators in conversations and meetings. For example, one community college produced videotapes and other training materials to use in faculty development workshops (Cooper, 1982). Kirk and Kirk (1995) developed a gaming simulation to help college counselors and administrators become more aware of the barriers and challenges that adult students face in the college environment.

SUMMARY

Increasing numbers of adults are returning to school to adapt to changes in life status and roles. Nontraditional students typically face responsibilities and developmental challenges that are quite different from those of most traditional-age college students. Although reasons for returning to school vary, it is clear that "more older students, taking more courses, will become the norm on many campuses" (Brazziel, 1989, p. 130). Although colleges benefit from the influx of nontraditional students, programs and services designed for traditional students frequently are not adjusted to meet the needs of this developmentally different population (Hruby, 1983).

Nontraditional students should be considered an asset to any higher education institution because of their level of maturity and the unique life experiences that they bring to the classroom. College counselors must help their institutions pay increasing attention to modifying (sometimes radically) their existing philosophies and approaches to instruction, administration, and services to meet the needs and demands of this "new majority" on campus.

REFERENCES

Aslanian, C. B. (1990, March). *The adult learner.* Paper presented at the annual meeting of the American College Personnel Association, St. Louis, MO.

Aslanian, C. B., & Brickell, H. M. (1980). *Americans in transition: Life changes as reasons for adult learning.* New York: College Entrance Examination Board.

Bauer, D., & Mott, D. (1990). Life themes and motivations of reentry students. *Journal of Counseling and Development, 68,* 555–560.

Brazziel, W. F. (1989). Older students. In A. Levine & Associates (Eds.), *Shaping higher education's future: Demographic realities and opportunities 1990–2000* (pp. 116–132). San Francisco: Jossey-Bass.

Butler, E. R., & Markley, H. D. (1993). *Developmental characteristics of nontraditional aged students.* Kansas City, MO: American College Personnel Association. (ERIC Document Reproduction Service No. ED 365 902)

Cass, V. (1979). Homosexual identity formation: A theoretical model. *Journal of Homosexuality, 4*(3), 219–235.

Champagne, D. E., & Pettipas, A. (1989). Planning developmental interventions for adult students. *NASPA Journal, 26,* 265–271.

Chickering, A.W., & Reisser, L. (1993). *Education and identity* (2nd ed.). San Francisco: Jossey-Bass.

Chickering, J. N. (1987). *Warmline training manual: Peer counseling returning adult students.* Memphis, TN: Memphis State University, Center for Student Development. (ERIC Document Reproduction Service No. ED 289 125)

Cooper, J. D. (1982). *Faculty development program on teaching adults.* Lansing, MI: Media Technology, Lansing Community College. (ERIC Document Reproduction Service No. ED 230 812)

Copland-Wood, B. A. (1985, November). *Older commuter students and the collegiate experience: Involved or detached?* Paper presented at the conference of the American Association for Adult and Continuing Education, Milwaukee, WI.

Creange, R. (1980). *Student support services: Re-entry women need them too. Field evaluation draft.* Washington, DC: Project on the Status of Women in Education, Association of American Colleges. (ERIC Document Reproduction Service No. ED 196 338)

Cross, K. P. (1980). Our changing students and their impact on colleges: Prospects for a true learning society. *Phi Delta Kappan, 61,* 627–630.

Devlin, M. (1996). Older and wiser?: A comparison of the learning and study strategies of mature age and younger teacher education students. *Higher Education Research and Development, 15*(1), 51–60.

Durnovo, M., & McCrohan, B. (1987, November). *Strategies for serving the neglected majority: An institutional framework for addressing students' needs over the next decade*. Paper presented at the annual conference of the California Association of Community Colleges, Santa Clara, CA.

Evans, N., & Wall, N. (1991). *Beyond tolerance: Gays, lesbians, and bisexuals on campus*. Alexandria, VA: American College Personnel Association.

Fisher, C. A. (1997). Identity and self-awareness for adult learners. *College Student Affairs Journal, 16,* 21–29.

Gianakos, I. (1996). Career development differences between adult and traditional-aged learners. *Journal of Career Development, 22,* 211–223.

Hagedorn, L. S. (1993, November). *Graduate retention: An investigation of factors relating to older female graduate students*. Paper presented at the annual meeting of the Association for the Study of Higher Education, Pittsburgh, PA.

Hayes, E. (1990, April). *Perceptions of adult men and women students in higher education*. Paper presented at the annual meeting of the American Educational Research Association, Boston.

Henry, M. D. (1985). Black re-entry females: Their concerns and needs. *Journal of NAWDAC, 48,* 5–10.

Hruby, N. (1983). MIA: The nontraditional student. *Academe, 71,* 26–27.

Hu, M. (1985). Determining the needs and attitudes of nontraditional students. *College and University, 60,* 201–209.

Jacobi, M. (1987, February). *Stress among re-entry women students: A contextual approach*. Paper presented at the annual meeting of the Association for the Study of Higher Education, San Diego, CA.

Kahnweiler, J. B., & Johnson, P. L. (1980). A midlife developmental profile of the returning woman student. *Journal of College Student Personnel, 21,* 414–419.

Kirk, J. J., & Kirk, L. D. (1995). *Night rehearsal: A gaming simulation for nontraditional students entering college.* (ERIC Document Reproduction Service No. ED 388 855; Available from James J. Kirk, Western Carolina University, Cullowhee, NC)

Lamb-Porterfield, P., Jones, C. H., & McDaniel, M. L. (1987). A needs assessment of re-entry women at Arkansas State University. *College Student Journal, 21,* 222–227.

Lauzon, A. C. (1989). Educational transition: A qualitative study of full-time married male students. *International Journal of University Adult Education, 28,* 34–46.

Levinson, D. J. (1978). *The seasons of a man's life.* New York: Ballantine Books.

Linder, F., Londoner, C., & Bauer, D. (1988, February). *Locus of control and values of adult learners in continuing professional education programs.* Paper presented at the annual meeting of the Eastern Educational Research Association, Miami Beach, FL.

MacKinnon-Slaney, F. (1994). The adult persistence in learning model: A road map to counseling services for adult learners. *Journal of Counseling and Development, 72,* 268–275.

Marino, C. A. (1997, March). *The student returns: Challenges of the returning student.* Paper presented at the annual meeting of the Conference on College Composition and Communication, Phoenix, AZ.

McCormick, C. (1995, July). *Focus groups: An active learning approach to identifying nontraditional students' needs.* Paper presented at the annual meeting of the American Psychological Society Institute on the Teaching of Psychology, New York.

McIlroy, J. H. (1984). Midlife in the 1980s: Philosophy, economy, and psychology. *Personnel and Guidance Journal, 62,* 623–628.

Morris, C. (1988). *Coming back to school: A profile of fall term 1987 transition center students* (Research Rep. No. 88-01). Miami: Miami–Dade Community College, Florida Office of Institutional Research.

Muench, K. E. (1987, October). *A comparative study of the psychosocial needs of adult men and women students in an adult degree program.* Paper presented at the annual meeting of the American Association for Adult and Continuing Education, Washington, DC.

Nordstrom, B. H. (1989). *Nontraditional students: Adults in transition.* (ERIC Document Reproduction Service No. ED 310 686)

Padula, M. A. (1994). Reentry women: A literature review with recommendations for counseling and research. *Journal of Counseling and Development, 73,* 10–16.

Porter, J. L. (1989, October). *Empowering the nontraditional student through adult-specific programming.* Paper presented at the annual convention of the Virginia Community College Association, Roanoke, VA.

Rawlins, M. E. (1979). Life made easier for the over-thirty undergrads. *Personnel and Guidance Journal, 58,* 139–143.

Redding, N. P., & Dowling, W. D. (1992). Rites of passage among women reentering higher education. *Adult Education Quarterly, 42,* 221–236.

Renzetti, C. (1992). *Women, men and society.* Boston: Allyn & Bacon.

Richter-Antion, D. (1986). Qualitative differences between adult and younger students. *NASPA Journal, 23,* 58–62.

Robertson, D. L. (1991). Gender differences in the academic progress of adult undergraduates: Patterns and policy implication. *Journal of College Student Development, 32,* 490–496.

Rogers, B. H., Gilleland, K. R., & Dixon, G. (1987, April). *Educational motivations of part-time adults as related to socio-demographic variables.* Paper presented at the annual meeting of the American Educational Research Association, Washington, DC.

Sagaria, S. D. (1989, March). *Teaching traditional and nontraditional age individuals: How should methods, expectations, and standards differ?* Paper presented at the annual meeting of the American Educational Research Association, San Francisco.

Streeter, R. B. (1980). Alternative financial resources for the nontraditional student. *Journal of Student Financial Aid, 10,* 17–22.

TIAA–CREF. (1998, March). Higher education: Enrollment trends and staffing needs. *Research Dialogues* [On-line serial], *55.* http://www.tiaa-cref.org/set-ar.html (September 10, 1999)

Trueman, M., & Hartley, J. (1996). A comparison between the time-management skills and academic performance of mature and traditional-entry university students. *Higher Education, 32,* 199–215.

Vacc, N. A., DeVaney, S. B., & Wittmer, J. (1995). *Experiencing and counseling multicultural and diverse populations* (3rd ed.). Bristol, PA: Accelerated Development.

Wall, V. A., & Evans, N. J. (Eds.). (in press). *Toward acceptance: Sexual orientation issues on campus.* Washington, DC: American College Personnel Association.

Wheaton, J. B., & Robinson, D. C. (1983). Responding to the needs of re-entry women: A comprehensive campus model. *NASPA Journal, 21,* 44–51.

Wilson, J., & Christian, C. (1986). Non-traditional female students tell what they want from a college. *The College Student Journal, 20,* 428–429.

Wortley, D. B., & Amatea, E. S. (1982). Mapping adult life changes: A conceptual framework for organizing adult development theory. *Personnel and Guidance Journal, 60,* 476–482.

9

College Counseling and the Needs of Multicultural Students

DORIS J. WRIGHT

FOCUS QUESTIONS

1. What are the academic, personal, and developmental experiences of multicultural students on college campuses today?

2. What challenges exist for college counselors in delivering culturally sensitive counseling and programming services to multicultural students?

3. How can college counselors most effectively address the needs of multicultural students?

ISSUES

Multicultural college students will experience developmental and daily dilemmas as they go through college in the new millennium. For many of these students, professional counseling can help them effectively resolve their problems so they can resume their academic progress. Finding the appropriate counseling intervention for multicultural students can be an arduous process if counselors are poorly equipped and insufficiently tooled to provide culturally relevant interventions. Moreover, college counselors who fail in their efforts to make their centers inviting to racial, cultural, and ethnic students will find their work with them a daunting task indeed. Those counselors who choose to remain ignorant about the cultural, racial, linguistic, and ethnic contexts of their multicultural clients are not practicing in keeping with reasonable standards of care and professional ethics. Providing effective multicultural counseling for multicultural students not only is practical in light of colleges' increasing diversity of enrollment but also is an ethical and moral duty for counseling in the new millennium.

The purpose of this chapter is to offer college counselors practical suggestions regarding how to work most effectively with multicultural student-clients. Using case vignettes, effective counseling with multicultural students is illustrated, and relevant professional skills for multicultural counseling are highlighted. I begin this discussion by first defining multicultural students and the characteristics of their cultural groups.

Characteristics of Multicultural Students

Who are multicultural students vis-à-vis campuses that are predominantly Eurocentric in their political and social structures? For the purposes of this chapter, the term *multicultural students* refers to those persons who are African American, Asian American, Native American, Hispanic, or Latino and those of mixed-race ancestries (Jenkins, 1999, p. 17). Over the years, multicultural students have been identified using a host of terms and phrases. Not all of these terms are accurate, nor do they offer favorable characterizations of multicultural persons. Among the terms used to describe multicultural students are the following: *students of color, diverse/diversified, cultural minority, underserved, mar-*

ginalized, indigenous, invisible, oppressed, culturally different, disen-franchised, numerical, and psychological minority. Multicultural students enroll in 2- and 4-year schools, large and small schools, and private and public institutions (U.S. Bureau of the Census, 1998). All 50 states have multicultural students enrolled in their universities. They are a significant presence in the fabric of college life.

It is important for counselors to understand three points about multicultural students' presence on campuses, especially in Eurocentric college environments. Jenkins (1999) noted that multicultural students (a) come from home communities that have been marginalized by color, class, or economic status; (b) have worldviews and cultural socialization patterns that vary from the traditional Eurocentric beliefs, socialization patterns, and practices found on college campuses; and (c) often represent poor, immigrant, and other marginalized people in world communities of the United States, Africa, Asia, and Central and South America. They bring heterogeneity to the college campus and to the counseling center in ways that have never happened before in the history of American colleges. This diversity of student enrollment is a permanent shift in the makeup of U.S. colleges and universities for which counselors must be prepared.

African Americans. The U.S. Bureau of the Census has projected that African Americans will exceed 35,469,000 by the year 2000 and 37,793,000 by the year 2005 (as cited in Baruch & Manning, 1999, p. 110). In 1995, 1,473,700 African Americans were enrolled in college, of which 917,000 were female (U.S. Bureau of the Census, 1998). Most African American college students attend public institutions (including historically Black colleges), according to U.S. Bureau of the Census (1998) data. Most African Americans reside in metropolitan areas such as New York, Chicago, and Detroit (U.S. Bureau of the Census, 1998). Recent housing trends, however, show an increase in the number of African Americans living in suburban areas.

Asian Pacific Americans. The term *Asian Pacific Americans*, which has been used since the 1960s, applies to 43 different cultural groups, including 28 Asian groups and 15 Pacific Island groups (Lee, 1996, as cited in Baruch & Manning, 1999, p. 163). These cultural groups are categorized into 4 major groups. East Asian (e.g., Chinese, Japanese, Korean), Pacific Island (e.g., Hawaiian, Samoan), Southeast Asian (e.g., Thai, Vietnamese), and South Asian (e.g., Indian, Pakistani) are the cultural groups represented (Baruch & Manning, 1999, p. 163). Combined across all groups, 75% of Asian Pacific Americans complete high school, and 20% earn a bachelor's degree. In 1995, almost 797,400 Asian American students were enrolled in colleges; most were enrolled in public institutions (U.S. Bureau of the Census, 1998).

Hispanic Americans. Hispanic Americans are the nation's largest language minority group (Baruch & Manning, 1999). They include a variety of Spanish-speaking cultures whose origins are from Mexico, Central and South America, Puerto Rico, Cuba, Guatemala, and El Salvador. Hispanics may best be described as Mexican Americans, Spanish Americans, Latin Americans, Chicanos, Puerto Ricans, Cubans, Guatemalans, and Salvadorians (U.S. Bureau of the Census, 1993, as cited in Baruch & Manning, 1999). Although these Hispanics share many values and goals, each group has distinct cultural goals. In 1993, 54% of all Hispanic Americans lived in two states—Texas and California (U.S. Bureau of the Census, 1993b). U.S. Bureau of the Census (1998) data reported that 1,093,800 were enrolled in U.S. colleges and universities in 1995. Of that group, more than 582,000 were enrolled in 2-year schools.

Native Americans. Native Americans are people with much diversity. They represent 252 languages, 505 federally recognized tribes, 365 state-recognized tribes, and many nations (Garrett, 1995, as cited in Baruch & Manning, 1999, p. 321). Almost half of all Native Americans live west of the Mississippi River in six states: Oklahoma, California, Arizona, New Mexico, Alaska, and Washington (U.S. Bureau of the Census, 1993a). Almost 9% of Native Americans have received a bachelor's degree or attained higher forms of education. In 1998, 131,300 Native American students were enrolled in colleges around the country (U.S. Bureau of the Census, 1998).

This brief demographic introduction to multicultural students reminds counselors that the multicultural groups represented on campus are heterogeneous. As such, it would be unwise for counselors to generalize across these racial and cultural groups. As a student population, their cultural heterogeneity challenges counselors to ask for clarity about racial and cultural issues before making assumptions and gross generalizations about a specific cultural group.

Case Vignettes

Two case vignettes are described below. Each case represents a typical counseling concern that college counselors might help students resolve. Throughout the remainder of this chapter, these two clients are used to illustrate multicultural elements of counseling. The cases are structured in such a way that no single past or current client could be identified so as to protect the anonymity of individual clients, the counseling centers, and the institutions involved.

The Case of Lynette. Lynette is a 19-year-old mixed-race sophomore. Her mother is African American, and her father is Cuban. She is bilingual, and Spanish was her first language spoken at home. She was raised in a middle-class, largely Caucasian suburb in a northeastern city. She graduated from a magnet school for the sciences and was a popular, intelligent student who earned a B+ average in her freshman year at a public institution as a premed/biology major.

Lynette was upset after she was not accepted into the Omega We Du sorority (a pseudonym), a popular Caucasian Greek organization, although the sorority had pledged two or three African American and Hispanic women in the past year. Now Lynette feels hurt, rejected, and devalued. This rejection comes just 2 weeks after she broke up with her boyfriend. She blames herself and believes she was rejected because she is biracial. Her grades are suffering, and she has withdrawn from friends. Lynette is depressed and despondent. She has contemplated suicide and has frequent thoughts about taking pills and alcohol. She mentioned her suicidal thoughts to a friend in the residence hall, who told the Director of Multicultural Services. It was the Director who walked Lynette over to the counseling center.

The Case of Michael. Michael is an African American engineering senior preparing to graduate in May. He is the eldest of four children.

Both of his parents are engineers. He has been interviewing for engineering jobs around the country for the past 2 months. Michael has been dating Angela for 1½ years, and they have become serious about their relationship. They have talked about Angela joining him when she finishes school next year. They have even spoken once about marriage.

Michael was out with some friends at a local bar when he spotted Angela seated at a table with another man. He was angry, hurt, and crushed. Later that evening, he phoned Angela and broke up with her. Two weeks have passed, and Michael is still moping around. He is sad and has withdrawn from his close friends. His grades are plummeting. He blew an interview with a big engineering firm. He has not told his anyone in his family about the breakup because he is ashamed and embarrassed about it.

His friends are tired of his moping around. As a last resort, his friends dragged him into the counseling center to see a counselor and demanded that he be seen that same day. Michael is reluctant to see a counselor because he thinks "counseling is for wussies." He tells the intake counselor that he's having academic difficulties and never mentions the relationship breakup with Angela.

Counseling Issues for Multicultural Students

Multicultural students, like Lynette and Michael, come to counseling with issues similar to those of other students: relationship difficulties, rejection, anxiety, depression, or hopelessness. However, in addition to these developmental issues, multicultural students must manage social and political oppression, economic disempowerment, and racial, cultural, and language discrimination—life experiences that Caucasian and traditional college students do not experience. These racial and language discrimination experiences, when coupled with age-specific developmental concerns, combine to create unique counseling issues for counselors. These special issues of multicultural students may be categorized in the following manner.

- Role overload
- Psychological or emotional support
- Career choice
- Systemic bias, discrimination, and prejudice
- Communication barriers

Role Overload. Multicultural students arrive on campus with role expectations and role obligations from their families, communities, and friends. Some multicultural students are obligated financially to their families while taking classes. It is not uncommon for multicultural students to have some financial duty to send money home for the care of younger siblings or other family members while supporting themselves. In addition, some students may be obligated to provide encouragement to younger siblings who look to them for moral and emotional support.

In the case of single-parent families, the adult multicultural student may be expected to provide emotional support to an overburdened single parent, an aging grandparent, or an ailing godparent. Still others are themselves single parents and, as such, have child-rearing and child-care responsibilities. These family and financial role expectations, when coupled with academic duties, combine to create overlapping roles that can overwhelm and overburden multicultural students, thereby reducing their time and energy for study and for personal rejuvenation.

Michael feels unspoken pressure to succeed, just as his parents did when they were in school. Also, it is possible he is refusing to confide in his family because he doesn't want his younger siblings to make fun of him and see him as a failure. These perceptions, whether real or imagined, can create unrealistic role expectations that contribute to role overload. Because African American families place a high value on getting an education and completing college, Michael feels the unexpressed family pressure to graduate. Fulfilling these familial role expectations can be overwhelming to him now as his college career ends. The breakup is an unexpected loss, and this change adds yet another role burden to his relocation after graduation.

Psychological Support. Multicultural students, like their Caucasian counterparts, need affirmation and emotional gratification to support their growth and to help manage the daily challenges of academic life. But unlike Caucasians, the college environment may not provide the necessary psychological or emotional support for multicultural students if the campus environment is culturally naive or insensitive to these students' emotional, developmental, and psychological needs. Without obvious support, multicultural students like Lynette and Michael feel alone and isolated and lack the sense of belonging that is so critical for academic success. Moreover, if multicultural students do not receive adequate psychological support, they begin to internalize the negative messages that come from difference (Jenkins, 1999, p. 7). Certainly, Lynette seems to have internalized the rejection messages and has been unable to discern and accept positive self-attributions. For Michael, his internalization of difference has been to feel alone and abandoned by his ex-girlfriend and by a campus community that does not understand his concerns. His feelings have become translated as shame and embarrassment.

Career Choice. The choice of a career is an important family decision for multicultural students. Career choice takes a special familial, cultural, and economic context for those students who are the first in their families to attend college. For these students, the choice of a major or a career is made with the approval of the family's head of household. It is not uncommon for multicultural students to consult their parents, godparents, and others concerning their choice of a major or a career. Counselors must recognize how cultural values and beliefs influence this significant developmental marker. How family and cultural context are considered when making career choices are factors that counselors must help multicultural students examine as they make their career choices. It is entirely possible that career choice is relational in nature. If such were true, then a healthy functioning multicultural student would effect a career decision within a larger social or cultural frame of reference. The counselor working with Michael about his job interview success (or lack thereof) must realize that he makes his decision within the context of familial values and beliefs. Moreover, Michael's parents, who are both engineers, shape his career perceptions. A nurturing and sensitive counselor must recognize the cultural importance that career choice has for Michael, Lynette, and other multicultural students.

Systemic Bias, Discrimination, and Prejudice. Multicultural students come to college from communities and families that have been victims of systemic bias, discrimination, and prejudice. Racial prejudice, language discrimination, and institutional biases have left an indelible mark on the young lives of these students. Counselors have an ethical and professional obligation to help multicultural students live through these violating acts and thrive despite these experiences. Multicultural students bring these recollections to college, and these recollections shape how these students perceive the campus environment and how they develop trust in the institution to support and nurture them throughout their college experience. Lynette's counselor must be careful not to dismiss Lynette's assertions that she was rejected because of her biracial identity status. The counselor must help Lynette process and rid herself of any negative self-attributions that have arisen from this perception so they do not stifle her personal and academic development. Counselors are challenged to respond to students' reports of such discrimination incidents with genuineness and belief so those multicultural students learn how to trust the college environment once again.

Communication Barriers. Language minority students come from families in which English was not their first language and is not currently the language spoken informally at home. These barriers pose two dilemmas for counseling these students. First, language minority students may feel the most comfortable sharing and disclosing in their primary language, such as Spanish, Korean, or Cantonese. Second, the translation of counseling terms, such as *empathy,* can alter their meaning significantly such that the counseling process is affected. Counselors who are not aware of these language translation changes in meaning may miss some valuable affective and cognitive content that can have an adverse effect on the efficacy of counseling interventions with linguistic multicultural students. Lynette's counselor should ask Lynette if she is comfortable discussing private matters in English. If not, her counselor is challenged to evaluate (a) how the linguistic differences affect one's ability to form a therapeutic alliance and (b) whether Lynette can work with a monolingual counselor (i.e., one who speaks and understands only the English language). Also, Lynette's counselor must be cautious in interpreting her suicidal expressions to be certain the cognitive and affective elements are understood clearly.

Five areas of concern are important to examine when counselors are working with multicultural students: role overload, psychological or emotional support, career choice, systemic bias and discrimination, and communication barriers. Counselors are asked to consider these areas when entering counseling relationships with multicultural students, whether they be individual or multiperson therapies. The likely outcomes are threefold: (a) increased awareness of cultural and racial components related to effective counseling; (b) recognition of cultural variables within the counseling process; and (c) creation of culturally relevant, meaningful therapeutic interventions.

RECOMMENDATIONS FOR ACTION

The final step in this discussion is to offer concrete suggestions to counselors for enhancing their counseling with multicultural students. Counselors must be careful not to stereotype cultural or racial groups on the basis of their own misperceptions or information they were taught in graduate school. Well-trained counselors have learned to refine their basic counseling techniques (e.g., paraphrasing, probing, summarizing) to explore students' cultural backgrounds. Just as counselors are taught to probe and question abuse survivors and trauma victims with care and sensitivity, they must exercise similar sensitivity when exploring a multicultural student's cultural, racial, or linguistic background.

Ethical Standards

Counselors are advised to reacquaint themselves with the American Counseling Association's (1995) *Code of Ethics and Standards of Practice* and give attention to its statements regarding diversity as an ethical imperative. The American Counseling Association's 1995 revision of the ethics code contains some of the most affirmative language regarding diversity and multicultural practice found anywhere. Several statements pertain specifically to multicultural or diversity issues and are highlighted below.

- The *preamble* encourages counselors to embrace a multicultural approach.
- *Standard A.2. Respecting diversity* contains two sections regarding diversity. *Standard A.2.a Nondiscrimination* states that counselors should not condone or engage in any discrimination. *Standard A.2.b Respecting differences* advises counselors to understand diverse cultural backgrounds and to examine their own values and beliefs.
- *Standard C.2.a Boundaries of competence* suggests that counselors should increase their boundaries of competence by gaining person-

al awareness, knowledge, and skills in working with culturally diverse populations.

- *Standard C.5 Public responsibility* contains two specific diversity guidelines. *Standard C.5.a Nondiscrimination* reaffirms counselors' obligation not to discriminate against students, clients, or supervisees in any manner. *Standard C.5.b Sexual harassment* states that counselors do not engage in sexual harassment.
- *Standard D.1.i Discrimination* says that counselors, as employers or employees, do not condone or engage in practices that are inhumane, illegal, or unjustifiable in hiring or promotion.
- *Standard E.5.b Cultural sensitivity* suggests that counselors should consider students' socioeconomic and cultural experiences when diagnosing mental disorders.
- *Standards E.6.b Culturally diverse populations* reminds counselors to be cautious when selecting tests for culturally diverse populations.
- *Standard E.8 Diversity in testing* asks counselors to use caution when using assessment techniques, making evaluations, and interpreting performance of culturally diverse populations not used in the standardization sample.
- *Standard F.1.a Counselor educators and trainers* encourages counselors as teachers to make an effort to include human diversity in their course curriculum.
- *Standard F.2.i Diversity in programs* says that counselors should be sensitive to diversity issues in recruitment and retention of students, faculty, and administrators.
- *Standard G.1.f Research responsibilities and diversity* guides counselors to be sensitive to diversity issues when conducting research with diverse populations.

Most counselors are genuinely and sincerely committed to offering culturally sensitive counseling interventions to their clients. However, not all counselors are clear about how best to achieve this counseling task. The following suggestions are practical ideas intended to help counselors enhance their relationships with multicultural students. They are applicable for beginning or senior clinicians and are designed for small and large counseling centers.

Diversity Protocol

Several basic questions are important to consider when counselors are working with multicultural students. A sampling of pertinent questions is described for use at five critical phases of counseling: (a) intake, (b) goal setting, (c) working phase, (d) solidifying growth and gains, and (e) closure and termination. Counselors should use the following questions to help guide their counseling with multicultural clients. These questions should be added to whatever questions counselors would ask in the course of therapy. They are not offered as a substitute for a standard clinical interview or an assessment protocol.

Intake

1. How does the student's cultural, racial, or ethnic background influence the presenting concerns? How do race and culture influence the student's desire to seek counseling?
2. How would you characterize the student's racial identity? What is the student's racial self-designation? How important is that racial self-designation to the presenting concern? How does the student assign value to his or her own racial or cultural group?
3. What are the client's familial or cultural views about counseling? How do religious views affect the presenting concerns or reasons for seeking counseling?
4. In what cultural context did the student's presenting concern occur?
5. How do racial and cultural factors influence the development of trust in you as a counselor?
6. What is the student's cultural worldviews about counseling and the helping process?

Goal Setting

1. How do racial, cultural, and ethnic variables influence the student's willingness to set workable counseling goals?
2. How will racial and cultural factors influence how counseling goals are set? How might the client's racial identity and worldview shape goal setting?
3. What views do you (the counselor) hold regarding cultural and racial factors in goal setting?

4. What cultural biases and beliefs do you (the counselor) hold about goal setting with multicultural students?
5. If you did not consider cultural and racial factors in goal setting, what important clinical information would be lost?
6. What is the cultural or racial context of your counseling center? Is that cultural context congruent with that of the multicultural student?

Working Phase

1. How will you (the counselor) adjust your counseling interventions to accommodate cultural and racial factors?
2. How do cultural and racial factors influence the client's openness to try out new interventions?
3. How do cultural and racial factors affect a client's resistance to working in therapy? How will you (the counselor) manage this culturally based resistance?
4. How will your own (the counselor's) values and prejudices restrict your ability to work effectively with this client? How do you know your proposed counseling interventions are culturally appropriate and ethically sound?
5. How does your counseling theoretical approach explain cultural factors within therapy?
6. What does cultural context have to do with your choice of counseling interventions?

Solidifying Growth and Gains

1. Into what cultural context will your client implement newly learned behaviors or awarenesses?
2. What social, cultural, or racial factors will help to solidify the new learning?
3. What cultural, gender, or racial factors might inhibit the maintenance of the new learning?
4. What other counselor responsibilities are necessary to extend this new learning into a cultural, social, or racial setting?
5. How does the multicultural client feel about the acquisition of this new insight, behavior, or belief? What reservations might the student have about continuing the new learning in either the home or the campus community?

Closure and Termination

1. What cultural factors are present within the closure or termination process?
2. What cultural or social beliefs do multicultural students have about being referred to another counselor on termination?
3. How does termination occur within the student's cultural or racial group? How has the student achieved termination within a culture different from his or her own group?
4. What are the counselor's cultural misperceptions and biases about termination with the multicultural client? How do they restrict or enhance the termination process?
5. How might cultural and social factors influence a student's resistance to termination?
6. How did the student's racial identity affect the student's participation in termination?
7. What changes have occurred in the student's racial and cultural identity, if any, since the beginning of counseling?

Multicultural Counseling Competencies

A further step in enhancing college counselors' practice with multicultural students is the use of multicultural competencies. These standards and guidelines assist counselors in examining their attitudes, beliefs, knowledge, and skills regarding counseling multicultural persons. An excellent place to start is with the Multicultural Counseling Competencies developed by Sue, Arredondo, and McDavis (1992) and further interpreted by Arredondo et al. (1996).

As colleges become culturally and racially diverse so will counseling centers. College counselors and other mental health professionals will be asked to confront cultural, racial, and ethnic issues within their counseling services if they are to remain open and viable support resources for multicultural students. College counselors cannot remain locked within the confines of their offices and believe they are providing effective and ethical counseling services. They must become integrated into the total fabric of their colleges. It becomes their duty to understand the college environment and its cultural milieu and then later to help multicultural students to live and thrive within the campus's social context. The message is a simple one: Effective multicultural counselors involve themselves outside their "50 minute" hour. They participate as full partners in the campus community. As such, they must become familiar with the cultural norms, beliefs, customs, and practices of the campus they serve. This awareness later becomes a useful skill as counselors support multicultural students in their academic and personal growth goals. Effective multicultural counselors are those persons who (a) are attuned to their own multicultural talents and limitations, (b) appreciate their clients' diversity, and (c) promote multiculturalism throughout the entire campus community.

Counseling in the next millennium will require counselors to broaden their professional roles beyond the 50-minute hour. They must develop a social consciousness and use it to strengthen their culturally appropriate interventions for all students. Is there an intended or likely outcome from this multicultural emphasis? For multicultural students, three benefits are clear.

- Counselors who step outside the "box" will discover a multicultural, multidimensional campus environment that enriches their service to multicultural students.
- Counselors who learn about social climate will create counseling interventions that are culturally framed to fit multicultural students' cultural contexts and worldviews.
- Counselors who accept diversity as an ethical imperative for the 21st century will lose their monolithic thinking and adopt pluralistic views of counseling. Multicultural clients will be viewed as adding value to the campus community and to the counseling process.

SUMMARY

One message resonates throughout this chapter: Multiculturalism is an integral aspect of the counseling process. Without such diversity, there is no practice of counseling. Counselors are challenged to find creative, ethically responsible, and culturally relevant professional counseling interventions for all students. College counseling in the new millennium is multicultural, multilingual, and multidimensional. It is grounded in theory, embellished by ethics, graced with diversity, and measured by social context. These outcomes are challenging to be sure, but they are not impossible for counselors and counseling centers to manage well. Together, these suggestions provide a template for working with multicultural students into the millennium and beyond.

REFERENCES

American Counseling Association. (1995). *Code of ethics and standards of practice.* Alexandria, VA: Author.

Arredondo, P., Toporek, R., Brown, S., Jones, S., Locke, D., Sanchez, J., & Stadler, H. (1996). *Operationalization of the multicultural counseling competencies.* Alexandria, VA: Association for Multicultural Counseling and Development.

Baruch, L., & Manning, M. (1999). *Multicultural counseling and psychotherapy: A lifespan perspective* (2nd ed.). Upper Saddle River, NJ: Merrill.

Jenkins, Y. M. (1999). Diversity in college settings: The challenge for helping professionals. In Y. M. Jenkins (Ed.), *Diversity in college settings: Directives for helping professionals* (pp. 5–20). New York: Routledge.

Sue, D., Arredondo, P., & McDavis, J. (1992). Multicultural counseling competencies and standards: A call to the profession. *Journal of Counseling and Development, 70,* 477–486.

U.S. Bureau of the Census. (1993a). *We the American . . . first Americans.* Washington, DC: Author.

U.S. Bureau of the Census. (1993b). *We the American . . . Hispanics.* Washington, DC: Author.

U.S. Bureau of the Census. (1998). *Statistical abstracts of the United States: 1998.* Washington, DC: Author.

10

College Counseling and International Students

JUN-CHIH GISELA LIN

FOCUS QUESTIONS

1. What are the main issues faced by international college students?

2. What are the characteristics of international students on U.S. college campuses today?

3. What challenges exist for college counselors in delivering counseling programs and services to international students?

4. What are the characteristics of culturally competent counselors and culturally effective programming when working with international college students?

ISSUES

Elena is from Yugoslavia. She was referred to the counseling center by a faculty member because of her depressed mood and suicidal feelings. She came alone to the United States and has not made many friends. She is not used to the food or the weather, and she feels homesick and lonely. Elena cries often, cannot sleep well at night, has little appetite, and has difficulty concentrating. She did not do well on her midterm examination and has lost her motivation in school. Elena wonders whether she made a mistake in coming to the United States. She is afraid of failure and of disappointing her family.

Sarah is from South Africa. She came alone to the United States 2 years ago and has not seen her husband since that time. Financial limitations have prevented her and her husband from visiting either in the United States or in South Africa. She is homesick, has problems sleeping, has a decreased appetite, and has difficulty concentrating on her studies. Sarah worries that her husband may not love her anymore because she receives fewer and fewer letters from him. She confided her concerns to her priest, who referred her to the college counseling center.

Ting is from Taiwan. She was self-referred to the counseling center. She learned from the Taiwanese Student Association's web site that a Taiwanese counselor works at the counseling center. She was accused of plagiarism on her dissertation by her adviser and has been asked to voluntarily leave the university or be formally charged. Ting told her dissertation committee members that she did not understand the concept of plagiarism, but no one believes her. When she was asked whether she copied material without appropriate citation, she admitted that she had copied her adviser's and other students' dissertations in the introductory chapter because the introduction was about historical events. She does not understand what she has done wrong because her research design and research data were her own works. Ting does not understand why her adviser did not correct her when she was preparing her initial draft.

International students, like Elena, Sarah, and Ting, are a significant presence on U.S. college campuses today. The term *international students* refers to individuals who are neither U.S. citizens nor permanent residents but who temporarily reside in the United States for educational purposes. Their cultural backgrounds often distinguish them from host country students (Paige, 1990). International students face similar academic, career, and nonacademic concerns (e.g., social, cultural, financial) as well as their own unique problems related to living in a foreign culture (Lin & Yi, 1997). Because of the cultural differences and international students' unique circumstances, the degree of the international students' concerns may be more severe. For example, adjustment problems are common among new college students. However, in Elena's case, her adjustment problems may be more serious than those of other freshmen because of the greater cultural gap and less social support. In Sarah's case, her problems are similar to those of other people who have long-distance relationships. However, because of greater physical distance, higher long-distance telephone rates, and more expensive airline costs between the United States and South Africa, she is less likely to have contact with her husband as often as those who have long-distance relationships within U.S. borders. In Ting's case, many students might plagiarize because of their lack of skills and knowledge; however, language difficulties and cultural differences complicate Ting's ability to respond appropriately to and negotiate effectively with her dissertation committee.

The purpose of this chapter is to offer college counselors practical suggestions on how to work effectively with international students. It examines the challenges that international students face on American campuses and the challenges that college counselors often face when working with international students. Factors to consider for service delivery, including the characteristics of culturally competent counselors and culturally effective intervention and programming, are examined. This chapter provides practical suggestions for modifying traditional counseling approaches to meet the needs and expectations of international students and discusses ethical dilemmas that may occur when providing these culturally effective services.

Characteristics of International Students

According to a report from the Institutes of International Education (Davis, 1997), there were 457,984 international students in the United States during the 1996–1997 academic year, a 1,200% increase since 1954. Among them, 59% were male, 41% were female, and 84.4% were single.

Undergraduates comprised 81.3% of the group, and 47.7% were graduate students who paid for their education with personal or family funds. Business and management (20.9%) and engineering (15.5%) were the two most popular majors; 41.5% were graduate students; 36.1% sought bachelor degrees; 11.6% sought associate degrees; and 10.7% came for practical training, nondegree, and intensive English programs. It is noteworthy that there was an 8.6% increase in the number of international students studying in community colleges from the previous 1995–1996 academic year. Community colleges tend to offer more personalized services through smaller classes and flexible course schedules. Community college is also more affordable (Davis, 1997, p. 116).

More than half of international students are from Asia (56.93%), followed by Europe (14.92%), Latin America (10.83%), Middle East (6.52%), North America (5.16%, excluding the United States), Africa (4.82%), and Oceania (0.81%). Japan has the largest subgroup (10.11%), followed by China (9.28%), South Korea (8.11%), India (6.69%), Taiwan (6.66%), Canada (5.02%), Malaysia (3.17%), Thailand (2.94%), Indonesia (2.72%), Hong Kong (2.39%), Germany (1.963%), and Mexico (1.959%). These numbers may change because of the Asian economic crisis, but Asian countries are still likely to represent the largest numbers of international students in the United States (Davis, 1997).

As previously mentioned, international students often face similar academic, career, and nonacademic concerns (e.g., social, cultural, financial) as well as their own unique problems related to living in a foreign culture (Lin & Yi, 1997). Common academic issues include understanding a different grading system, selecting courses, learning relevant study skills, feeling more comfortable reading, writing and speaking in English, understanding the lectures and the different expectations of the instructors, and getting used to the competitiveness of their classmates. Even the basic approach to learning provides a formidable challenge. Many international students are used to memorizing course material, so learning to synthesize and draw conclusions from the material is a new experience (Wehrly, 1988). Plagiarism is an often overlooked but serious problem, as shown in Ting's case.

International students experience career-related problems as well. They must find a major that is relevant to their own interests yet still meet their family's expectations about an acceptable career direction.

They must obtain practical training opportunities in the United States and then find employment in their home countries. Some international students even find themselves, following graduation from U.S. universities, overqualified for the job markets in their home countries (Leong, 1984).

High expectations to succeed and fear of failure frequently lead to symptoms of anxiety and depression. Sometimes students' difficulties are manifested in "psychotic and neurotic reactions and psychosomatic complaints" (Salem, 1985, p. 54). Adjustment issues include effectively communicating and interacting with U.S. citizens; getting used to the food, climate, campus, and local community; being far away from home; studying long hours; and coping with loneliness, social isolation, and relationship difficulties, as in the cases of Elena and Sarah. Maintenance of their cultural identity may be a challenge for some international students. Non-Christians find it difficult to find a place to practice their religion, especially if they live in small communities. International students often encounter overt and covert prejudice and discrimination in the classroom, in their community (e.g., housing), or in both because of the differences in their appearance, dress, accents, or customs. These differences make for cultural clashes. For example, an Asian student complained about the excessive noise his neighbors' made while those same neighbors complained about the smell of the student's cooking.

Financial pressure is another source of stress for most international students. They usually have to pay out-of-state tuition, have limited work opportunities because of immigration laws, and are not eligible for U.S. federal assistance such as financial aid. Their funding is unstable because the exchange rates vary. For example, the bundle of five major currencies (dollars, marks, yen, francs, and pounds) increased 64% from March 1996 to March 1998. Many students from Indonesia, Malaysia, Philippines, South Korea, and Thailand were significantly affected because of the Asian economic crisis.

International students who have good English language skills, who have more social support, and who have more contacts with U.S. students report more satisfaction in their study experiences in the United States (Leong, 1984). There are group differences in the concerns among international students because they are a diverse group. For example, in my own experience, undergraduate students tend to report more problems with language barriers, choice of majors, and identity crisis, where-as graduate students tend to have more complaints about homesickness, dating, and marital problems.

Challenges in Counseling International Students

International students underuse counseling services despite their diffi-culties (Al-Qusem, 1987; Brinson & Kottler, 1995; Salem, 1985). The rea-sons are likely to be related to their negative attitudes toward help seek-ing and their unfamiliarity with counseling services and counselors' roles (Oredein, 1988). Because of the stigma often attached to mental health issues (e.g., crazy people go to counseling, weak people ask for help with their personal problems) and the cultural constraints of not dis-cussing personal matters with strangers (Hayes & Lin, 1994), internation-al students may perceive counseling as an untrustworthy and inappro-priate way to address personal problems. Instead, these students might seek help from a co-national friend, relative, spouse, academic adviser, faculty member, or American friend before they would seek profession-al help (Salem, 1985). International students often believe it to be more culturally acceptable to have physical or academic problems than psy-chological problems (Lin & Yi, 1997). Because they tend to wait to seek professional help, when they do come, they may be experiencing a sig-nificant subjective crisis (Lin, 1996). These students may seem very demanding at that point because they are highly stressed, expect to be seen immediately, and desire fast relief.

The major challenges for counselors when working with international students are overestimation or underestimation of the influence of cul-ture; cultural differences in assessment and intervention strategies; lan-guage barriers; an understanding of the different cultural norms, values, worldviews, religions, customs, and political beliefs; verbal and nonver-bal communication styles; financial ability; and an understanding of clients' immediate needs and expectations. In my experience, interna-tional students seldom self-refer to counseling. Counseling may not be part of their cultural practice, especially those who are from non-Western countries. Even when they seek counseling, they may not be familiar with what counseling is and what counselors do. International students tend to respond best to directive, active influencing (Sue, 1990) and to a concrete, structural, problem-solving counseling style (Lin, 1996). However, these expectations and preferences may be inconsistent with counselors' training, cultural beliefs, or personal style. If counselors overemphasize Western cultural values (e.g., individualism, competitiveness), hold rigid stereotypes, exhibit cultural and communication barriers, or are unable or unwilling to adopt a different counseling style, they will tend to be less effective with international students (Leong, 1984; Sue, 1990).

International students, by virtue of cultural and language differences, may have difficulty articulating their problems to a counselor. They may have difficulty expressing their feelings; they may not understand why dealing with feelings is important; and they may be unwilling to disclose personal information, especially if that information is not relevant to their presenting concerns. If counselors do not seem to understand international students' subjective experiences, or if they are inflexible or unwilling to meet the needs of these students (e.g., offer advice to address their immediate concerns), international students may not return for further services.

RECOMMENDATIONS FOR ACTION

Counselor characteristics play a major role in effective intervention. International students prefer counselors who are honest, genuine, trustworthy, accepting, concrete, warm, interpersonally skilled, and empathic (Bradley, Parr, Lan, Bingi, & Gould, 1995). They seek those who can address immediacy and provide structure in counseling interactions and who are flexible in approach, respectful of cultural differences (Al-Qusem, 1987), nonjudgmental, and personal (Lin, 1996). In addition, culturally competent counselors are culturally aware and knowledgeable of assumptions, values, and biases of both counselors and students; open and respectful to different value systems; tolerant of ambiguity; and willing to learn about cultural differences (Cadieux & Wehrly, 1986).

It is important that college counselors adopt multiple helping roles when serving international students (Sue, Ivey, & Pederson, 1996). This often means moving beyond the confines of the counseling office to be

actively involved in assisting students. These multiple roles include adviser, advocate, teacher, consultant, problem solver, facilitator of indigenous
support systems, mediator, resource person, referral agent, case manag-
er, expert witness, mentor, and role model. For example, in Ting's case,
the counselor took on multiple roles to help her appeal the charge of
academic dishonesty. In addition to a traditional counseling role, the
counselor served as an expert witness and advocate for the appeals committee and provided consultation to faculty members. She served as a
resource person to identify sources of advice for university rules and
regulations, immigration questions, and legal questions. She also encouraged Ting to seek the help of her indigenous support system (i.e.,
spouse, co-nationals) to help with the difficult yearlong process. Ting's
appeal was successful.

Effective Intervention and Programming

Effective intervention and programming that modify traditional counseling approaches and make them more flexible are most helpful in
counseling international students (Lin, 1996). Early education about the
availability of counseling services, types of services, locations, and
effective marketing strategies are important factors when counseling
services are being delivered to international students. Because international students do not usually self-refer to counseling, working with
other university and local groups, such as the international students
office, admissions office, residence halls, English as a Second Language
departments, faculty, academic advisers, student organizations, and religious organizations, is important for referral resources and collaborative
programming (Lin & Yi, 1997). For example, counseling center information could be sent out in new student information packages with the
I-20 (a required documentation from the attending college or university in order to get a student visa) and could be advertised again during
the campus immigration check-in period and orientation.

International students may be reluctant to visit a place with a name
associated only with mental health services. They are more likely to visit
a counseling center that also provides academic and career services.
Marketing strategies could include self-help materials and referral infor-

mation using refrigerator magnets, flyers, bookmarks, and campus newspapers. It is culturally friendly to advertise in various languages, including the location with the building name or with a reference to a campus map, the phone number with instructions on how to make appointments, the different types of services offered and whether there is a charge, and a note about confidentiality. It is also helpful to decorate the building and counseling offices with culturally diverse artwork or photos. Having magazines or newspapers in different languages could provide a welcoming physical environment for international students.

Counseling strategy is another important factor in service delivery. Culturally appropriate counseling styles could help engage students who come for help. Sue (1990) pointed out that culturally different clients often prefer counselors who use directive, active, and influencing skills. For those students who have never been to counseling, it may be helpful to explain what counseling is and to find out what their expectations about counseling are. When international students present with very specific problems, it is most helpful to collect only necessary relevant information and to address their immediate concerns by using a direct, concrete approach. Counselors should acknowledge cultural differences, allow longer silences, and normalize their problems as bicultural or bilingual whenever appropriate (Lin, 1996).

Culturally specific counseling and programs are important when supporting international students (Pederson, 1991). Nontraditional counseling groups are different from traditional counseling or support groups in at least one of the following aspects: psychoeducational or educational in nature; structured or semistructured; flexible in location, attendance, and record keeping; and a mixture of native English speakers and people with international backgrounds. The nontraditional counseling group might have the nature of a support group, but it should avoid using the term *support* because many international students may misunderstand the word in that context (e.g., Do you give me money? Am I weak?).

Nontraditional counseling groups focus on psychoeducation to address international students' needs and concerns or on training in certain skills. These groups often provide various degrees of structure with clear goals so students know what to expect. These groups can be coled by multidisciplinary professionals and peer helpers so as to reduce the stigma generally associated with using counseling services. The use of professionals from various offices who interact with international students and who are likely to understand the students' issues offer several benefits. Students are provided exposure to more people, thus maximizing referral opportunity. The use of international student peer helpers can allow sharing of common experiences, build confidence through their successful experiences, and increase network opportunities with other students. The use of native speakers can help non-English speakers to practice their English speaking skills. Minimizing paperwork will provide the most flexibility for students as well as easy access to services. Drop-in groups are more appropriate than groups that have set agendas so students can come only to meetings in which they are interested. It should be noted that a major difficulty with drop-in groups is the lack of stable attendance; thus, retention of the group members is a major task for this type of group. Providing food at meetings may attract more consistent attendance. An E-mail bulletin board and a student organization listserv advertising various campus and group activities could also serve as a useful reminder.

It is important that college counselors reach out to and consult with the international student community. Outreach and consultation require counselor competency in specific areas of knowledge about cultural differences, the unique needs and interests of international students, and factors preventing international students from using counseling services. Using peer counselors and working collaboratively with the international student community in marketing the services are often effective methods in reaching the international community. College counselors could increase awareness and use of campus counseling services by international students by providing formal outreach programs (e.g., making presentations) and, more informally, by attending international student functions.

Proactive programs, seminars, workshops, and groups could help prevent problems before they arise. Programs that target the needs and interests of international students are likely to increase the use of counseling services (Brinson & Kottler, 1995). It is my experience that some international students do not understand the purpose of a workshop (e.g., biofeedback workshop). Therefore, when counselors are offering proactive programs, it may be better to use the word *seminar* (e.g., relaxation techniques seminar).

Sample academic seminar topics include the following:
- Cultural Differences in Learning Styles
- Taking Notes When English Is Not Your First Language
- Overcoming Test Anxiety
- Too Much to Do But Not Enough Time
- Speed Reading
- Speaking in the Classroom
- Writing Skills

Possible career seminar topics include the following:
- How to Find a Mentor
- Culturally Appropriate Career Decision Making
- Job Interview Skills
- Resume Writing
- Job-Hunting Strategies

Potential personal seminar topics include the following:
- Cultural Adjustment
- Return-Home Adjustment
- Friendship With U.S. Citizens
- Social Skills
- Communication Skills
- Relaxation Skills
- Achieve a Balanced Lifestyle
- Avoiding Harassment

Nontraditional ways to help international students include offering walk-in services, telephone counseling, on-line counseling, or a question-and-answer newspaper column or developing culturally appropriate computer-assisted programs. A counseling center's web site can provide information specific to international students' needs and direct them to other helpful web sites. Walk-in services set no limits on time, and no appointment is needed, thus overcoming some time and cultural issues (Lin, 1996; Sue & Sue, 1990).

Other nontraditional approaches include training peer helpers who speak different languages as peer counselors or translators; offering self-help materials such as handouts, audiotapes and videotapes, and educational slides in different languages; or providing an automated tele-phone line with recordings on self-help topics. For example, CounseLine at Texas A&M University Student Counseling Service offers short 3–5 minute recordings on various self-help topics. Students can call around the clock for a menu of topics (e.g., dealing with loneliness, helping a depressed friend, helping international students) as well as find out the different services available in the counseling center. Information about resources should be offered through a variety of approaches, such as telephone messages, web sites, telephone help-lines, public service announcements on radio and television, and newsletters (Lin, 1996).

Ethical Dilemmas for Service Delivery

Counselors are likely to encounter ethical dilemmas when modifying traditional counseling approaches in order to work effectively with inter-national students. Nontraditional counseling approaches are problematic because the current professional ethical guidelines inadequately address nontraditional service delivery issues. Thus, some counselors may feel uncomfortable offering food to students (it is unethical to "bribe" clients), meeting outside of the counseling center, or doing minimal assessments. Counselors who fulfill nontraditional multiple roles (e.g., mediator, expert witness) may struggle with the question of whether these students are actually "clients." If the counselor attends various international func-tions, the international students may consider the counselor a friend. The students may invite the counselor to their house for dinner, give gifts, ask for rides, ask for their home phone number, or ask to call or visit when-ever they need. They might not understand why a counselor avoids mul-tiple relationships (e.g., being a friend and a counselor at the same time) while the counselor fulfills multiple roles. International students might not understand the issue of confidentiality if they refer their family or friends for help but the counselor cannot tell them how they are doing. These types of boundary issues may be perceived by international stu-dents as rigid and distrustful. Thus, it is important to inform the students about ethical standards as defined by appropriate professional organiza-tions (e.g., the American Counseling Association) at the outset to minimize problems and misunderstandings. Furthermore, if peer counselors or translators are used during the counseling process, they are bound by the same ethical standards. It is the counselors' responsibility to communicate these standards to the peer helpers. Finally, it is important that counselors do not practice outside their areas of competence. It is the counselors' responsibility to understand what their limits are as far as working with students from different cultures. College counselors should consult or make referrals whenever appropriate.

SUMMARY

This chapter provides practical information to help college counselors more effectively serve international students. The characteristics of international students on U.S. college campuses, the challenges college counselors face in delivering culturally effective services, and the characteristics of culturally competent counselors are discussed. International students' use of college counseling services can be increased by providing culturally competent counselors and culturally specific counseling services and outreach programming. Culturally competent college counselors, working actively with campus and community resources, are in a unique position to dramatically improve opportunities for international students to succeed academically and to increase their satisfaction with their scholastic stay in the United States.

REFERENCES

Al-Qusem, N. F. (1987). *Perceptions of Western Michigan University international students regarding seeking personal counseling.* Unpublished doctoral dissertation, Western Michigan University.

Bradley, L., Parr, G., Lan, W. Y., Bingi, B., & Gould, L. J. (1995). Counselling expectations of international students. *International Journal for the Advancement of Counselling, 18,* 21–31.

Brinson, J. A., & Kottler, J. (1995). International students in counseling: Some alternative models. *Journal of College Student Psychotherapy, 9,* 57–70.

Cadieux, R. A. J., & Wehrly, B. (1986). Advising and counseling the international students. In K. R. Pyle (Ed.), *New directions for student services* (pp. 51–63). San Francisco: Jossey-Bass.

Davis, T. M. (Ed.). (1997). *Report on International Educational Exchange, 1997. Open Door 1996/97.* New York: Institutes of International Education.

Hayes, R. L., & Lin, H.-R. (1994). Coming to America: Developing social support systems for international students. *Journal of Multicultural Counseling and Development, 22,* 7–16.

Leong, F. T. L. (1984). *Counseling international students: Relevant resources in high interest area.* Ann Arbor, MI: ERIC Clearinghouse on Counseling and Personnel Services. (ERIC Document Reproduction Service No. ED 250 649)

Lin, J.-C. G. (1996). Counseling college students from Taiwan. In P. D. Pedersen & D. Locke (Eds.), *Cultural and diversity issues in counseling* (pp. 51–53). Greensboro, NC: ERIC Counseling and Student Service Clearinghouse.

Lin, J.-C. G., & Yi, J. (1997). Asian international students' adjustment: Issues and programs suggestions. *College Student Journal, 31,* 473–479.

Oredein, O. O. (1988). *Differences among international students on a measure of attitudes toward seeking professional counseling help.* Unpublished doctoral dissertation, Mississippi State University.

Paige, M. (1990). International students: Cross-cultural psychological perspectives. In W. J. Lonne & J. W. Berry (Series Eds.) & R. Brislin (Vol. Ed.), *Cross-cultural research and methodology series: Vol. 14. Applied cross-cultural psychology* (pp. 161–185). Newbury Park, CA: Sage.

Pederson, P. B. (1991). Counseling international students. *The Counseling Psychologist, 19,* 10–58.

Salem, E. A. (1985). *Attitudes of international students from developing countries toward campus professional psychological services.* Unpublished doctoral dissertation, Southern Illinois University at Carbondale.

Sue, D. W. (1990). Cultural specific techniques in counseling: A conceptual framework. *Professional Psychology: Research and Practice, 21,* 424–433.

Sue D. W., Ivey, A. E., & Pederson, P. B. (1996). *A theory of multicultural counseling & therapy*. Pacific Grove, CA: Brooks/Cole.

Sue, D. W., & Sue, D. (1990). *Counseling the culturally different: Theory and practice* (2nd ed.). New York: Wiley.

Wehrly, B. (1988). Cultural diversity from international perspective, Pt. 2. *Journal of Multicultural Counseling and Development, 16,* 3–14.

PART III

TODAY'S COLLEGE COUNSELOR AND THE INSTITUTION

11

Life–Career Development Counseling

DENNIS W. ENGELS, BONITA C. JACOBS, AND CAROLYN W. KERN

FOCUS QUESTIONS

1. What are some key issues affecting life–career planning and development in higher education today?

2. How are college counselors involved in life–career planning and development?

3. How do college counselors provide effective life–career planning and development services?

4. What are some key career planning and development strategies for college counselor service delivery in the 21st century?

ISSUES

After graduating from college in 1964, a friend of one of the authors started a continuous 30-year employment, culminating in 1994 with retirement as a national president of the same major U.S.-based multinational company that he started with in 1964. Except for one child who is still in college, all of this friend's young adult children work as temporary contract workers, with little prospect of ever holding one job for longer than 5 years. These children's more varied career paths seem as typical today as this friend's career path of long-term, incrementally upward employment with one employer seemed typical yesterday. Today's conditions and future labor market projections (Bridges, 1994; Ettinger, 1996; Feller & Walz, 1997; Rifkin, 1995) suggest that career development matters in new and unprecedented ways (Engels & Harris, 1999). As previous expectations of mutual employer–employee loyalty shrink and traditional safety nets and benefits commensurate with long-term continuous employment erode, college counselors have to help students and others find appropriate means and strategies for owning and caring for their own careers. With continuous increases in new knowledge, current information and knowledge are perishable and at risk of obsolescence, and the general concept of a turnkey college "diploma for life," such as this friend got in 1964, seems a mere historical artifact.

Today and for the foreseeable future, workers will need high-level workplace skills and knowledge, especially skills for continued learning throughout their lives ([Labor] Secretary's Commission on Achieving Necessary Skills [SCANS], 1991, 1992a, 1992b). Individuals also will need to depend increasingly on themselves and their personal resources and assets for career stability. Seen in the light of global and technological change as dominant constants and life–career development as essential to individual survival and prosperity, educators at all levels need new and creative ways to attend to career development. This chapter is aimed at helping college counselors consider new paradigms for promoting and providing individual career development programs and life–career counseling for all students.

A report entitled *America's Choice: High Skills or Low Wages!* from the Commission on Skills of the American Workforce (1990) says that the United States must have workers with high-level skills and knowledge to compete in a global and high-wage market in which new technologies, emerging communications, and other factors radically change the means and strategies for work and successful competition. Cochairing of this study by Ira Magaziner, William Brock, and Ray Marshall, of the Clinton, Reagan, and Carter presidential administrations, respectively, suggests how the fundamental importance of this report transcends political, economic, and philosophical perspectives. *America's Choice: High Skills or Low Wages!* is profound, fundamental, and universal. The stakes are high, we all are shareholders, and everyone in our colleges and universities needs these high skills.

From both policy and operational standpoints, how do college counselors and educators promote career development across the life span? What special roles do counselors play in building visions and goals, addressing current trends, and implementing programs that are both nationally sensitive and locally appropriate in scope, focus, and thrust? In view of the major economic, technological, and other changes cited above, college counselors should consider their willingness to seek new ways to recommit energy and resources to such a vision and goals.

Policy and Other Factors

While the visionary *Goals 2000* (National Education Goals Panel, 1993; White House, 1991) idealized educational and competency programs of the Bush and Clinton administrations and *America's Choice: High Skills or Low Wages!* (Commission on Skills of the American Workforce, 1990) addressed general public and private policy issues, little of the attention has focused on the direct, dramatic impact on individuals. Today, individuals should depend less on external forces and policies and more on internal resources. In times of shrinking job duration and increasing job shifts and changes, global markets, and the many other factors noted in the references cited above, individuals must be good owners and stewards of their own careers, and it all starts before kindergarten and remains a major responsibility throughout life. Implications of this perspective for educators are varied, but good strategies and resources that lend themselves to implementation are readily available. At the college level, these issues seem to require some new thinking and applications.

Knowledge and Skills for the Future

In the competencies identified by the SCANS (1991), we find the knowledge and skills identified by representatives of major businesses, industry, labor, and education that constitute specific individual components of the more general goals listed in the vision of *Goals 2000* (National Education Goals Panel, 1993; White House, 1991). SCANS (1992a) competencies greatly expand the basics of education to encompass a three-part foundation of necessary skills. They include (a) the "3 *Rs*" plus speaking and listening; (b) thinking skills, such as reasoning, decision making, problem solving, and learning to learn; and (c) personal qualities, such as integrity, respect for self and others, and honesty.

Beyond this three-part foundation of (a) the revised basics, (b) thinking skills, and (c) personal characteristics, SCANS (1991) leaders identified five areas of additional competencies that will be required for successful participation in a smart or high-skills workforce: resources, interpersonal, information, systems, and technology. These general competencies encompass the following:

- Resources—identifying, organizing, planning, and allocating time, money, material, and human resources;
- Interpersonal—working with others as a team member, a teacher, a service provider, a leader, and a negotiator who works well with men and women from diverse backgrounds;
- Information—using computers and other means for acquiring, evaluating, maintaining, interpreting, communicating, and using information;
- Systems—understanding, monitoring, correcting, designing, and improving social, organizational, technological, and other complex interrelationships;
- Technology—selecting, applying, and maintaining technological tools and equipment.

Although some educators and counselors have been familiar with many of these necessary knowledge and skill components for a long time (Foster, 1979; Hartz, 1978a, 1978b; National Occupational Information Coordinating Committee [NOICC], 1989, 1997; Texas Advisory Council for Technical–Vocational Education, 1975, 1985), mainstream education has only selectively attended to these competencies, primarily in vocational, career, and technical education, with minimal and marginal focused attention on career development in the preparation of most students. At issue is how attainment of these necessary skills can be widespread, mainstream, and infused within and throughout the curriculum, with major increased mastery of appropriate aspects of these necessary skills and knowledge by all students at all levels of education. Current deficits and voids in the education of far too many highlight major aspects of the challenge of empowering Americans with high skills and knowledge (Isaacson & Brown, 1997; National Alliance of Business, 1990).

Seeking Solutions, Direction, Strategies, and Approaches

Seen in light of so many and such sweeping changes, career planning and development strategies and actions for college counselor service delivery in the 21st century may be facing some of the most critical factors ever. Contemporary workforce challenges, demands, and necessities militate against the compartmentalization common for so long in most educational settings. Eventually, everyone needs to earn a living, and skill building for that purpose has unprecedented urgency today. Without early and focused attention on fundamental and advanced workplace knowledge and skills such as the SCANS (1992a) competencies, many of today's students, even college students who drop out, will be at risk of limited and sporadic employment in dead-end jobs at poverty level and lower incomes with limited or no benefits (Hoyt & Lester, 1995; Rifkin, 1995), to say nothing of the quality-of-life issues attendant to low income, especially for high school and college dropouts. Marshaling resources and identifying and creating opportunities to meet challenges, problems, and barriers are a perennial top priority for educators, but where does one look for resources to address this vital issue of preparing students for empowerment in tomorrow's marketplace?

In the *National Career Development Guidelines (NCDG)* produced by the NOICC (1989, 1997) comes a very strong potential blueprint for facilitating acquisition and mastery of the SCANS (1992a) competencies across the entire life span and across a wide spectrum of institution and agency settings. Acknowledging that no one size fits all, the *NCDG* are designed for state and local adaptation to accommodate, accentuate, and tailor the guidelines to local needs and circumstances, and many state career development guidelines reflect the efficacy of adapting the *NCDG*.

Although labor and workforce development bills and laws, such as the Workforce Investment Act of 1998, are referred to as careers bills, a more precise term might be *jobs bills,* reflecting the narrow and dominant accountability criterion of job placement. From a policy standpoint, college counselors and other educators should promote the lifelong career development of all individuals, rather than merely emphasizing employment manifested in first jobs and next jobs. Additionally, we need career information aimed at both users and developers, rather than mere labor market information.

Redefining Career

In view of the turbulence, constant change, and instability in the world of work today, the world may be ready for a long-standing concept of career counselors who note that each person has one career that is lifelong. Seen in this light, one's career starts in duties and exposure to and experience with work at home, followed by work habits and requirements at school, and then is manifested in a variety of tasks and settings throughout one's life. If each person has one career that is lifelong, policies and programs need to help people get and keep jobs. College counselors should also help people with planning for future careers and balancing and integrating life–work roles and responsibilities with other life roles and responsibilities, for example, family membership, parenting, and citizenship (Hansen, 1997). In addition to definition and integration issues, other issues such as identifying, analyzing, and disseminating appropriate individualized career information and appropriate inclusion of computer-based interactive guidance information systems are vital parts of an overall college counseling program. Although career counselors have been attuned to this message, college counselors may have to reframe to fully embrace and model these and related concepts of definition and integration.

Yet another paradigm shift for some college counselors will be escaping the false dichotomy implicit in the compartmentalization of career counseling. Career literature is replete with the message that career and personal counseling are inseparably linked (Betz & Corning, 1993; Davidson & Gilbert, 1993; Haverkamp & Moore, 1993; Isaacson & Brown, 1997; Krumboltz, 1993; Lucas, 1993; Subich, 1993; Super, 1993; Tolsma, 1993), so college counselors should emphasize the personal and career connections in their services. Career development is not merely about jobs; it is very much about a core area of life that affects other areas of life to such an extent that college counselors should embrace the widest array of integrated service provision. Additionally, career development is so vital and so fundamental that college counselors should consider how best to embrace life–career counseling for its pivotal importance. By extension, college counselors should address issues long ago resolved by public school counselors about whether and how to provide clinical mental health services in an institution whose primary mission is educational. The public school response was to drop clinical counseling services and simply to refer. Although this issue merits entire journals and books, suffice it to say that college counselors should engage themselves and the entire university community in assessing the priority level of life–career counseling.

Contemporary and Future Life–Career Development Issues and Strategies

Clearly the issues and choices are profound. By almost any measure, individual and societal career development have never had greater importance for human life—ours and our children's. To address these issues, college students and others need career information aimed at both users and developers. Labor market information, useful for macroeconomic private and public sector planning, needs sifting, winnowing, and distilling to become career information suitable for individual use.

In the 1960s, the United States was not ready for the reform movement called career education, and implementation efforts were sporadic and largely fleeting (Herr & Cramer, 1996; Hoyt, 1977; Isaacson & Brown, 1997). In the face of many factors, college counselors should find ways to meet the career readiness and life–career development needs of all students. Today, this goal should be integrated into the mission of all education. College counselors must be ready for career education today, if students' life–career needs are to be addressed. We have the vision in *Goals 2000* (National Education Goals Panel, 1993; White House, 1991), the goals in the SCANS (1992a) competencies, and the blueprint and tools in the NOICC's (1989, 1997) *NCDG* and the *Professional Standards* of the National Association of Colleges and Employers (1998). Because of college counselors' educational backgrounds and their familiarity with the resources mentioned here and in view of their dedication to promoting the worth, dignity, uniqueness, and potential of human beings (American Counseling Association, 1997), college counselors are well prepared and may be well positioned to serve as major catalysts in helping to build and implement comprehensive developmental life–career programs, with a healthy dedication to the individual career development of today's and tomorrow's students.

RECOMMENDATIONS FOR ACTION: ONE UNIVERSITY'S LIFE–CAREER DEVELOPMENT INITIATIVE

Selected ideas and anecdotal information from a current initiative in developing a model life–career development program at a metropolitan 25,000-student university are offered here to illustrate aspects of the points covered above; to describe a major undertaking aimed at building a model life-career development program; and to encourage college counselors to entertain possible new paradigms, strategies, programs, and service delivery modes.

As the University of North Texas Career Center Task Force addressed the charge of creating a vision, a mission statement, guiding principles, and related aspects of a world-class career center, task force members worked to understand the context of our times and the possibilities available in envisioning a major career center for the 21st century. To address the charge, task force members formed two work teams, with one team reviewing external models, philosophies, strategies, and related matters and the other team reviewing existing internal services and resources and assessing needs and desires of students, staff, faculty, and other constituencies. The external work team relied heavily on professional literature and World Wide Web resources in identifying philosophies and model career centers at universities throughout the United States, and the internal work team concentrated on seeking input from and assessing needs of students, faculty, staff, and other current and potential constituent groups. The model that was finally selected was Pennsylvania State University's Career Services Center, and the work team initiated communication with Pennsylvania State University's Career Services Director (J. R. Rayman, personal communication, January 26, 1999).

Throughout the task force's work, the entire task force was guided by many issues to afford a contextual perception regarding career and personal development in the 21st century. Central among these issues were rapid demographic and economic changes, with subsequent impact on the career choices of individuals throughout their lifetimes; the ambiguous nature of the emerging information-oriented, high-technology society; and requirements for program accountability as key factors influencing higher education, student retention, and individual career development. Attention to the whole person, to a one-owner, lifelong career, and to the need to balance and integrate work roles and responsibilities with other life roles and responsibilities were driving foci as the task force worked to find ways to consciously link personal and career development services. To these ends, the career center task force developed vision and mission statements, struggled to find a sufficiently encompassing title, and identified some strategies for planning and implementation by the life–career center team in concert with the entire learning community. On concluding its work, the task force presented a model, vision and mission statements, guiding principles and strategies, findings of internal needs assessments, and a list of director qualifications. Following the presentation, the Vice President for Student Development arrived at a model that combined what had been the Career Opportunities Center and Student Employment Office and sought a close integration of that revised center with the Counseling and Testing Center by creating a direct chain of authority line with a newly created position. The new Dean of Life–Career Development has direct supervisory responsibility for both the newly expanded Career Opportunity Center and the Counseling and Testing Center. This new position is designed to provide students and other constituents with a seamless array of life–career development services and to reflect and complement a newly heightened priority level of career development throughout all aspects of the university learning experience.

One major disclaimer regarding the process was that circumstances required carrying out the entire task force's charge within 4 months rather than the 12 or more months recommended in the *NCDG* (NOICC, 1989, 1997). Although this time crunch did limit the "learning curve" and some important aspects of democratic give-and-take, the overall activity yielded some encouraging outcomes and possibilities, as illustrated below.

Vision Statement

Help students and others maximize career, academic, and personal development throughout the University of North Texas experience and beyond.

Mission Statement

The Office of the Dean of Life–Career Development supports a major goal of facilitating career, academic, and personal development as a life-long learning process. Career development involves (a) understanding the role of career in the larger perspective of individual human development and life roles and responsibilities; (b) self-exploration in terms of academic and career options; (c) understanding and mastering job-market requirements, competencies, and trends; and (d) making initial and subsequent career decisions.

Having vision and mission statements helped with determining a name, but the process was complicated by various views and issues, perhaps most notably, some of the issues attended to earlier, "turf" issues and even basic concerns about the need for primacy of the word *career* in the title.

Name

Although no unanimous choice emerged, a compromise consensus yielded the office of the Dean of Life–Career Development as an appropriately descriptive title. Among alternative titles were Center for Career and Personal Development; Career, Academic, and Personal Development Center; Life–Career Development Center; Career Opportunity Center; and Career Services. The Vice President's decision to establish a dean's position to coordinate life–career development as a top priority assuaged these differences.

Structure

As noted above, the new office of the Dean of Life–Career Development merged two existing colocated centers providing services in employability skills and employer interaction and student employment, respectively, while promoting a seamless interface with and a clear priority on life–career development in the counseling and assessment center. The Learning Center and Cooperative Education Programs also seem to lend themselves to close collaboration with the office of the Dean of Life–Career Development. This model was designed to modestly expand the Pennsylvania State University career center model by including a fuller counseling emphasis devoted to helping students and others with personal, academic, and career development—in effect, a life–career development emphasis. This expansion seems highly consistent with professional practice and literature noting the close connections between personal and career counseling, as noted earlier (Betz & Corning, 1993; Davidson & Gilbert, 1993; Haverkamp & Moore, 1993; Isaacson & Brown, 1997; Krumboltz, 1993; Lucas, 1993; Subich, 1993; Super, 1993; Tolsma, 1993).

Implementation Strategies

The office of the Dean of Life–Career Development assists students and other designated clients in developing, evaluating, or implementing career, education, and employment decisions and plans. The various units are dedicated to achieving this mission by continuing to provide traditional employability and career and personal development services while expanding to a more holistic emphasis promoting life–career development. Among its reorganized priorities, this model's new emphasis requires greater attention to the following areas:

- Assessing student and other constituent needs through grassroots input and working to see matters from student and other constituent perspectives;
- Planning for and providing resources and services that help students develop self-knowledge related to career and life opportunities, choices, and work performance;
- Providing outreach and other catalytic services for extended constituents and conducting ongoing program evaluations and appropriate modifications.

Specific Services and Strategies

The coordinated units are committed to helping students and others in the following ways:

- See themselves as individual owners and stewards of their own lives and careers;
- Identify, understand, and assess their competencies, interests, values, and related personal characteristics;
- Plan their short-term and long-term career development;
- Balance and integrate work roles and responsibilities with other life roles and responsibilities;
- Take responsibility for developing career decisions, graduate-professional school plans, employment plans, or job-search competencies;
- See connections among and between experiences in student activities, community service, student employment, research projects, cooperative education, internships, and other opportunities;
- Obtain educational and occupational information to aid career and educational planning and to develop an understanding of the world of work;
- Select personally suitable academic programs and experiential opportunities, such as entry–progression in an appropriate educational, graduate, or professional program designed to optimize future educational and employment options;
- Prepare for finding suitable employment by developing job-search skills, effective candidate presentation skills, and an understanding

of the fit among personal attributes, competencies, and occupational requirements;

- Effectively manage careers after graduation;
- Link with alumni, employers, professional organizations, and others who will provide opportunities to develop professional interests and competencies, integrate academic learning with work, and explore future career possibilities.

Outreach Strategies

All individual and group processes in the office of the Dean of Life–Career Development are to be integrated into the mainstream of the total program for all students, with the support and participation of students, administrators, faculty, staff, people from business and industry, and others. Central among the strategies for this effort are

- Helping academic departments emphasize internships and field-based experiences in both graduate and undergraduate courses and curriculum design and cultivate alumni and other community resources to form a variety of such partnerships to enhance career relevance.
- Encouraging each academic department to emphasize internships and other community partnerships in curriculum design.
- Providing students in all disciplines with career models through, among other means, a database of alumni profiles via the World Wide Web and other means of dissemination.
- Promoting student, faculty, and adviser awareness of existing personal and career counseling and personal–career development resources.
- Helping faculty infuse aspects of career education into all courses as a complement to existing curricula.
- Systematically enhancing connections with the community and the collective and respective community structures for mutual benefit.
- Encouraging and providing workshops and other services to help faculty, staff, and administrators be more involved in all aspects of the career development process.

- Providing workshops and other services to help and encourage faculty, staff, and administrators with referrals to appropriate resources.
- Encouraging and providing workshops and other services to help faculty, staff, and administrators in all introductory and survey courses in specific areas to discuss the potential career value of such a major.
- Encouraging and providing workshops and other services to help faculty, staff, and administrators help students translate their course work and degree into the world of work.

Qualifications for the Dean of Life–Career Development

The position requires an earned doctorate in counseling, counseling psychology, higher education, or a closely related field and a minimum of 5 years of administrative experience in higher education, career services, or related areas. Also required are excellent interpersonal, communication, human resource management, and leadership skills; strong theoretical and practical knowledge of life–career development; and proven ability to lead and translate ideas and concepts into successful career and personal development programs and services.

This is a glimpse at aspects of an ongoing process aimed at addressing many issues related to life–career development and college counseling. We hope that providing one institution's approach to helping college counselors and other career development professionals deliver life–career development services, through traditional and more holistic approaches, adds a pragmatic dimension to the discussion regarding the need for new paradigms for college counselors today and in the future.

SUMMARY

Starting with a rationale for a transition from career counseling to "life–career development counseling" while focusing on career development as a vital, integral, and infused component at all levels of education, this chapter identifies common issues and concerns, such as conceptualizing, planning, funding, and implementing a university life–career development program. Following selected allusions to public and private policy issues, insights are offered regarding a vision of career development and life–career development resources and strategies for attaining that vision. This chapter also incorporates anecdotal experiences in launching a life–career development center at a large public university. In view of major paradigm shifts, the emphasis is on conceptual and programmatic issues and strategies, rather than specific techniques for enhancing traditional approaches.

REFERENCES

American Counseling Association. (1997). *Ethical standards.* Alexandria, VA: Author.

Betz, N. E., & Corning, A. F. (1993). The inseparability of "career" and "personal" counseling. *The Career Development Quarterly, 42,* 137–142.

Bridges, W. (1994). *Job shift.* New York: Addison-Wesley.

Commission on Skills of the American Workforce. (1990). *America's choice: High skills or low wages!* Rochester, NY: National Center on Education and the Economy.

Davidson, S. L., & Gilbert, L. A. (1993). Career counseling is a personal matter. *The Career Development Quarterly, 42,* 149–153.

Engels, D. W., & Harris, H. L. (1999). Career development: A vital part of contemporary education. *National Association of Secondary School Principals Bulletin, 83,* 70–76.

Ettinger, J. M. (1996). *Improved career decision making in a changing world* (2nd ed.). Garrett Park, MD: Garrett Park Press.

Feller, R., & Walz, G. R. (Eds.). (1997). *Career transitions in turbulent times.* Greensboro: University of North Carolina Educational Resource Information Clearinghouse.

Foster, D. E. (1979). *Assessment of knowledge acquired in an employability skills training program.* Unpublished doctoral dissertation, University of North Texas, Denton.

Hansen, L. S. (1997). *Integrative life planning: Critical tasks for career development and changing life patterns.* San Francisco: Jossey-Bass.

Hartz, J. D. (1978a). *Employability inventory: Findings and analysis.* Madison: University of Wisconsin Vocational Studies Center.

Hartz, J. D. (1978b). *Instructor's guide to employability skills.* Madison: University of Wisconsin Vocational Studies Center.

Haverkamp, B. E., & Moore, D. (1993). The career–personal dichotomy: Perceptual reality, practical illusion, and workplace integration. *The Career Development Quarterly, 42,* 154–160.

Herr, E. L., & Cramer, S. H. (1996). *Career guidance and counseling through the lifespan* (5th ed.). Needham Heights, MA: Allyn & Bacon.

Hoyt, K. B. (1977). *A primer for career education.* Washington, DC: U.S. Department of Education.

Hoyt, K. B., & Lester, J. L. (1995). *Learning to work: The NCDA Gallup survey.* Alexandria, VA: National Career Development Association.

Isaacson, L. E., & Brown, D. (1997). *Career information, career counseling, and career development* (6th ed.). Boston: Allyn & Bacon.

Krumboltz, J. D. (1993). Integrating career and personal counseling. *The Career Development Quarterly, 42,* 143–148.

Lucas, M. S. (1993). Personal aspects of career counseling: Three examples. *The Career Development Quarterly, 42,* 161–166.

National Alliance of Business. (1990). *Employment policies: Looking to the year 2000.* Washington, DC: Author.

National Association of Colleges and Employers. (1998). *Professional standards.* Washington, DC: Author.

National Education Goals Panel. (1993). *Goals 2000.* Washington, DC: U.S. Department of Education.

National Occupational Information Coordinating Committee. (1989). *National career development guidelines.* Washington, DC: Author.

National Occupational Information Coordinating Committee. (1997). *National career development guidelines* (2nd ed.). Washington, DC: Author.

Rifkin, J. (1995). *End of work: Decline of the global labor force and the dawn of the post-market era.* New York: Putnam.

Secretary's Commission on Achieving Necessary Skills. (1991). *What work requires of schools.* Washington, DC: U.S. Department of Labor.

Secretary's Commission on Achieving Necessary Skills. (1992a). *Learning a living.* Washington, DC: U.S. Department of Labor.

Secretary's Commission on Achieving Necessary Skills. (1992b). *Skills and tasks for jobs: A SCANS report for America 2000.* Washington, DC: U.S. Department of Labor.

Subich, L. M. (1993). How personal is career counseling? *The Career Development Quarterly, 42,* 129–131.

Super, D. E. (1993). The two faces of counseling: Or is it three? *The Career Development Quarterly, 42,* 132–136.

Texas Advisory Council for Technical–Vocational Education. (1975). *Qualities employers like and dislike in job applicants: Final report of a statewide employer survey.* Austin: Texas Board of Education.

Texas Advisory Council for Technical–Vocational Education. (1985). *Qualities employers like and dislike in job applicants: Final report of a statewide employer survey.* Austin: Texas Board of Education.

Tolsma, R. (1993). Career or noncareer? That is the issue: Case examples. *The Career Development Quarterly, 42,* 167–173.

White House. (1991, April 18). *Goals 2000.* Washington, DC: Author.

12

Outreach Programming From the College Counseling Center

CAROLYN W. KERN

FOCUS QUESTIONS

1. What is the purpose of outreach programming on college campuses?

2. What are the challenges and pitfalls of outreach programming on diverse college campuses?

3. What are the ingredients of an effective outreach program?

ISSUES

Counseling services on college and university campuses fulfill three essential roles according to the accreditation standards of the International Association of Counseling Services:

- a counseling role to assist students in personal and psychological adjustment,
- a preventive role to assist students in developing skills that meet their educational and life goals, and
- a contributive role to the campus environment that facilitates the growth and development of students (Kiracofe et al., 1994, p. 38).

Although most college counseling centers successfully fulfill their counseling role, they are sometimes less successful in addressing the preventive and contributive roles outlined by the International Association of Counseling Services. A primary means by which college counselors can enhance these roles on college campuses is through the implementation of effective outreach programming. This chapter examines the purpose of outreach programming, suggests theoretical underpinnings, explores challenges encountered in outreach program delivery, and recommends strategies for implementing effective outreach programs.

Outreach programming is a series of intentionally planned presentations and interactional experiences provided to students by college counselors. Effective outreach programming complements the educational mission of higher education by providing programs that are supportive of academic success. Moreover, effective outreach programming enhances the total college experience by providing programs that encourage holistic personal and interpersonal growth, support healthy life choices, and minimize ineffective or harmful behaviors. Thus, outreach programming fulfills the preventive and contributive roles by supporting both the curricular and the cocurricular experiences of today's college students.

Using Theories to Build Effective Outreach Programming

Psychological theories provide a sound basis for effective outreach programming. These theories help counselors focus on transitional experiences, common concerns, and specific problems experienced by both traditional-age and nontraditional-age college students. Most helpful are theories of psychosocial development, cognitive development, typological perspectives, and campus environment (Chickering & Reisser, 1993; Creamer & Associates, 1990; Evans, 1996; Huebner, 1990; King, 1978; Knefelkamp, Widick, & Parker, 1978; Smith, 1978).

Psychosocial development theories support the view that individuals develop essentially through a process that involves the accomplishment of a series of developmental tasks. Partly as a consequence of age progression and partly as a consequence of sociocultural or environmental influences, individuals over the life span are confronted by a series of developmental challenges to their current identity or developmental status that require some form of response (Cass, 1984; Chickering & Reisser, 1993; Gilligan, 1982; Josselson, 1978, 1996; Pascarella & Terenzini, 1991; Schlossberg, 1984). Thus, psychosocial theories provide direction for outreach by suggesting programs that challenge students to expand their current developmental level to new levels. For example, an outreach program that involves a rescue scenario in which students must make decisions about who is rescued and who is not is designed to challenge students' values, beliefs, and moral decision making, thereby stimulating growth to new developmental levels.

Cognitive development theories also provide direction and focus for campus outreach programming. Cognitive development occurs as a result of accommodation and assimilation of new ideas and information. Therefore, outreach programming can be designed to provide new information and constructive methods by which students can evaluate and incorporate those new ideas. Additionally, outreach programming suggests strategies by which students can transfer their learning to other decision-making areas in their lives. It is important that college counselors recognize individual differences in regards to cognitive development. Students are not all in the same place and may not develop in the same way (Gilligan, 1982; King, 1978; Piaget, 1971; Smith, 1978).

Campus environment and typology theories also suggest direction for outreach programming. Student organizations, residence life, and fraternities and sororities can benefit from outreach programming that uses activities and learning opportunities based on environment theory. Leadership styles, personality types, and experiential learning opportunities can all assist students in developing broader insights into individual differences (Holland, 1985; Kolb, 1984; Myers & McCaulley, 1985; Strange, 1996). For example, college counselors used typology theory to provide a program for a campus Panhellenic association. Students completed the Myers-Briggs Type Indicator (Myers & McCaulley, 1985), which was scored prior to the program. At the program, students were given their results, and the counselor provided a detailed explanation of types. This was followed by an activity designed to demonstrate type differences and how those differences could affect communication and understanding within this campus organization.

Specific Issues and Student Populations

Outreach programming encourages positive, constructive behaviors (Ellis, 1994) and provides college counselors with a proactive, preventive approach for addressing problematic issues for students and the larger campus community. Interest in these problem areas may arise from current news events or may reflect concerns common to college student development and experiences. Therefore, effective outreach programming typically addresses prevention of problems, such as sexually transmitted diseases, substance use and abuse, date rape, violence, or eating disorders.

Knowledge of the concerns of specific student populations is also beneficial in planning outreach programming. Although many college students share certain common challenges, there are experiences unique to diverse populations. The concerns of traditional-age college students often differ from those of nontraditional-age students, international students have concerns specific to their needs, and multicultural students exhibit concerns unique to their situations. Thus, college counselors should be knowledgeable about these and other groups on campus as they plan outreach programs. For example, some students may especially benefit from programs that address dealing with oppression or the minority experience within a majority campus. Gay, lesbian, or bisexual students might benefit from programs on relationship building that are specific to their needs. The reader is referred to Chapter 7, "Traditional-Age College Students"; Chapter 8, "Nontraditional College Students"; Chapter 9, "College Counseling and the Needs of Multicultural Students";

and Chapter 10, "College Counseling and International Students," for further discussion of specific student populations.

RECOMMENDATIONS FOR ACTION

An active and innovative outreach-programming component is an integral part of college counseling centers' service to students. The following recommendations for action are provided to assist college counselors in developing outreach programs that will be meaningful and successful on their campuses.

Understanding Unique Campus Needs

Each college campus has unique and diverse needs regarding outreach programming. The wide variety of ages, nationalities, ethnicities, and lifestyles demands specific attention to difference while recognizing the common concerns of all students. The needs of students at a commuter-oriented institution may differ from those at a residential institution. The needs of nontraditional-age students are likely to differ from those of more traditional-age college students. The needs of native students and international students are likely to differ as well. The needs of distance learners, whose connection to campus is more "virtual" than real, may differ yet again from students in other settings. It is important that college counselors consider the distinctive factors that each campus and student body represents as they design effective programming for their individual institutions.

Students typically attend only programs that correlate with their needs. Therefore, college counselors should thoroughly investigate their student population (Astin, 1998) to identify the needs and issues most relevant to those students. It is critical that outreach program designers consider students' needs, not just the perceived needs of administration or counseling center staff. Students' needs may vary from concerns about personal safety to coping with the overwhelming stress of family and school pressures. Periodic assessment of the student population is the most useful way to determine students' needs. Students can be surveyed through campus newspapers, campus television or radio, and campuswide E-mail systems. Outreach programming is also more likely to meet students' needs when it reflects current issues on a particular campus or nation-wide campus concerns, for example, relationship violence, racism, depression, and alcohol abuse. College counselors must be proactive in developing a strong needs-assessment foundation on which to build their outreach-programming efforts.

Planning an Outreach Program

Planning and organizing an effective outreach program should not be left to chance. Several models are available to assist in the planning process, including attending to theoretical underpinnings (Andreas, 1993; Barr & Cuyjet, 1991; Hurst & Jacobson, 1985; Morrill, 1990). Morrill presented a very detailed model that facilitates effective planning, presentation, and evaluation. The model includes four stages with several steps.

Stage I: Initiating the Program includes five steps—the germinal idea; the planning team; assessment of needs, resources, and con-straints; identification of alternative program targets and purposes; and program selection.

Stage II: Planning Program Objectives, Delivery System, and Evaluation Methods includes four steps—selecting program goals, devel-oping the training methods or delivery system, planning the method of intervention, and planning for program evaluation.

Stage III: Presenting and Evaluating a Pilot Program includes three steps—planning program publicity, implementing the pilot program, and assessing evaluation data along with making decisions about the pro-gram's future.

Stage IV: Program Refinement includes four steps—refining training pro-cedures and materials, planning for continued evaluation, training leaders, and offering the program on a regular basis (Morrill, 1990, pp. 426–437).

Planning and designing programs for an entire academic year is helpful and recommended. This process assures that diverse topics are being cov-ered and facilitates appropriate timing and location. For example, an out-reach program on homesickness is best offered early in the school year, whereas a program on test-taking skills might be most useful shortly before midterm or final examinations. It is important to allow for additions or changes on the basis of issues that arise during the year. Program designers might even have several programs "in the can" that are implemented only in response to specific problems. For example, a completely planned outreach program on grief could be implemented following a campus death.

Topic Selection. Selecting topics for outreach program presentations is an important early decision. As I stated earlier, a needs assessment can provide information from students on topics of concern or interest to them. Specific campus and national issues also suggest potential topics of interest, and there are a variety of developmental and educational concerns for college students that could be the focus of outreach programs. Some useful topics for outreach programs include (a) educational–career: study skills, test taking, note taking, textbook reading, time management, learning styles, career decision making, the freshman experience, the senior experience, job hunting, resumes, and interviewing strategies; (b) personal–social: relationships, dating, financial wellness, date rape, depression, anxiety disorders, addictions, anger management, conflict management, understanding personality characteristics, personality styles, leadership skills, and decision making; and (c) health-related: drug and alcohol abuse, sexually transmitted diseases, HIV/AIDS, diet and exercise, and pregnancy concerns. Programming for nontraditional students, minority students, and international students may include topics related to specific needs, for example, living in the college campus culture.

Timing and Location. Timing is another important success strategy. College counselors must know what activities are happening on campus to avoid potential conflicts with major or traditional campus events. It is important to know when sporting events are being held, particularly if sports are a major campus activity. Similarly, college counselors who are planning outreach programs must take into account the routines of the students on campus regarding mealtimes, social nights, and weekend involvement. An outreach program that is planned for Friday night on a predominantly commuter campus or that conflicts with an important basketball game is likely to fail. Creating a college counseling center web site on the Internet is a valuable strategy in regards to timing and location because it allows students to review outreach materials any time that is convenient for them.

The location of an outreach program also can dramatically affect its success. Successful programs are offered where the students are located, whether in the student union, residence halls, fraternities or sororities, or on-line. The term is *outreach* programming, so college counselors must be willing to reach out beyond their offices and counseling centers to find those places where students are most likely to congregate and will feel most at ease.

Collaboration and Coordination. Most college counseling centers have limited staff, so collaboration with diverse campus entities (e.g., peer leaders and advisers, residence hall staff, student organization leaders) can expand outreach offerings (Hatcher, 1995). At Oklahoma State University, the counseling center counselors held a workshop in which hall staff taught them how to present an effective program. Necessary information and materials were provided along with an opportunity to practice workshop delivery skills. This freed up the staff at the counseling center so they could focus on programs that required a more professional level of counseling skills and knowledge.

Counselors can also be resources for other units on campus because of their unique education and orientation. Through partnerships and collaboration, the knowledge that counselors possess can be shared with the whole campus. At Appalachian State University, the counseling center teams with the student-run campus radio station to offer a weekly radio program called Love Talk. The program is presented before a live audience, and students can E-mail or call in questions about relationships that are answered by a panel of counselors. Thus, the particular training and talents of college counselors are used to deliver innovative outreach programming and to provide communications majors with valuable practical experience.

Another important consideration when planning an outreach program is coordination with other units on campus offering similar presentations. Coordinating services will enhance effectiveness and reduce duplication. Working together for a comprehensive campuswide outreach program will dramatically enhance success.

Advertising. Another essential component is advertising. The speaker may be dynamic and the information relevant and timely, but no one knows the outreach program is occurring. Necessary questions to ask include where and how should the advertising be displayed? Is the information correct, and does it draw attention? Is it appropriate to the target audience? Campus E-mail provides an excellent avenue to notify students, faculty, and staff about outreach programs. Bulletins, flyers, and television and radio announcements are useful. Timeliness of advertising is also important. If done too early, everyone forgets; if done too late, students are doing other things. A good rule of thumb for most types of outreach programs is to begin advertising 1 week before the program.

Presenters. Effective presenters are a critical component to a successful outreach program. Key skills and talents for a presenter include knowledge and understanding of the subject area, genuineness, confidence, effective presentation skills, interest in the program topic, openness to questions and interaction with participants, and a desire to help students. Staff may have different strengths where programming is concerned. One counselor may be very effective with a live audience, and another may be more effective in responding to a chat room or designing the program. It is wise to consider staff's strengths in the total programming process.

Materials. Effective programs will provide handouts (or downloads), efficaciously display information, or provide food. Students are drawn to programs for many reasons, and food is frequently used to gather a group. An overhead projector, computer-generated information, or flip charts provide a focal point for participants' attention. Today's students benefit from opportunities to be actively involved in the learning process, so including an action component through a group project helps students put information to work during a program. Providing paper and markers helps participants use multiple modes for learning. College counselors should seek resources to help develop effective programs and provide effective handouts and information (Brooks-Harris, 1998). One such resource is the Counseling Center Village, a web site sponsored by the American College Personnel Association Commission. The web site provides workshop design strategies, program outlines, and even handouts. Links to Internet sites that are useful for outreach programming are included as well (http://ub-counseling.buffalo.edu/ccv. html).

Outcomes Assessment. Finally, assessing the effectiveness of a program provides insight for future presentations. It allows presenters the opportunity to refine or change any part of a program, whether it be the time, topic, content, or style of the presentation. Participant surveys are helpful ways to assess outreach programs. Staff evaluations provide additional insight. Assessment should be done shortly after the program is complete so the most accurate information is collected. An overall evaluation at the end of the year should take place annually to determine what changes are appropriate for the following year. Outcome assessment is a critical component of successful outreach programming.

Outreach Programming in Cyberspace

The emerging emphasis on distance learning and the tremendous growth and availability of Internet services on campuses offer college counselors new and innovative challenges for outreach program delivery. A college counseling center's web site can provide diverse information relevant to outreach, including program topics, schedules, and locations. Prepared outreach programs can be adapted for the web site, or new programs can be developed specifically for this delivery method. Chat rooms organized around specific outreach topics (e.g., study skills, career planning, procrastination) offer a unique service delivery option. A good example of a web site developed specifically to meet the needs of distance-learning students is that of the Bureau for Student Counseling and Career Development at the University of South Africa, a distance-teaching university. This web site provides an extensive listing of helpful Internet sites around the world on a variety of topics for its students. Another innovative outreach service is provided by the Counseling and Psychological Services Center at Appalachian State University. Students submit anonymous questions to "Ask Uncle Sigmund" that are answered by counseling center staff and posted for the campus to view on the center's web site. A college counseling center's web site also can provide links to other useful Internet resources on topics relevant to students' concerns; for example, a site sponsored by the University of Chicago provides "virtual pamphlets," submitted by college counselors across the nation, on a variety of topics of interest to students. The pamphlets can

---

Box 3

Web Sites for Outreach Programming

Appalachian State University:
www.appstate.edu/www_docs/student/sigmund/index.html

University of Chicago virtual pamphlets:
uhs.bsd.uchicago.edu/scrs/vpc/vpc.html

University of South Africa:
www.unisa.ac.za/dept/sdb/bsccd/index.html

Edinboro University of Pennsylvania:
edinboro.edu/cwis/studaff/services/counseling/broeh.html

University of Dayton:
www.udayton.edu/cc

URLs available September 10, 1999

---

be copied to a counseling center's own web site or a link provided. Clearly, outreach programming is no longer campus-bound. The Internet offers college counselors wonderful opportunities for expanded and creative outreach programming. URLs for these and examples of other college counseling centers' web sites are provided in **Box 3.**

Case Study

The following case study describes an outreach program presented at a major southwestern university. Program-planning successes and challenges are discussed to provide college counselors with an example of how outreach programming may be developed and implemented. Planning and pitfalls are included.

Date rape was identified as an important outreach program topic by students, college counselors, and residence hall staff. College counselors teamed with residence life staff to present a program on date rape in one of the large residence halls on campus. Advertisement was done through posters and signs located in the lounges, cafeteria, and hallways. Residence hall staff also encouraged students during floor meetings to attend the program.

A large group of more than 100 participants attended the program. Men and women were asked to situate themselves on opposite sides of the room. The program began with a videotape of several interactions between male and female students. Male and female presenters then attempted to facilitate a discussion that highlighted communication styles and patterns and focused on the underlying messages of the videotape interactions. Shortly after the discussion began, a derogatory comment was made by a female participant, and in response, several male participants became angry. The male and female participants began verbally attacking each other across the room. Program presenters attempted to intervene in the evolving dispute by pointing out communication errors but could not reduce the emotional intensity. At that point, the program presenters decided it was best to end the program and simply concluded with some closing comments.

Program evaluation suggested alternative means for more effectively addressing this topic. Presenters found that a focus on the role of communication patterns and misunderstandings remained integral to an outreach program on date rape. However, they recognized that the means of presentation, especially the group dynamics, should be changed for the next program. Smaller, mixed-gender groups or separate programs for men and women would be more manageable and offer sufficient opportunity for all participants to be heard. Ground rules for discussion should be established early. The program presenters recognized that some participants may have already been directly affected by date rape; thus, the program may have activated especially strong reactions from them. Warning participants about this possibility before the program would be helpful. Additionally, presenters should encourage participants who may be adversely affected to debrief with a college counselor directly after the program. Program presenters found that these changes resulted in a more successful program on this critical topic.

SUMMARY

This chapter has discussed the purpose and theoretical foundations of outreach programming and offered college counselors concrete suggestions for establishing effective programming on their unique campuses. Outreach programs take personal and social development out of the college counseling center, where, typically, limited numbers of students receive services, to the larger student population. The effect can influence students' lives and perhaps prevent decision making that would lead to detrimental life experiences. Outreach programming helps students gain the enhanced interpersonal skills needed in today's lifestyle and even more in demand in the workforce. Effective outreach programming requires that counselors leave their offices and meet students out in the campus community, in a manner some counselors may not be accustomed to doing. The results may not always be dramatic, but if even one student is positively influenced by programming outside of the customary counseling setting, then the efforts are worthwhile. Outreach programming offers college counselors a new and different strategy to significantly influence students in positive life directions.

REFERENCES

Andreas, R. E. (1993). Programming planning. In M. J. Barr & Associates (Eds.), *The handbook of student affairs administration* (pp. 199–215). San Francisco: Jossey-Bass.

Astin, A. (1998). The changing American college student: Thirty-year trends. *The Review of Higher Education, 21,* 115–135.

Barr, M. J., & Cuyjet, M. J. (1991). Program development and implementation. In T. K. Miller, R. B. Winston, Jr., & Associates (Eds.), *Developing effective student services programs: Systematic approaches for practitioners* (pp. 1–14). San Francisco: Jossey-Bass.

Brooks-Harris, J. (1998, December 18). *Workshop central* [On-line]. Available: http://ub-counseling.buffalo.edu/wc.html

Cass, V. C. (1984). Homosexual identity formation: Testing a theoretical model. *Journal of Sex Research, 20,* 143–167.

Chickering, A. W., & Reisser, L. (1993). *Education & identity* (2nd ed.). San Francisco: Jossey-Bass.

Creamer, D. G., & Associates. (1990). *College student development* (Media Publication No. 49). Alexandria, VA: American College Personnel Association.

Ellis, D. (1994). *Becoming a master student.* Boston: Houghton-Mifflin.

Evans, N. J. (1996). Theories of student development. In S. R. Komives, D. B. Woodard, Jr., & Associates (Eds.), *Student services: A handbook for the professional* (3rd ed., pp. 164–187). San Francisco: Jossey-Bass.

Gilligan, C. (1982). *In a different voice.* Cambridge, MA: Harvard University Press.

Hatcher, S. L. (1995). Peer helping for prevention on the college campus. In S. L. Hatcher (Ed.), *Peer programs on the college campus* (pp. 417–421). San Jose, CA: Resource.

Holland, J. L. (1985). *Vocational Preference Inventory (VIP): Professional manual.* Odessa, FL: Psychological Assessment Resources.

Huebner, L. A. (1990). Interaction of student and campus. In U. Delworth & G. R. Hanson (Eds.), *Student services: A handbook for the profession* (2nd ed., pp. 165–208). San Francisco: Jossey-Bass.

Hurst, J. C., & Jacobson, J. K. (1985). Theories underlying students' needs for programs. In M. J. Barr, L. A. Keating, & Associates (Eds.), *Developing effective student programs: Systematic approaches for practitioners* (pp. 113–136). San Francisco: Jossey-Bass.

Josselson, R. (1978). *Finding herself: Pathways to identity development in women.* San Francisco: Jossey-Bass.

Josselson, R. (1996). *Revising herself: The story of women's identity from college to midlife.* New York: Oxford University Press.

King, P. M. (1978). William Perry's theory of intellectual development. In L. Knefelkamp, C. Widick, & C. A. Parker (Eds.), *Applying new developmental findings* (New Directions for Student Services No. 4, pp. 35–51). San Francisco: Jossey-Bass.

Kiracofe, N. M., Donn, P. A., Grant, C. O., Podolnick, E. E., Bingham, R. P., Bolland, H. R., Carney, C. G., Clementson, J., Gallagher, R. P., Grosz, R. D., Handy, L., Hansche, J. H., Mack, J. K., Sanz, D., Walker, L. J., & Yamada, K. T. (1994). Accreditation standards for university and college counseling centers. *Journal of Counseling and Development, 73,* 38–44.

Knefelkamp, L., Widick, C., & Parker, C. A. (Eds.). (1978). *Applying new developmental findings* (New Directions for Student Services No. 4). San Francisco: Jossey-Bass.

Kolb, D. A. (1984). *Experiential learning: Experience as the source of learning and development.* Englewood Cliffs, NJ: Prentice Hall.

Morrill, W. H. (1990). Program development. In U. Delworth & G. R. Hanson (Eds.), *Student services: A handbook for the profession* (2nd ed., pp. 420–439). San Francisco: Jossey-Bass.

Myers, I. B., & McCaulley, M. H. (1985). *Manual: A guide to the development and use of the Myers-Briggs Type Indicator.* Palo Alto, CA: Consulting Psychologists Press.

Pascarella, E. T., & Terenzini, P. T. (1991). *How college affects students.* San Francisco: Jossey-Bass.

Piaget, J. (1971). *Psychology and epistemology.* Harmondsworth, England: Penguin.

Schlossberg, N. K. (1984). A model for analyzing human adaption to transition. *Counseling Psychologist, 9*(2), 2–18.

Smith, A. F. (1978). *Lawrence Kohlberg's cognitive stage theory of the development of moral judgement.* In L. Knefelkamp, C. Widick, & C. A. Parker (Eds.), *Applying new developmental findings* (New Directions for Student Services No. 4, pp. 53–68). San Francisco: Jossey-Bass.

Strange, C. C. (1996). Dynamics of campus environments. In U. Delworth & G. R. Hanson (Eds.), *Student services: A handbook for the profession* (2nd ed., pp. 244–268). San Francisco: Jossey-Bass.

13

Building Effective Campus Relationships

ROBERT MATTOX

FOCUS QUESTIONS

1. Why is networking so important for college counselors, and what campus relationships are valuable to develop and maintain?

2. What strategies can counselors use to build successful campus relationships?

3. How can college counselors remain integral to institutions?

Successful college counselors recognize that positive campus relationships are essential in promoting the mission of counseling centers and solidifying the presence of college counseling on campuses. If college counseling is to thrive in the new millennium, counselors and counseling centers must initiate, cultivate, and maintain meaningful ties with academic affairs and the academic mission of institutions. Likewise, they must educate the campus community about the integral contributions that college counselors make on a daily basis. This chapter examines the importance of networking for college counselors and offers strategies counselors can use to build productive campus relationships. Sample documents are also provided.

ISSUES: THE VALUE OF NETWORKING

Effective networking with campus groups promotes the integral role that college counselors play within institutions. Negative relationships, or those simply undeveloped because of perceived lack of time and attention, may hinder or even harm the efforts that college counselors make to effectively serve their students. Establishing effective working relationships with campus constituencies, whether by design or by opportunity, is important to the success of college counseling on any campus. Consider the following examples:

Patty Littlebear, a college counselor at a small 2-year institution in South Dakota, was covering evening hours at the college counseling center. She looked up to see a student standing in her doorway. The student asked Patty to come quickly to Dr. Clatt's classroom because a student was behaving strangely. Patty, on entering the classroom, discovered a student weeping uncontrollably at a desk in the center of the room. The other students had vacated the room and were standing in the hall with the professor. Patty quickly assessed the situation and suggested that Dr. Clatt move the class down the hall to a vacant classroom. Patty began talking with the student, and after about an hour, the student felt well enough to go home. A few days later, Dr. Clatt called to thank Patty for her quick response and assistance. Dr. Clatt indicated that the student had returned for the next class and was maintaining a good class standing. Additionally, Dr. Clatt invited Patty to give a presentation about counseling services at the next faculty meeting, and soon after, the Dean of Education asked Patty to attend a collegewide meeting and discuss the services her office provides. This case illustrates how college counselors can transform an opportunity into a networking success.

Phil, a community college counselor in Michigan, overheard several female students discussing their concerns about lighting on the west end of campus. Some areas were dimly lit or not lit at all, and several of the building lights needed replacement. Phil asked the physical plant director what could be done about the lighting problem. The director acknowledged that there was a problem but fixing the lights was too expensive. Unwilling to let the subject rest, Phil contacted several faculty and staff that he knew were student advocates and requested their support in finding a solution for this lighting problem. Additionally, Phil consulted with the community college system attorney about the Campus Safety and Security Act. Armed with knowledge of this legislation and supportive colleagues, Phil requested a meeting with the physical plant director, the director's supervisor, and the college president. Phil and his colleagues presented their concerns, recognized the budget limitations, reviewed the relationship of the lighting problem to potential crime and liability issues, and requested that the campus develop a plan to address the problem. Shortly after the meeting, Phil received notification that a plan was adopted to make the necessary repairs and address long-term lighting needs. The president thanked Phil and the others for their concerns about students' safety and potential liability problems. This intentional networking on Phil's part had a profound long-term campus impact.

These two case studies are real situations. In each scenario, the counselor was effective in finding a solution to the presenting problem. Had each counselor not been assertive in providing assistance, a less helpful message about the benefits and soundness of college counseling services might have been received. As it was, influential members of the campus community were enlightened about the benefits of college counseling, resulting in additional support and visibility for counseling services. In both cases, by opportunity and by design, opportunities for networking came about as a direct result of the college counselor responding proactively to specific needs.

Intentional networking by college counselors should include developing relationships with several particularly important campus constituencies. Solid working alliances with these people can enhance counseling service delivery, boost referrals, and solidify college counselors' role within institutions.

Senior Administrators

Institutional financial concerns and student academic success are two priorities for most senior university administrators. In an effort to reduce costs, some institutions have experimented with outsourcing their counseling services to private agencies off campus (Phillips, Halstead & Carpenter, 1996). Interestingly, many of those institutions discovered outsourcing was actually more expensive and provided less service to the student population than a campus counseling service and reinstated their counseling centers.

These outsourcing experiments underscore the importance of college counselors working proactively with senior administrators at their institutions. If college counselors are to avoid the "outsourcing experiment," then they must be proactive in raising awareness and educating senior administrators about the critical role that college counseling plays on campus. When the topic of college counseling comes up, these administrators want to know about the effectiveness of counseling (Rickinson, 1997), especially in regards to promoting student retention and academic success (Rickinson & Rutherford, 1995). College counselors must provide the research that supports their value to institutions.

Faculty

Faculty are one of the most influential groups on any campus. They have contact with large numbers of students and carry significant political clout. College counselors who establish effective relationships with faculty reap many benefits for students, counseling centers, and themselves. Likewise, those who ignore the faculty often experience negative consequences and isolation from this important campus resource. Faculty members who are knowledgeable about the benefits of counseling services and who have confidence in the counseling staff are an outstanding conduit between counseling centers and students. Often, they detect students who need assistance and refer them to a counselor whom they have come to trust. Likewise, faculty often allow college counselors into their classrooms to make presentations, thus increasing the visibility of counseling centers and their services. Some counseling centers have been spared outsourcing and major budget reductions, at least in part, because of strong advocacy by supportive faculty members.

Campus Police

One of the better relationships that counselors can develop is with the campus police department. It is true that counselors are wise to keep a distance from the punitive side of campus police work; however, many campus police departments maintain an educational and developmental focus that fits effectively with counseling programs. Networking with the campus police department has many benefits, including assistance in working with suicidal or homicidal clients, transportation services for students who require hospitalization, first aid, emergency medical services, and escort services.

Campus Legal Services

Many college campuses have their own legal services or college attorneys, whereas some institutions contract their legal services or rely on state-appointed legal representation. Sometimes college counselors find that they require legal advice (Anderson, 1996).

Effective college counselors take the initiative to meet and establish relationships with institutional attorneys. Attorneys can provide college counselors with copies and interpretations of applicable institutional, state, and federal policies and statutes regarding critical issues (e.g., confidentiality, mandatory-reporting criteria, and involuntary commitment). Their assistance can be invaluable when college counselors are working with a student who is facing legal problems in a local jurisdiction. Additionally, if a counselor experiences harassment by a student or some other campus person, university attorneys can provide support and advice regarding on-campus and local authority assistance.

Attorneys need to understand how the counseling center works within the institution's framework, the reporting hierarchy, types of counseling provided, and how clients' records are maintained (Jenkins, 1997). They should be advised of the professional training of college counseling staff and the ethical guidelines followed by diverse professional orientations within that staff. Also, if there are certification or state licensure laws, it is a good idea to provide the attorneys with copies of them. Positive relationships with campus attorneys can prove vitally important at a later date.

Personnel Office

On most campuses, the gatekeeper for hiring, promotion, and personnel action is the personnel office. Developing positive relationships with this office has significant merit for college counselors who are involved in staffing. When a position is available and must be filled quickly, the personnel office can facilitate a rapid recruitment process. Additionally, many personnel offices offer employee assistance programs designed to provide a variety of services (e.g., counseling and mental health services) for faculty and staff (Mattox, 1986). College counselors can offer consultation services that will benefit faculty, staff, and counseling centers.

Campus Staff

An essential role on any college campus is played by the staff, especially secretaries and office administrators. College counselors should network frequently and effectively with campus staff. A secretary who understands counseling services and knows how to make effective referrals is a good resource for students and faculty. Additionally, campus staff can keep college counselors up-to-date on what is happening on campus and can streamline college counselors' access to influential decision makers on campus.

Recognizing important campus constituencies and providing effective networking with campus groups promote the integral role that college counselors play within institutions. The following recommendations for action offer specific strategies for college counselors wishing to build or enhance successful campus relationships.

RECOMMENDATIONS FOR ACTION

Involve to Solve

Sometimes students, faculty, and staff are unaware that counseling is available on campus. There are several strategies that counselors can implement to inform the campus community that counseling services are available (Glennen, 1976). One highly successful strategy is the development of some type of "Involve to Solve" program. Involve to Solve strategies are intentionally designed programs that facilitate campus community input into campus counseling policies and procedures. These strategies open the door for counselors to inform the campus community about counseling services provided during the past semester and gather information from various areas about campus needs that could be addressed by the counseling center. Examples of Involve to Solve programs include referral guides, semester reports, classroom activities, and marketing strategies.

Campus Counseling Referral Guide. Each counselor and counseling center should have a "Campus Counseling Referral Guide." This guide is designed to provide faculty and staff with information on how best to handle an emergency involving psychological issues. For example, if a student walks into a faculty member's office, states that he has broken up with his significant other, is not doing well in school, and is considering suicide, what should that faculty member do? The Campus Counseling Referral Guide provides faculty and staff with suggestions and procedures that are immediately helpful in this type of situation. College counselors should provide copies of their Campus Counseling Referral Guide to individual faculty and staff members and should solicit assistance from these constituencies in future updates of the guide.

When counselors are developing a Campus Counseling Referral Guide, they should keep in mind that the guide is most effective if it meets individual campus needs and scenarios. **Box 4** offers suggestions to help counselors begin developing their own guides.

Semester or Quarterly Reports. Sometimes all of the good work that counselors do on a daily or yearly basis is lost in the mainstream of

---

Box 4

Outline of Campus Counseling Referral Guide

1. Outline the purpose of the guide.
2. Provide a case example of a distraught student that outlines how the faculty–staff members can help the student and how the faculty–staff members can refer the student.
3. Outline the emergency procedures for faculty–staff.
4. Provide information on how the faculty–staff members can recognize a student who is under stress.
   a. What is stress?
   b. When a student says he or she is stressed.
   c. Unusual changes in behavior.
   d. Rapid onset of illness.
   e. Traumatic changes in personal relationships.
5. Provide information on recognizing drug and alcohol abuse.
6. Dealing with a suicidal student.
7. How can I refer a student for further help?

---

academe. Using effective communication methods is an excellent way to communicate college counselors' contributions to the community. A semester or quarterly report is a valuable communications tool. Depending on the size of the campus, a copy of this report can be provided to various faculty and campus administrators and even can be made available to students. This report will keep the campus up-to-date on counseling activities and services and provide an outstanding marketing and networking tool. **Appendix B** offers a suggested outline for a college counseling semester or quarterly report.

Classroom Activities. Counselors have many responsibilities, and in most cases, administrators and faculty are aware of their fine work. However, some faculty, students, and administrators are not aware of the contributions that college counselors make to the campus community. Being a guest speaker in classes or volunteering to teach a course in their specialty area provides college counselors with excellent networking opportunities. Counselors can pick a department for the year and volunteer to guest lecture or to substitute if a faculty member must be out of class. One method that works very well is for counselors to E-mail or to send a written memorandum to all faculty in a particular department indicating their willingness to assist in these ways. I do not recommend sending this memorandum or E-mail campuswide, because the response could be overwhelming.

Marketing. Students cannot appreciate or use the services of the college counselor if they do not know where the counseling center is or what it does. Just sitting in the office waiting for students to show up does not work. It is critical that college counselors take an aggressive approach to spreading the word about themselves and their services. **Box 5** identifies a list of strategies for marketing counseling services to faculty, staff, administrators, and students.

Diversify to Survive

Some college counselors are fortunate to work for institutions that are financially stable and fully recognize the need for and importance of college counseling. However, those college counselors who do not have that luxury must be prepared to justify the need for their counseling services and programs. There are numerous ways that counselors can make themselves indispensable to the function of their institutions. It may require some additional training and continuing education, but the rewards far exceed the effort.

Many colleges would like to increase services to their students without hiring more staff. If the opportunity arises, counselors can approach administration with a proposal to assume additional or modified responsibilities. An important condition of any adjustment must be the availability of continuing education required to perform any new responsibilities. The following support services are especially well suited to the talents and training of college counselors.

Disability Support Services. Many counseling centers are assuming responsibilities in disability support programs. These required (by law) and worthwhile services are a very large responsibility and

---

Box 5

Marketing Strategies for College Counseling Centers

- Campus publications (e.g., newspapers)
- Campus television and radio stations
- Development of and involvement in campus crisis response teams
- Teaching
- Flyers posted around campus
- E-mail
- Counseling center web site
- Sponsor anxiety, depression, and eating disorders screening days
- Sponsoring and programming for Counseling Awareness Week
- Place table tents in the cafeteria
- Place banners in the student center
- Write a weekly column for newspapers
- Teach a senior seminar course
- Place advertisements on television in the student center
- Provide and sponsor workshops for faculty and staff, including continuing education credit
- Sponsor Career Counseling Week
- Develop a relationship with the college's foundation and alumni office
- Development of and involvement in campus committees
- Guest speaking for classes and organizations
- Distribute brochures around campus
- Sponsoring and programming for Mental Health Awareness Month
- Develop mental health "theme of the month" campaigns
- Invest in giveaways, such as refrigerator magnets that suggest designated drivers
- Teach a freshman seminar class
- Place counseling advertisement kiosks in heavy traffic areas around campus
- Have an open house

---

require substantial continuing education to implement and support. However, they present an ideal opportunity for college counselors to provide services.

Academic Advising. Every campus has students with undeclared majors. Counselors or counseling centers can offer to serve as advising centers for these students. Counseling centers are a logical place for students with undeclared majors because professional counselors can offer career and life development services that might assist them. A secondary benefit of this strategy is the development of closer relationships with the academic side of the institution.

Institutional Testing. There are many counseling centers that have testing as part of their responsibilities. The administration of tests (e.g., American College Test, Scholastic Aptitude Test, College Level Examination Program, Advanced Placement Test, Graduate Record Examination, Graduate Management Admissions Test) ties counseling centers to various other departments, such as admissions, graduate schools, and academic departments. Testing is a necessary function in higher education, and college counselors, by training and function, are excellent campus resources for this area.

International Students. One area of opportunity for college counselors who are interested in diverse student groups is working with international students. This work requires additional training in federal and state policies affecting these students as well as familiarity with various cultural groups on campus. The reader is referred to Chapter 10, "College Counseling and International Students," for a more in-depth discussion of this topic.

Career Placement. Adding career placement responsibilities allows college counselors to use their skills in new ways and is a natural extension of the career counseling services that most college counselors provide. Career placement may require travel and training in additional skills (e.g., marketing). Chapter 11, "Life–Career Development Counseling," offers additional insights into college counselors' role in career development.

Alcohol and Drug Prevention Education. Substance abuse prevention offers yet another opportunity for counselors to use their skills and diversify their services. Alcohol and drug prevention education is mandatory for institutions receiving federal funds. Sometimes college counselors can develop partnerships with the campus health center or other departments or programs (e.g., counseling program) to create and implement effective alcohol and drug prevention education. College counselors may require some additional training to learn governmental reporting requirements or grant writing specifications and should exhibit effective presentation skills for this work (see Chapter 12, "Outreach Programming From the College Counseling Center").

Campus Committees. There are tremendous benefits when counselors involve themselves in various campus committee assignments. For example, one college counselor, on hearing rumors about privatization of counseling services on his campus, volunteered for a regional accreditation preparation committee and became chair. He used his leadership position to stop the rumors. Another counselor chaired a campuswide safety committee composed of faculty, staff, and students. The visibility for counseling services was very positive. When the committee won a state award for its campus communication efforts, the campus president personally recognized the counselor for her contributions to the institution. This recognition had lasting, positive ramifications for the college counseling efforts on that campus.

Developing Campus Relationships

Successful college counselors and counseling services work hard at developing positive campus relationships that will benefit the counseling center and the campus. There is no better way to endear oneself to campus administration than to be the person who finds the workable solution to a difficult problem. For example, the president of a small private college in the Rocky Mountains was concerned that the institution was not following regulations with regard to alcohol and other drug education and prevention. The president was worried that the college would become ineligible to receive federal financial aid if it did not improve its drug and alcohol prevention efforts. The college counselor, hearing of the president's concern, developed a viable alcohol and drug prevention and education plan at little or no cost to the institution and presented the plan to the president. Obviously, the president appreciated the counselor's proactive attitude in finding a positive solution, and benefits flowed from this appreciation to the counseling center.

One of the key words in academe today is *collaboration*. How can one or more services of the campus work together to make the campus programs stronger? College counselors can invite faculty in the counseling, social work, or psychology department to present workshops on various issues for students, sponsored by the counseling center. College counselors can provide programming for the athletic department, the adult learners' office, and the campus health or wellness center. These types of relationships and collaboration bring together the campus community and help cross boundaries that exist between some offices. The result is increased visibility and support for college counseling.

Most institutions have campus newspapers and other means to communicate what is happening on campus. These publications provide a prime opportunity for college counselors to inform campus colleagues of professional contributions to local, state, and national professional organizations, professional publications, awards, presentations, and activities. Wise networking also includes informing the editors of the campus publications, program directors of campus radio stations, and campus and local television stations when the counseling professionals are providing a specialty workshop or event. Every networking effort is cumulative and ultimately enhances the college counselors' visibility.

Research and Retention

It is important that college counselors make campus administration aware of the unique contribution that counseling makes to student retention. There are several ways to do this. College counselors can provide senior administrators with copies of research that corroborates the effectiveness of counseling in student retention. Two good examples are research studies by Bishop and Walker (1990) and Wilson, Mason, and Ewing (1997). It is even more useful to demonstrate the effectiveness of counseling by creating a personalized departmental study (Illovsky,

1997), directed specifically to the counseling services on a particular campus. The combination of this departmental study and the research gathered from others provides powerful evidence that college counseling is a critical tool in student retention.

There does not seem to be a single standardized survey instrument available to measure the effectiveness of college counseling services and how counseling may be useful in retaining students. Counselors and counseling centers should develop their own surveys. A sample of a self-designed counseling survey is provided in **Appendix C**.

SUMMARY

This chapter has explored key issues regarding college counselors' relationships with the campus community. Recommendations for action suggest ways that college counselors can enhance their presence on campus, develop effective campus relationships, market their services, and diversify their responsibilities. Further recommendations regarding the value of conducting research on student retention were offered.

College counseling and, indeed, the counseling profession should double their efforts to ensure that the profession takes its proper role as an important partner in the health care strategy of this country. College counselors can lead this effort on their respective campuses by using and developing networks and collaborations among the different campus policy makers. Also, by diversifying their services and becoming solution-oriented campus change agents, college counselors can position themselves as integral components of the campus community. Finally, I encourage college counselors to become professionally involved in the American College Counseling Association. Campus, state, and national networking and professional advocacy are critical activities to promote college counselors' effectiveness in the new millennium.

REFERENCES

Anderson, B. S. (1996). *The counselor and the law* (4th ed.). Alexandria, VA: American Counseling Association.

Bishop, J. B., & Walker, S. K. (1990). What role does counseling play in decisions relating to retention? *Journal of College Student Development, 31,* 88–89.

Glennen, R. E. (1976). Intrusive college counseling. *School Counselor, 24,* 48–50.

Illovsky, M. E. (1997). Effects of counseling on grades and retention. *Journal of College Student Psychotherapy, 12,* 29–44.

Jenkins, P. (1997). *Counseling, psychotherapy and the law.* Thousand Oaks, CA: Sage.

Mattox, R. J. (1986, April). *Counselor roles in business and industry.* Paper presented at the annual meeting of the American Counseling Association, Los Angeles.

Phillips, L., Halstead, R., & Carpenter, W. (1996). The privatization of college counseling services: A preliminary investigation. *Journal of College Student Development, 37,* 52–59.

Rickinson, B. (1997). Evaluating the effectiveness of counseling interventions with final year undergraduates. *Counseling Psychology Quarterly, 10,* 271–285.

Rickinson, B., & Rutherford, D. (1995). Increasing undergraduate student retention rates. *British Journal of Guidance and Counselling, 23,* 161–172.

Wilson, S. B., Mason, T. W., & Ewing, M. J. (1997). Evaluating the impact of receiving university-based counseling services on student retention. *Journal of Counseling Psychology, 44,* 316–320.

APPENDIX B

Outline of Counselor Semester Report

COUNSELOR:_____SEMESTER:_____DATE:_____

TYPE OF COUNSELING   **Sessions**   **Individuals**
Academic _____
Career _____
Personal _____

SUPERVISION/CONSULTATION
Student _____
Group _____
Individual _____
Faculty _____
Staff Parent_____
Advising _____
General_____
Total_____

COUNSELING GROUPS
Name of Group   Day and Time   Number of Members

WORKSHOPS/SEMINARS
Title   Day and Time   Number of Members

CLASS PRESENTATIONS
Class   Instructor   Title   Day and Time

STUDENT ACTIVITIES
Organization   Responsibility

CAMPUS SERVICES
Committee/Council   Responsibility

PROFESSIONAL SERVICE *(Positions held, councils, committees)*

PROFESSIONAL ACTIVITIES *(Conference attendance, program participation)*
Conferences   Participation   Date   Location

COMMUNITY SERVICE *(Off campus: civic, church programs, etc.)*
Organization   Program   Date

COMPLETED RESEARCH PROJECTS OR PUBLICATIONS

APPENDIX C

Counseling Services Student Satisfaction Survey
Counseling and Advising Program Services (CAPS)
Kennesaw State University

Thank you for taking a moment to respond to this survey. Your comments will be invaluable to us, as we strive to continually improve services.

College Classification: ☐ Freshman ☐ Sophomore ☐ Junior ☐ Senior ☐ Graduate

Age: _____   Gender: ☐ Male ☐ Female___

Ethnicity: ☐ African American ☐ Asian American/Pacific Islander ☐ Latino
☐ European American/Caucasian ☐ Native American ☐ Other_____

How many counseling sessions have you attended at CAPS?
1____   2–10_____   11–20_____   20+_____

For what reason did you come to the CAPS Center? (Check as many as apply)
☐ Personal Counseling ☐ Academic Counseling
☐ Career Counseling ☐ Readmit Counseling

PLEASE CIRCLE THE NUMBER TO THE RIGHT OF EACH STATEMENT, WHICH INDICATES YOUR LEVEL OF AGREEMENT WITH IT (1 = Least Agreement; 5 = Highest Agreement).

1. I was treated courteously by the front office staff.
   1   2   3   4   5   N/A
2. I was treated courteously by the counselor I saw.
   1   2   3   4   5   N/A
3. I felt the counselor was appropriately concerned about my problem.
   1   2   3   4   5   N/A
4. The counselor seemed well-trained and skilled in helping me with my problems.
   1   2   3   4   5   N/A
5. I felt comfortable in the waiting area.
   1   2   3   4   5   N/A
6. My counselor helped me to develop better ways of coping with my concerns.
   1   2   3   4   5   N/A
7. I felt there were too many forms to fill out.
   1   2   3   4   5   N/A
8. If the need to speak to someone arises again, I would return to CAPS.
   1   2   3   4   5   N/A
9. I would recommend CAPS to others.
   1   2   3   4   5   N/A
10. The career inventories were helpful to me.
   1   2   3   4   5   N/A
11. As a result of counseling, I believe that I am more likely to stay in school.
   YES____   NO____
12. As a result of counseling, I believe that I will do better academically.
   YES____   NO____
13. The length of time to schedule an appointment with a counselor was too long.
   YES____   NO____
14. When waiting in the Career Resource Room to meet with my counselor, I am usually seen in a timely manner.
   YES____   NO____

If "No" to Question 14, how many minutes, on average, did you have to wait? _____
Please comment on any suggestions that you feel can assist us in improving our services.

Thank you, for taking the time to complete this survey. Please place your completed survey in the designated drop box.

14

Strategies for Small Staff College Counseling Centers

JOYCE R. THOMAS

FOCUS QUESTIONS

1. What is a small staff college counseling center, and how does it differ from larger centers?

2. What are the unique challenges of working in a small staff college counseling center?

3. How can a small staff college counseling center offer comprehensive, quality services without overextending itself?

4. What guidelines can assist the small staff college counselor in providing quality counseling services?

ISSUES

When students find their way to their college counseling center, it will not be readily apparent to them how large the counseling staff is or how wide its range of services is. In both large and small staff centers, students will see other students coming in and out, will hear phones ringing, may see students working at computer terminals or making appointments, and may see office doors closed with "session-in-progress" signs hanging from doorknobs. Indeed, smaller and larger staffed counseling centers share many common features. For the purposes of this chapter, the essential features of the small staff college counseling center are explored. A small staff counseling center is defined as a distinct campus entity providing professional counseling services and staffed by less than three full-time counselors. One might think that it would be more advantageous to work in or make use of services from a larger staffed center rather than one with such a small counseling staff. And yes, there can be unique challenges to providing comprehensive counseling services within a smaller staff office. However, as I explore in this chapter, small staff college counseling centers are not necessarily disadvantaged and can offer a multitude of services to support students and staff.

A small staff college counseling center can be found on any campus of any size in any location. The size of an institution's counseling center does not seem to be determined by whether it is private or public, has a liberal arts focus or is technically focused, or has residence halls or is a commuter campus. Rather, staffing seems to be determined by the unique priorities, budget, and mission of each institution.

Small staff college counselors have a wide variety of backgrounds and fulfill diverse roles on their campuses. Their academic credentials include both master's and doctoral degrees in counseling, social work, psychology, and college student personnel. Small staff college counselors pursue the various board certifications and appropriate licenses for their professional orientation. Small staff college counselors assume a variety of roles on their campuses. These most often include personal counseling, career testing and exploration, academic advising, public and campus outreach, consultation services for the campus community, and crisis intervention. Small staff counselors may also coordinate disability services for their campuses, provide national testing services, manage employee assistance programs, oversee drug and alcohol awareness programs, and direct peer educator and residence life training. For further information about college counseling roles and settings, see Chapter 1, "The College Counseling Environment," and Chapter 3, "College Counseling Today: Changing Roles and Definitions."

The most obvious reason for the existence of small staff centers is that some schools have a low enrollment. However, a steady increase in enrollment at institutions of higher education is expected to continue through 2007 (*Digest of Education Statistics 1997,* 1998). In some instances, these significant enrollment increases have caused colleges and universities to institute or expand counseling services. Many of these new opportunities will involve small staff college counseling centers.

Although a few higher education institutions have added counseling services, the overall trend is a shrinking demand for college counseling services despite a steady increase in enrollment, a rise in the number of student visits and the severity of issues, and a strong link between the use of counseling services and students' success and retention (Bishop, 1990, 1995; Coll, 1995; Dean & Meadows, 1995; Geraghty, 1997; Harris & Kranz, 1991; Heppner & Johnson, 1994; Paul, 1997; Sharkin, 1997; Tentoni, 1997; Wilson, Mason, & Ewing, 1997). There are numerous reasons for the shrinkage of college counseling services in both large staff and small staff settings. Existing counseling services may lack the necessary support from administration, despite heavy and consistent use of those services by students. Counseling services may be considered low-priority items and, under budget cuts, are sometimes downsized or eliminated altogether. Personal mental health counseling may be outsourced as well, so that college counselors are doing less personal counseling and more crisis management, career counseling, and academic advising. These trends and circumstances present substantial challenges for small staff college counselors. Their survival depends on the implementation of creative, proactive strategies for counseling service delivery within the college community.

RECOMMENDATIONS FOR ACTION

There are many ways that college counselors can provide creative, proactive services for the college community without the luxury of a large counseling staff. This section suggests 10 diverse strategies for successful implementation of services at a small staff college counseling center.

1. Enhance your background experience. Because the small staff counselor must often function as a generalist within a growing population with diverse needs (Paul, 1997), it is helpful to have a broad base of knowledge. A background in both counseling and college student personnel is helpful. This might include course work in higher education administration and college student development. Small staff college counselors also should be well-grounded in various counseling approaches and responsive to the unique demands of their institution and students: "If one's therapeutic approach is crystallized in one counseling orientation, be open and prepared for change. I think the setting can almost demand it" (M. Lillard, personal communication, September 16, 1998). The reader is referred to Chapter 4, "Professional Preparation for College Counseling: Quality Assurance," for additional discussion about preparing for a college counseling career.

Exposure to and involvement in a variety of counseling and college-related experiences that go beyond the textbook (i.e., workshops, additional reading) can be beneficial. Training in group facilitation, computer use, public speaking, assertive communication, time management, and leadership is essential. A background in abnormal psychology, mental health diagnosis, and brief therapy approaches is suggested (Archer & Cooper, 1998; Chandler & Gallagher, 1996). Leadership skills are essential. Counselors who are self-starters and who consistently demonstrate the traits of effective leadership—enthusiasm, creativity, and autonomy (Krulak, 1998)—are likely to be successful in small staff settings.

2. Develop essential counseling documents. It is important for the small staff college counselor to develop and implement a mission statement that will guide service delivery. The mission statement reveals the underlying philosophy and goals of the counseling center and clarifies the center's relationship to the larger institution. The reader will also have an enhanced understanding of collegewide goals because the counseling center's mission will be consistent with those of your institution (Bishop, 1995; May, 1992). Guidelines for writing effective mission statements for college counseling centers can be found in the Accreditation Standards of University and College Counseling Centers (Kiracofe & Donn, 1994). Two excellent examples of mission statements for small staff college counseling centers appear in **Box 6**.

Box 6

College Counseling Centers' Mission Statements

Southern Polytechnic State University, Marietta, Georgia, Two Counselors, 4,000 Students

The Counseling Office shares the university's commitment to recruit and retain students and to provide them with a teaching/learning environment both inside and outside the classroom. Programs are designed to assist students in discovering and realizing personal, educational, and career planning goals. Services include developmental, remedial, and preventive components in order to meet the needs of well-adjusted students, students with personal adjustment problems, and students requiring special services because of learning disorders and/or physical disabilities.

Castleton State College, Castleton, Vermont, One Counselor for 1,800 Students, 4-Year Liberal Arts

Castleton State College Wellness Center is committed to fostering the development of all members of the Castleton community. We strive to promote healthy life choices in all aspects of living. We encourage the exploration of positive self-growth experiences that enhance an individual's overall life process. We offer services through the unification of two offices. Health services and counseling and testing services work in conjunction to offer holistic and comprehensive services to our community. Counseling services strives to meet the psychological needs of students, alumni, faculty, and staff by providing a safe, supportive, and confidential environment that empowers them to explore personal and interpersonal concerns. In keeping with the educational mission of our institution, we promote self-awareness, teach effective coping strategies, and encourage responsibility and respect. The office of alcohol and drug education is open to students for information or answers to questions regarding substance abuse or related problems. The office provides training and information on a variety of topics related to alcohol, tobacco, and other drugs via classroom presentations, residence hall programs, peer outreach, and campuswide awareness events.

In addition to a mission statement, other counseling documents should be developed for the organization and implementation of services. These might include a complete policies and procedures guide (Patton, 1998; Stoy & Cordle, 1999), a policy and consent form, a brochure, an intake form, a counseling contract, release of information forms, and termination summary forms. Not all of these documents may be necessary for every center. For professional and ethical reasons, however, at least two are essential: the consent to treat and release of information forms (Kiracofe & Donn, 1994). The consent to treat (and professional disclosure) form explains the parameters of counseling, describes student–client rights, and defines confidentiality limits. The release of information form allows for student–client authorization for information exchange among appropriate parties. See **Appendixes D, E,** and **F** for examples of these forms.

3. Communicate with influential players at your institution. It is important that the small staff college counselor communicates with the influential players at his or her institution. These are the "top" people who should know what the college counselor does so that they can advocate for and possibly use his or her services. They may include administrators, board members, faculty, and security officers (Bishop, 1990, 1995; Heppner & Johnson, 1994; Kiracofe & Donn, 1994; May, 1992). Communication with the influential players should include education on the profession of counseling, information on the counselor's background experiences as a helping professional and leader, and the college counselor's vision or mission for the institution's counseling center. An effective way to educate and create productive relationships with these influential players is to develop specific proposals for counseling center services. Submit these proposals in writing, and seek counsel and input from your administrators about your plans. It is also helpful to keep all of the influential players up-to-date on your services by sending relevant, regular correspondence. This correspondence might include end-of-semester reports, thank-you notes for referrals, and reminders of upcoming events. See Chapter 13, "Building Effective Campus Relationships," for further recommendations regarding college counselors' associations with campus constituencies.

4. Make yourself visible to the campus community. The issue of visibility for a college counselor can be a tricky one. This is especially true on a smaller college campus or when there are only one or two college counselors; the counselor's face eventually becomes quite familiar. On the one hand, it is important to foster this familiarity so students know their college counselor and the services that he or she provides (Tentoni, 1997). On the other hand, there is the ethical concern that comes from being so widely known and recognized all over campus. This may cause some students to worry about the safety of their anonymity and confidences (Grayson, 1986). Grayson pointed out a powerful difference, however, between "visibility as a professional tactic" (p. 188) and the counselor who tries to be in the spotlight without having enough sensitivity to its implications. Grayson suggested several specific efforts that counselors on small college campuses can undertake to maintain clients' privacy and confidentiality. These efforts include (a) not initiating acknowledgment of clients in public; (b) not alluding to cases while talking to friends or colleagues; (c) developing prudent and clear-cut policies in regards to release of information, consultations with college employees and parents, and procedures during crises; and (d) keeping and referring to "detailed process notes to avoid transposing the content of patients whose lives are intertwined" (Grayson, 1986, p. 190).

Still, students should know about the services on campus if they are going to use the services, and therefore, counselors within large and small staff counseling centers must make themselves visible. Within the parameters of the policies mentioned above, there are many ways to ethically, professionally, and sensitively enhance your visibility.

- Introduce yourself and your services. Do this through regular, brief correspondence with appropriate faculty and staff; at student orientation sessions; and by submitting articles in faculty, student, and alumni publications.
- Visit classrooms. Briefly introduce yourself and your services in classrooms, and leave copies of your business card and brochure so students can learn more about their college counseling center. Offer to present mental health-related programs for faculty when they are absent from their classroom.
- Become involved on your campus. Serve on diverse college committees. Be visible at and actively participate in student functions. Be

aware of the pursuits and concerns of your student population. Attend college functions (e.g., dedications, graduation, and socials).

- Use technology whenever possible. Provide your campus E-mail address, and encourage students to use it for general educational inquiries and to schedule appointments. Use and keep current your voice mail and outgoing message system. A college counseling center's web site can provide an infinite amount of information for students and employees. Three particularly impressive and comprehensive web sites of small staff college counseling centers can be found at the following Internet addresses (available September 10, 1999): http://www.csc.vsc.edu/wellness/well.html (Castleton State), http://admin.acadiau.ca/counsel/ (Acadia University), and http://www.centenary.edu/centenar/campusrv/counse/ (Centenary College).

5. Be sensitive to ethical dilemmas. Ethical practice is no different within a small staff counseling center than within one that is larger. However, there are some particularly sensitive ethical issues that arise for small staff counselors. The first is the unavoidable occurrence of dual relationships. When only one or two counselors are available to counsel students, and these same counselors also teach courses, do academic advising, chair committees, and participate in college social functions, there is no doubt that dual relationships will occur (Grayson, 1986). A second ethical dilemma is confidentiality. A counselor may be working with the spouse of an advisee. A counselor may have a close friendship with an instructor who recently referred a student for counseling. A client may greet the counselor in the hallway and begin discussing his or her concerns about a roommate, who also happens to be a client. As stated so succinctly by Grayson, "A reputation for confidentiality is a cornerstone of a student mental health service. If it is damaged, usage of the service declines, and patients become guarded in their communications to therapists" (p. 187). It is crucial to develop appropriate policies and procedures to follow in regards to handling dual relationships and confidentiality. Two excellent examples of small staff counseling center policies and procedures manuals that address ethical issues have been developed at Southern Polytechnic University in Marietta, Georgia (Stoy & Cordle, 1999) and Southern State Community College in Hillsboro, Ohio (Patton, 1998).

The ethics section in each manual is quite comprehensive and specifically relevant to the ethical concerns of small staff college counselors. The reader is referred to Chapter 5, "Practicing Ethically as a College Counselor," for a more in-depth discussion of various ethical issues.

6. Ease your load without compromising services. College counselors are dedicated professionals with a passion for helping students succeed. This dedication, however, can be problematic when college counselors try to provide large staff center services with small staff resources. Small staff college counselors can find themselves following a short road to burnout by continuously overextending themselves. The following strategies are suggested for small staff counselors who could benefit from easing their work demands without compromising the quality of services.

- Develop your center as an internship site for local graduate programs in counseling education (Bishop, 1990). This strategy does not suggest that there is no work involved in supervising an intern. Nor is it intended to suggest that the intern can assume all of the office responsibilities while the counselor rests. Supervising an intern is an enormous responsibility, one that requires tremendous time, talent, and care if it is to be done ethically and effectively (Kiracofe & Donn, 1994). Interns can, however, allow for more students to be seen in the center and possibly free the primary counselor's schedule for other projects.
- Use a brief therapy approach (Archer & Cooper, 1998; P. J. Kitzman, personal communication, September 18, 1998; M. Lillard, personal communication, September 16, 1998). Bishop (1995) stated that brief counseling approaches may be necessary (and naturally occur at college counseling centers given the time increments of semesters and terms) to allow counselors more time to focus on preventative and developmental roles.
- Continue to review and follow your counseling center's goals and mission. Are you doing what is indicated in your mission? Are you setting appropriate boundaries so as not to overextend yourself? Should the mission be revised?
- Make a commitment to regular staff meetings with colleagues. This is especially important for small staff college counselors. Staff meet-

ings can enhance the counselor's knowledge, improve counseling skills, expand resources, prevent isolation, and reduce burnout.

7. Develop a community referral network. College counselors have a professional and ethical responsibility to refer clients whose needs surpass the counselors' resources. Small staff counselors should identify referral sources for things like housing, domestic abuse counseling, legal assistance, medical care, inpatient substance abuse treatment, and similar needs. As the severity of problems and the number of students seen increase, college counselors must have community referrals in place so that they can offer students the best care possible (Bishop, 1990; Kiracofe & Donn, 1994). K. Paulson (personal communication, September 10, 1998), the sole counselor at Centenary College (in Shreveport, Louisiana), stated,

> I needed to have a referral list for students. . . . I got out the phone book and started calling people: counselors, psychologists, and psychiatrists. When possible I talked to the mental health professionals themselves. I requested addresses, telephone numbers, rates, issues [for which] they had expertise, and recommendations for other counselors. I also [received] good information on who NOT to refer to. . . . I visited several mental health hospitals and picked two that I would work with.

M. Stoy (personal communication, September 18, 1998), Director of Counseling at Southern Polytechnic State University (in Marietta, Georgia), has developed a comprehensive referral network for her students that includes psychiatric care: "Establishing good referral procedures is crucial. I have been able to obtain psychiatric referrals at a fairly low cost for students without insurance. The school reimburses the doctor for up to two visits." Whenever possible, spend time getting to know the helping professionals within your referral network. The personal time and effort invested in establishing such relationships can increase the number of referrals you have within your network and, possibly, enhance the effectiveness of the resources available to students.

8. Explore alternative modes of service delivery. There are a variety of ways to provide mental health services to students. If small staff college counselors want to reach the majority of students in an effective and proactive way, they often must move beyond the confines of the counseling center. Providing various group support and group counseling services is one way to move beyond the office. It seems that more structured psychoeducational groups (e.g., relaxation training or study skills improvement) fair better than long-term personal growth or therapy groups (Archer & Cooper, 1998; Kinkade, 1995). Obviously there are exceptions to this rule, and each college counseling center must explore the unique needs of its students to determine what group or groups could be the most beneficial.

Providing miniseminars for dissemination of information can also be quite helpful. My counseling center cosponsors "Lunch Break Seminars" on a variety of topics from "Navigating Financial Aid" to "Test Taking Success." My center includes a bag lunch for participants, which helps increase attendance. Some counselors have found that offering these types of seminars is neither time- nor cost-effective because of poor attendance and have had stopped offering them. Instead, they present to larger groups of students by invitation (e.g., at campus organizational meetings, for residence hall floor meetings, during new student orientation). Other counselors use peer educators or peer leaders (P. J. Kitzman, personal communication, September 18, 1998; R. J. Kline, personal communication, January 29, 1999). With intensive screening and training, peer educators can be an effective resource for counselors to assist in outreach services on campus. The reader if referred to Chapter 12, "Outreach Programming From the College Counseling Center," for recommendations regarding this topic.

A third mode to reach more students is to provide national mental health screenings at your institution (D. Ellis, personal communication, September 15, 1998). Excellent materials are provided by national organizations at a minimal cost for such issues as depression, anxiety, eating disorders, and alcohol awareness. Contact information for three national organizations can be found in **Box 7**.

Box 7

National College Student Screening Organizations

Freedom From Fear
National Anxiety Disorders College Screening Project
308 Sea View Avenue
Staten Island, NY 10305
718-351-1717

National Mental Illness Screening Project
National Depression Screening Day
One Washington Street, Suite 304
Wellesley Hills, MA 02481-1706
781-239-0071

Eating Disorders Awareness and Prevention
603 Stewart Street, Suite 803
Seattle, WA 98101
206-382-3587

---

9. Use resources for consultation and professional development.
There are so many ways that counselors can enhance their skills, knowledge, and professionalism. With the advent of electronic listservs and the ease of Internet access, even isolated counselors can easily connect with other professionals. With demands on the small counseling center to do more with less, it can be quite easy for a lone counselor to "forget" to take time for himself or herself, to develop professionally, and to reach out to other colleagues. "Counselors may feel especially pressured due to increasing demands for services. . . . It is even more important for these counselors to build professional networks with others in similar positions. Sharing concerns, brainstorming alternatives, and supporting each other are invaluable experiences" (Harris & Kranz, 1991, p. 87). It is essential that counselors participate in professional organizations, attend counseling- and college-related conferences, and take part in regular consultations or staff meetings with colleagues (Kiracofe & Donn, 1994). A small staff counselor can easily become isolated.

> Being the only counselor on campus . . . one can easi-
> ly feel isolated from other collegiate professionals. Even
> though I am a member of several professional organi-
> zations and attend state and national conferences, noth-
> ing can really replace the ability to walk across the hall
> and chat with a colleague. (E. Patton, personal commu-
> nication, February 8, 1999)

Indeed, that "across the hall" connection cannot be replaced. Yet, small
staff college counselors still must find avenues to connect that are satisfying, productive, and both personally and professionally enhancing.
Membership in professional counseling and college-related organizations
has the benefits of providing necessary personal connections, leadership
opportunities, and opportunities for knowledge and skill development.

Examples of helpful organizations for small staff college counselors
include the American Counseling Association, the American College
Counseling Association, the American College Personnel Association, the
National Career Development Association, and state and local branches
of these organizations. Many of these organizations also have their own
electronic mail listservs, which can provide not only personal connections but also a never-ending supply of current information. Identifying
and seeking out colleagues in your institution or community with whom
you can consult are also essential. Mentoring is another effective way to
foster development as a counselor. Phelps (1992) discussed how seeking
out and forming a relationship with a mentor could greatly enhance a
new professional's postgraduate counseling effectiveness: "Mentoring
relationships can . . . provide an additional dimension of personal support in the quest for professional identity, establishing priorities, making
adjustments, and finding one's niche in the profession" (p. 31).

10. Evaluate your services. Counseling services, like any other service on a college campus, must be regularly evaluated (Kiracofe & Donn,
1994). The challenge is how to evaluate services for which the value may
be quite subjective (Wilson et al., 1997). It is essential, of course, to objec-
tively evaluate (exactly how many students did you see?), but this alone

is not enough (Wilson et al., 1997). T. Lane (personal communication, February 9, 1999), Director of Counselling and Employee Assistance Services at Acadia University in Wolfville, Nova Scotia, made the point very well: "Some support services become grimly attached to counting customer contacts but a skeptical senior administrator may not be convinced that a popular service necessarily contributes anything worth institutional [dollars]." A thorough evaluation must also assess what effect counseling services have had on students' health and whether this effect has contributed to improved academics and retention (Wilson et al., 1997). Studying the current literature linking counseling services with student retention can provide helpful information. It is also important to document how many of the students served by the counseling center actually stayed in school (retention). For example, staff at my institution are currently tracking students on academic probation who participate in a series of "student success seminars" sponsored jointly by the counseling office and the academic achievement center. Data will be gathered on the basis of participation, grade point average before and after the seminars, and scores on a learning behaviors inventory before and after the seminars.

Most counseling centers have standard evaluation forms for students who use the counseling services. These evaluations help small staff counseling centers to gather evidence directly from students as to what benefit, if any, they received from counseling and what suggestions they may have for improvement of services. An example of a small staff college counseling center evaluation is included in **Appendix G**.

Another good way to educate the campus about college counselors and the small staff counseling center is to provide a one-page report to the institution that summarizes services for the past year. This end-of-year report can go to any college employee who had contact with the center as well as those previously identified as "influential players." An example of this kind of report is provided in **Appendix H**.

SUMMARY

Single or small staff college counseling centers are found on many different types of campuses, and they exist for as many different reasons. Low enrollment, downsizing, budget cuts, and outsourcing are just a few of the reasons why a college may use a small counseling staff. Small staff college counselors, like their large staff counterparts, are trained professionals who seek appropriate licensure and certification relevant for their professional orientation.

Working within a small staff college counseling center can be a career filled with great personal and professional satisfaction. The position calls for autonomy, leadership, and personal creativity. The most effective "small staffers" are those who have a clear mission, can communicate well and often with their cohorts, find ways to become known and respected on their campus, use traditional and creative means to meet the needs of students, and regularly evaluate the outcomes of their services.

Satisfied small staff counselors are also aware of the importance of taking good care of themselves. They do this by practicing ethically, staying connected professionally, reaching out for support, and continuously updating their skills as professional counselors. The small staff counseling center is an immensely rewarding employment environment for college counselors who have a passion for extensive and varied student contact and who embrace the key strategies of visibility, involvement, creativity, and flexibility.

REFERENCES

Archer, J., Jr., & Cooper, S. (1998). *Counseling and mental health services on campus*. San Francisco: Jossey-Bass.

Bishop, J. B. (1990). The university counseling center: An agenda for the 1990's. *Journal of Counseling and Development, 68,* 408–413.

Bishop, J. B. (1995). Emerging strategies for college and university counseling centers. *Journal of Counseling and Development, 74,* 33–38.

Chandler, L. A., & Gallagher, R. P. (1996). Developing a taxonomy for problems seen at a university counseling center. *Measurement and Evaluation in Counseling and Development, 29,* 4–12.

Coll, K. M. (1995). Career, personal, and educational problems of community college students: Severity and frequency. *NASPA Journal, 32,* 270–278.

Dean, L. A., & Meadows, M. E. (1995). College counseling: Union and intersection. *Journal of Counseling and Development, 74,* 139–143.

Digest of Education Statistics, 1997. (1998). Washington, DC: National Center for Education Statistics.

Geraghty, M. (1997, August 1). Campuses see steep increase in students seeking counseling. *The Chronicle of Higher Education, 43,* pp. A32–A33.

Grayson, P. A. (1986). Mental health confidentiality on the small campus. *Journal of American College Health, 34,* 187–191.

Harris, S. A., & Kranz, P. (1991). Small college counseling centers: Changing trends for a new decade. *Journal of College Student Psychotherapy, 5,* 81–89.

Heppner, P. P., & Johnson, J. A. (1994). New horizons in counseling: Faculty development. *Journal of Counseling and Development, 72,* 451–453.

Kinkade, E. A. (1995, March). Group work in college counseling: A balancing act. *Visions, 3*(1), 13–14.

Kiracofe, N. M., & Donn, P. A. (1994). Accreditation standards for university and college counseling centers. *Journal of Counseling and Development, 73,* 38–44.

Krulak, C. C. (1998, September–October). The fourteen basic traits of effective leadership. *About Campus, 3*(4), 8–11.

May, R. (1992). Severe psychopathology in counseling centers: Reaction to Gilbert. *Journal of Counseling and Development, 70,* 702–703.

Patton, E. (1998). *Policies and procedures manual.* Hillsboro, OH: Southern State Community College, Counseling and Career Resources Center.

Paul, N. C. (1997, August 12). College students seek more counsel. *The Christian Science Monitor,* p. 12.

Phelps, R. E. (1992). University and college counseling centers: One option for new professionals in counseling. *Counseling Psychologist, 20,* 24–32.

Sharkin, B. S. (1997). Increasing severity of presenting problems in college counseling centers: A closer look. *Journal of Counseling and Development, 74,* 275–282.

Stoy, M., & Cordle, T. (1999). *Policies and procedures.* Marietta, GA: Southern Polytechnic State University, Counseling Services.

Tentoni, S. C. (1997). A marketing technique to increase visibility and use of health center counseling services. *Journal of American College Health, 46,* 93–96.

Wilson, S. B., Mason, T. W., & Ewing, M. J. M. (1997). Evaluating the impact of receiving university-based counseling services on student retention. *Journal of Counseling Psychology, 44,* 316–320.

APPENDIX D

Sample Consent to Treat Form

Professional Disclosure Information and Consent
Ozarks Technical Community College (OTC)
Springfield, Missouri

The OTC Counseling and Career Development Service adheres to the accepted ethical and professional standards of the American Counseling Association. OTC's short-term personal counseling services are available for those students currently enrolled at OTC. Short-term career counseling is also available for currently enrolled and prospective OTC students. There is no charge for these services. Personal counseling relationships are professional, and contacts between clients and counselors are expected to be of a professional nature.

No personal counseling information will be released to those outside of OTC's Counseling and Career Development Office without your explicit authorization unless there is substantial or immediate danger of physical harm to yourself or others.

During a short interview, you will have an opportunity to discuss the reasons you are seeking our services. Although your counselor will work with you to achieve the best possible results for you, it is impossible to guarantee any specific results regarding your counseling goals.

You have the right to ask questions about your counselor's credentials and approach. You may also accept or reject any suggested counseling interventions. You and your counselor may choose to contract for follow-up sessions to discuss your issues more fully. Since this is a short-term counseling service, referral to outside counseling agencies may be recommended if your counselor believes you could benefit from assistance beyond the scope of our services.

You have the right to report any complaint about our services to the Director of Counseling or to the Vice President of Student Development.

Joyce R. Thomas
Nationally Certified Counselor
Licensed Professional Counselor

Consent to Treat

I have read and understand the information presented above. I give my consent for counseling, testing, and other services that may be deemed necessary and appropriate by my counselor at Ozarks Technical Community College.

Signature_____Date_____

APPENDIX E

Sample Release of Information Form

AUTHORIZATION TO RELEASE INFORMATION
TO THE OTC COUNSELING & CAREER
DEVELOPMENT OFFICE

I,_____ authorize _____
    Printed name of client   *Name of referring person and/or agency*

_____ to send any report, statement,
    Address of referring person and/or agency

analysis, diagnosis, or any professional record to Joyce Thomas, NCC, LPC,
Ozarks Technical Community College, Office of Counseling and Career
Development, Information Commons Building 112A, 1001 E. Brower,
Springfield, MO 65801.

_____   _____

    Client Signature   *Date*

_____   _____

    Witness Signature   *Date*

This consent for release of confidential information will expire on_____.

Additional Comments:

Prohibition of redisclosure: This information has been disclosed to you from
records whose confidentiality is protected by federal law. Federal regulations
(42 CFR Part 2) prohibit you from making any further disclosure of this information except with the specific written consent of the person to whom it per-
tains. A general authorization for the release of medical or other information if
held by another party is not sufficient for this purpose. Federal regulations
state that any person who violates any provision of this law shall be fined not
more than $500.00, in the case of the first offense, and not more than
$5,000.00 in the case of each subsequent case.

APPENDIX F

Sample Consent for Release of Confidential Information Form

I, _____ authorize Ozarks Technical Community College Counseling and Career Development Services to release information to the following:

_____

NAME of person and/or agency to receive this information

_____

ADDRESS

_____   _____

CITY AND STATE   PHONE

_____   _____

Client's Signature   Witness

_____

Date Signed

I authorize the counseling staff of OTC's Counseling and Career Development Services to release only the following confidential information about me:

( ) Summary of Treatment   ( ) Dates of Counseling Appointments
( ) Summary of Academic Progress ( ) Testing Results
( ) Other

This consent for release of confidential information will expire on _____.

APPENDIX G

Sample Counseling Services Evaluation Form

Southern State Community College
Counseling & Career Resources Center

Our records indicate that you have recently used the services provided by Southern State's Counseling & Career Resources Center. To help us improve services, we are interested in your feelings about your experience with the center and our staff. Please complete the following anonymous survey by answering each question.

After completing the survey, simply return it to us in the enclosed preaddressed envelope. No additional postage is necessary.

Please indicate your sex: ____Male   ____Female

Which of the following describes you best?
___ college freshman
___ college sophomore
___ community adult
___ high school student
___ other_____

DIRECTIONS: Circle the appropriate response to each question or statement below.

SECTION I

1. The amount of time I waited to get a counseling appointment was
     a. excellent   b. good   c. acceptable   d. not acceptable

2. The convenience of the location of the office was
     a. excellent   b. good   c. acceptable   d. not acceptable

3. Getting through to the center by phone was
     a. easy   b. acceptable   c. difficult   d. not acceptable

4. The treatment I received from the clerical staff was
     a. very good   b. good   c. fair   d. poor

5. I have not returned for additional counseling sessions because
     • I received the assistance I was seeking and did not need additional help.
     • I want to come back but haven't had time.
     • Counseling was not helpful, so I didn't return.
     • Other_____

6. If I needed help again, I would return to the Counseling & Career Resources Center.
     a. yes   b. maybe   c. probably not   d. no

7. Based on my overall experience, I consider the center's services
   a. very good   b. good   c. acceptable   d. not acceptable

SECTION II

8. How would you rate the assistance you received from your counselor?
   a. very good   b. good   c. fair   d. poor

9. How thoroughly did you feel your concerns were addressed?
   a. excellently   b. well   c. fairly   d. poorly

10. On the whole, did your counselor behave as though you were important?
    a. always   b. often   c. sometimes   d. rarely

11. To what extent do you agree with the statement, "My counselor understood my problems and me."?
    a. strongly agree   b. agree   c. disagree   d. strongly disagree

12. To what extent do you agree with the statement, "My counselor helped me understand myself better."?
    a. strongly agree   b. agree   c. disagree   d. strongly disagree

13. To what extent to you agree with the statement, "My counselor provided information or assistance to help me make the needed decision or change."?
    a. strongly agree   b. agree   c. disagree   d. strongly disagree

14. How satisfied are you with the progress you made in counseling?
    a. completely   b. for the most part   c. somewhat   d. not at all

15. Would you recommend the Counseling & Career Resources Center to a friend with a problem or concern?
    a. strongly recommend   b. perhaps recommend
    c. not recommend   d. strongly not recommend

16. Please share, in the space below, any additional comments or suggestions that might help us improve services in the Counseling & Career Resources Center.

Thank you for participating in our follow-up satisfaction survey. If you would like to resume your work in the Counseling and Career Resources Center, or if you have other questions or concerns, please call us at 1-800-628-7722 extension 624 or 625.

Thanks again!

APPENDIX H

Sample End-of-Year Report

1998–1999 End-of-Year Report
Ozarks Technical Community College Counseling
& Career Services
Joyce R. Thomas, Counselor

OTC's Office of Counseling and Career Development has completed its second full year of offering counseling services for the OTC community. Counseling is one of three OTC student services that fall under the supervision of the Counseling and Career Development Director, Karla Gregg (the other two are New Traditions [formerly New Perspectives] and the Vocational Evaluation and Assessment Center). The primary functions of OTC's counseling service are to provide short-term personal counseling for OTC students and career counseling and assessment for currently enrolled and prospective OTC students. Through utilization of these free and confidential services, students are assisted in working through social, emotional, and academic issues, which may be negatively affecting their success at OTC.

Some of the most common issues for which students seek our confidential services are test anxiety, grief, relationship and communication struggles, career indecision, depression, academic struggles, domestic abuse issues, and time management.

In addition to students, numerous OTC employees also utilized services. Approximately 95 contacts (up from 56 the previous year) were initiated by employees for the following reasons:
- to discuss concerns about working with challenging students
- to request special programs for the classroom
- to refer a student for counseling services
- to find information about local social service and/or mental health services.

The goals during this second full year of counseling were all achieved. They were to (1) purchase and implement computerized career assessment tools to enhance our career counseling services for currently enrolled and prospective OTC students; (2) actively seek out new local social and mental health services to expand our student referral network; (3) continue providing self-help programs for students and community members; (4) develop OTC's counseling office as one suited for field experience by master's-level counseling students; (5) assist in the development of the counseling and career development portion of our web site; (6) research methods to provide more proactive, creative services within a small staff college counseling center; (7) provide national exposure for OTC by presenting a program for the American Counseling Association Annual Conference (these last two items were achieved in large part through the researching assistance and equipment availability from our LRC). Data substantiating the accomplishment of these goals can be found on the back of this report.

To further enhance OTC's counseling services, the following are the primary goals for the 1999–2000 academic year.
1. Continue supervision of one counseling intern per semester.
2. Assist in the hiring and supervision of a part-time licensed counselor.
3. Improve skills as a leader and college counselor by
    a. pursuing a leadership position within the American College Counseling Association.
    b. attending and presenting at a national counseling association conference.
4. Purchase materials for and implement the National Depression Screening for the OTC campus community (this will take place on October 7, 1999).
5. Offer one personal growth group for OTC students during the Spring 2000 semester.
6. Working closely with the Office of Research and Assessment, develop and implement a client satisfaction survey for the counseling center.

As indicated on the opposite page, there was a significant increase over last year in the number of students served within the Counseling and Career Development Office. Specifically, we saw a 32% increase in the total number of one-on-one contacts, a 43% increase in career assessments given, and a 35% increase in the number of students reached through classroom presentations. This increase is due in part to the relocation of the counseling office to the Information Commons, the assistance received through master's-level counseling interns, and the expansion of counseling services (i.e., group counseling and career assessment). This increase is also due in large part to the efforts of each of our faculty and staff. Many students with whom I met were referred by a concerned staff member or remembered me as being an invited speaker in one of their classes. More extensive and specific information about the level of student satisfaction with OTC's Counseling and Career Development Services will be gathered from the client satisfaction surveys (see goal #6 above). The summary of results will be sent to each of you as soon as the survey process is complete.

Ozarks Technical Community College Counseling
& Career Services Statistics for 1998–1999

(Unless otherwise indicated, the number of clients reported does not reflect students who came in more than once. The numbers indicate students seeking services for the first time.)

1.

	1997–1998	1998–1999
TOTAL FIRST TIME STUDENT CONTACTS	170	250
Academic Advising (Number does not include students seen during general registration periods)	40	50
Personal Counseling	44	65
Career Counseling	72	105
Crisis Intervention	01	02
Group Counseling	00	10
Combination of Any of the Above	10	18
Students seeking any of the above services more than once	101	135
Average number of sessions per student	2.4	2.4
Average length of each session	1.25 hours	1.5 hours
Total number of one-on-one student contacts made (new and continuing)	404	599
Career assessments given (CAPS, IDEAS, MBTI, CAI-V, CAI-E)	181	323
OTC employee consultations	56	95

2. TOTAL SEEN IN SEMINARS/PRESENTATIONS = 811 (530 seen during 1997–1998)

Test Taking Success
OTC A & P Classes
OTC Reading Comp. Class
OTC Surgical Tech. Class
OTC Lunch Break Seminars
OTC Student Success Seminars
OTC Practical Nursing Students
OTC PTA Class
OTC Pre-Algebra Class

OTC Career Development
SMSU Counseling Class
Healthy Body Image
OTC Lifetime Wellness Class
OTC Nutrition Class

Personality Preferences
OTC Office Systems Tech. Classes
OTC Student Services Employment

Career Exploration
Strafford High School
King's Chapel Students

Grief & Bereavement
OTC Pathophysiology Class

Depression
OTC Lunch Break Seminar
OTC Lifespan Psych. Class

Building Personal Resilience
Ozarks Literacy Council
Job Council of the Ozarks
OTC Sociology Class
OTC Lifespan Psych. Classes
OTC U.S. History Class
American Counseling Association Conference

3. COLLEGE ACTIVITIES/COMMITTEE PARTICIPATION

Fall Campus Picnic
New Student Orientation
Student Outcomes Assessment Committee
Student Forum Luncheon

Graduation
Student Services Retreat Committee
Crisis Management Committee

4. PROFESSIONAL DEVELOPMENT ACTIVITIES

OTC In-Services
Threat Management Seminar
"The Network" Women in Higher Education
MVA Conference
Student Success Seminars

American Counseling Association Conference
PowerPoint Workshop
Stress & Disease Seminar
Communication Skills Seminar
Family Violence Seminar

5. MENTAL HEALTH CENTER/COMMUNITY VISITS

Vocational Rehabilitation
Carol Jones Recovery Center

Job Council of the Ozarks-Branson
OTC Mansfield

6. NATIONAL PRESENTATION & RESEARCH

- Developed and presented a 90-minute PowerPoint program entitled "Building Personal Resilience to Manage Stress" for the American Counseling Association's 1999 World Conference in San Diego.
- Researched and wrote the chapter "*Strategies for Small-Staff College Counseling Centers*" to be published in a counseling textbook for college counselors in Spring 2000.

PART IV

COLLEGE COUNSELORS AND THE FUTURE

15

College Counselors' Well Being

DEBORAH C. DAVIS AND
BARBARA L. MARKLEY

FOCUS QUESTIONS

1. What is counselor well being, and how can a well being approach help prevent counselor impairment?

2. What strategies can help college counselors achieve a wellness focus in their professional practice?

3. How can college counselors use their preparation in developmental interventions to help themselves, their clients, and the profession achieve wellness?

ISSUES

College counseling is a dynamic and stimulating profession. College counselors work in diverse higher education environments in which learning and personal growth are valued and expected. Counselors' opportunities to help students achieve their personal and academic goals are practically limitless. Counselors' career ladders are diversified and accessible. Direct counseling and clinical services, teaching, administration, training, outreach, and supervision are only a few of the many career paths that counselors may pursue. Many counselors operate from a developmental foundation, which allows them to integrate clinical approaches within a holistic life framework. College counselors are change agents with the power to influence campus climates and shape institutional policies. College counseling, as a profession, is increasingly recognized as an integral service for campuses today.

Despite all of the goodness associated with college counseling, some counselors experience increasing levels of stress and anxiety, disenchantment with their roles, and frustration with their supervisors and institutions. How can college counselors maintain the zest and enthusiasm for their work in the face of declining budgets, escalating demands, increasing severity of student problems, and the assorted stresses associated with the helping profession?

This chapter examines the concept of counselor well being from the holistic perspective of wellness. Burnout is described, and counselors' stories, collected by us, are shared to illustrate what happens when one's life is out of balance and impairment is imminent. Wellness is contrasted with health, and the developmental partnership between counseling and wellness is discussed. Counselors are encouraged to use an integrated developmental approach, focusing on self-care and well being, in their private lives and professional practices. Recommendations are offered to guide college counselors who are beginning or renewing a wellness commitment.

Counselor Burnout

"The purpose of wellness is to maximize human potential for our clients and ourselves" (Witmer & Young, 1996, p. 152). The following quotations, which were shared with us by college counselors describing how they felt about their work in higher education, illustrate counselor burnout in action.

> A college counselor is like a car battery. At the beginning of the school year, all the students/clients are plugged in and drawing current. At the end of the school year, the battery is worn down and must be recharged. And each time the battery is recharged, it has more difficulty holding its charge, and eventually it must be replaced. That is when complete burnout has taken place.

> When I try to describe my experience to someone else, I use the analogy of a teapot. Just like a teapot, I was on fire, with water boiling—working hard to handle problems and do good. But after several years, the water had boiled away, and yet I was still on the fire— a burned-out teapot in danger of cracking.

Burnout was recognized as a serious cause of impairment among helping professionals in the late 1970s and is still a matter of concern in the literature associated with impairment among helping professionals (Capner & Caltabiano, 1993; Farber, 1990; Figley, 1993; Schaufeli, Maslach, & Marek, 1993). Although no single concept or definition of *burnout* is accepted as standard, Freudenberger (1974), considered by many to be the term's originator, described it as "failing, wearing out or becoming exhausted through excessive demands on energy, strength, or resources" (p. 159). Maslach (1982) stated that burnout is "a syndrome of emotional exhaustion, depersonalization and reduced personal accomplishment that can occur among individuals who 'do people work' of some kind" (p. 1). College counselors certainly face the chronic emotional strain of dealing intensively with other human beings, particularly when these individuals are troubled or having problems.

Maslach (1982) further identified common threads in the varying definitions of burnout, with general agreement that burnout is a negative internal psychological experience involving feelings, attitudes, motives, and expectations. Burnout can be considered one type of job stress. Although it has some of the same deleterious effects as other stress responses, burnout is unique in that the stress arises from the social interaction between the helper and the recipient. At the heart of the burnout syndrome is a pattern of emotional overload and subsequent emotional exhaustion. For example, a college counselor might become emotionally overinvolved with students' problems, overextend himself or herself, and then feel overwhelmed by the demands imposed by other people. The counselor feels drained and used up, lacking the energy to face another day. Emotional resources are depleted, and there is no source of replenishment in sight. These additional quotes help the reader understand the experience of emotional exhaustion.

> Everyday I was knocking myself out at the college—for the students particularly, but also to prove to others (and myself) that I was a good college counselor. Before the day was even over I was exhausted and emotionally drained. I just wanted to go home and sit on the couch and cry. I needed a rest, but couldn't seem to get away from the endless demands for my time. I felt so alone.

This emotional exhaustion is a common condition associated with the burnout syndrome. Once the emotional exhaustion sets in, counselors often feel like they are unable to give anymore of themselves.

> It's not that I don't want to help, but that I just can't motivate myself to feel compassionate about anything.

Attempting to cut back on involvement with others is one coping strategy that some counselors use to lighten this heavy emotional burden. Cutting back involvement is difficult in the college setting. Rather than proactively addressing the problem, some counselors report retreating from the intrusions. Sometimes they seek the minimum amount of contact with students that is necessary to "get by." They may stop any extra commitments with students and limit their availability to only office hours. Occasionally, they retreat to a "by the book" attitude and begin speaking of students in categories rather than as individuals. By applying a standard formula response, they avoid recognizing students individually and thus avoid becoming emotionally involved.

This development of a detached, indifferent response and disregard for others' needs and feelings marks a second characteristic of the burnout syndrome: depersonalization. Maslach (1982) reported that when an individual becomes soured by the press of humanity, he or she wishes, at times, that other people would "get out of my life and just leave me alone." As the following counselor quote illustrates, sometimes this wish is acted on, and the other people are literally shut out:

> I found myself putting students and student groups
> down in ways I never would have imagined. Sometimes
> I'd just refer students, even with little things I could han-
> dle, just so I didn't have to deal with them because I just
> knew they wouldn't do what I suggested.

In the college counseling environment, it is not uncommon for counselors to encourage students to stop in anytime and discuss what's going on with them. Additionally, they may attend numerous programming and extracurricular events with students. For a counselor who is experiencing burnout, the almost constant contact with students and hearing one student's problems replayed over and over by many others become too much. Seriously impaired counselors begin to resent the students from whom there seems to be no escape.

> I began to get extremely frustrated when students
> would want to see me beyond office hours, or when the
> director asked me to give another workshop in the res-

> idence halls. I found myself caring less and developing
> an extremely negative attitude. I wanted to hide when I
> saw students who, only months before, I'd given huge
> amounts of time and attention.

It is understandable why students would be confused by this change of behavior from a counselor who, until recently, had been so friendly and helpful.

Feelings of negativity toward others can progress until they turn to feelings of being down on oneself. Caregivers often feel disgrace or guilt about the way they have treated or thought about others. They sense that they are becoming the uncaring, cold type of person whom no one, especially themselves, wants to be around. This is the third factor of burnout: a feeling of reduced personal accomplishment. College counselors may begin to develop a sense of inadequacy about their ability to relate to students, which may result in the belief that they are a failure. With this decline in self-esteem, depression may follow. Some counselors will seek counseling themselves or will be fortunate enough to have caring colleagues who intervene and help them gain perspective and balance. Others may leave their positions and abandon the work that they thought they'd love so much. Sadly, the problem may well be that they loved their work too much and lost sight of and perspective on the critical and holistic balance so necessary for counselors' well being.

Counselors' Well Being

The terms *wellness* and *well being* are used interchangeably in this chapter. Clinebell (1992) suggested that people are well, or have well being, to the degree that the center of their lives is integrated and energized by love and healthy spirituality. Wellness is not a new concept for the counseling profession. As early as 1947, the World Health Organization defined *health* as "physical, mental, and social well being, not merely the absence of disease or infirmity" (World Health Organization, 1958, p. 3). In the early 1990s, "spiritual well being" was added to this definition. Jung (1958) observed that the human psyche seeks integration and that there is an instinctual drive toward wholeness and health. Maslow (1970) noted that growth, self-actualization, and the pursuit of health must be accepted as a widespread and perhaps universal human tendency. The relationship between spiritual, mental, and physical well being is increasingly discussed in the professional and popular literature (Dossey, 1993; Hafen, Karren, Frandsen, & Smith, 1996; Koenig, 1999; Perls & Silver, 1999).

Wellness Models

Several different wellness models have been proposed, the most basic being the tripartite definition of wellness as the holism resulting from consideration of physical, mental, and spiritual aspects of function. Hettler (1984) conceptualized wellness as consisting of six major dimensions: intellectual, emotional, physical, social, occupational, and spiritual. Ardell (1988) described eight areas of wellness: psychology and spirituality, physical fitness, job satisfaction, relationships, family life, nutrition, leisure time, and stress management.

Witmer and Sweeney (1992) offered an integrated model to illustrate the characteristics of a healthy person over the life span. They proposed that the characteristics of wellness are expressed through five life tasks: spirituality, self-regulation, work, friendship, and love. These life tasks dynamically interact with the life forces of family, community, religion, education, government, media, and business and industry. Global events, both natural and human, have an impact on and are affected by the life forces and the life tasks. Witmer and Sweeney's model demonstrates the interconnectedness of the characteristics of a healthy person, the life tasks, and the life forces that interact for the well being or detriment of the person.

Review of the literature suggests that a multidimensional model for wellness should include the influences of differences related to gender, race, culture, and economic status (Crose, Nicholas, Gobble, & Frank, 1992). Jackson and Sears (1992) found evidence of race as a factor in wellness. Their study indicated that stress-related diseases occur more frequently in African American women than in European American women, with more than 63% of the African American women who participated in their study reporting moderate to severe levels of stress.

African American women reported the lowest level of emotional well being across gender and racial lines (Jackson & Sears, 1992). Neighbors, Jackson, Bowman, and Gurin (1983) found that the coping skill most often used by African Americans was prayer. The aforementioned research illustrates the importance of a holistic well being model.

Myers, Witmer, and Sweeney have continued to expand wellness research and have developed an increasingly sophisticated model that incorporates research and theoretical concepts from a multitude of disciplines, including anthropology, education, medicine, religion, psychology, and sociology. The Wheel of Wellness (Myers, Witmer, & Sweeney, 1997) holds great promise for providing college counselors with an exciting instrument, which is well grounded in theory, to assist them in assessing well being and educating themselves and clients about this multidimensional model.

Well Being and Health Are Not Synonymous

Traditionally, health education has focused primarily on physical wellness, whereas counseling has focused primarily on emotional, social, and occupational wellness. However, over the past two decades, the concept of wellness has been developed in several disciplines to describe the "whole person" or well being view of quality-of-life issues. Ardell (1988) defined wellness as "a conscious and deliberate approach to an advanced state of physical and psychological/spiritual health" (p. 5).

It is important to distinguish between health and wellness or well being. Health has often been described as the absence of illness. Myers (1991) suggested that wellness goes far beyond this point and emphasizes a zest and enthusiasm for life. She explained that, with a holistic focus, wellness incorporates not only the whole person but the whole person throughout the totality of the life span.

> Wellness is not a one-shot effort, a here-and-now philosophy. It promises an enhanced life-style, beginning at any point when deliberate conscious choices toward wellness are made. Given the integrated nature of

human functions, any positive changes in any one aspect of functioning will lead to enhanced functioning in all areas. (Myers, 1991, p. 185)

Today, bookstores are brimming with a myriad of self-help books, tapes, guides, and resources to support anyone seeking a well being perspective. Physical health issues have received more attention than other areas, in part, because physical illness is often the consequence of neglecting physical and other health and wellness activities. As symbols of a growing popularity, health clubs, personal trainers, weight loss groups, and promotional activities such as walks and races are expanding across the nation. Increasingly, the popular and professional literature emphasizes the important roles that spirituality, mental health, social adjustment, and other wellness dimensions play in a healthy and balanced lifestyle. Considerations of wellness and well being are strong in the population at large and require the attention of college counselors.

The Developmental Partnership: Counseling and Wellness

The focus of developmental college counseling interventions is on helping students negotiate and cope with normal developmental challenges and tasks. The goal is to help students learn and integrate the skills necessary to effectively cope with life, with the ultimate goal of optimizing the developmental potential for each human. Likewise, just as the developmental college counseling model does not ignore clinical concerns, the wellness model does not negate or ignore pathology. Individuals experiencing significant dysfunction may need illness-oriented forms of treatment. However, from a well being perspective, the goals of intervention should focus on holistic development, positive choices, and satisfying lifestyles.

Again, the absence of illness is not the goal but rather optimum functioning across the life span. Therefore, there is not a time in life when the choices for well being will not have positive benefits because these choices empower individuals to make decisions that are in their own self-interests. This is a significant point for students and counselors.

Wellness choices have a multiplying effect. "The wellness paradigm incorporates a developmental emphasis stressing prevention, the phenomenon of choice, and the optimization of human functioning" (Myers, 1991, p. 188). If counselors understand these dynamics, counseling and human development services will be more holistic for growth and learning over the life span.

Of special interest to us is the role of wellness and wellness education in counselor education programs. Witmer (1997, 1998) outlined a wellness program for students and faculty based on the assumption that counselor education programs, while espousing the virtues of developmental counseling, have neglected to address the vital role of wellness in curriculum and program development. We express similar concerns and encourage counselor education programs and professional organizations to explore this concern as a priority for the new millennium.

Witmer and Young (1996) proposed that the purpose of wellness is to maximize human potential for clients and college counselors. It is their belief that college counselors are uniquely positioned to help themselves, their students, and society as a whole by embracing a well being lifestyle and adopting a practice of extreme self-care.

RECOMMENDATIONS FOR ACTION

Everyday, thousands of college counseling professionals juggle work and home responsibilities, trying to get ahead and keep up with the escalating pace of life. They work long hours and fit personal errands, like shopping and banking, into limited lunch hours and hectic weekends. They take continuing education classes required for professional development and counseling licensure and certification renewal. E-mail, voice mail, regular mail, and faxes—the things that are supposed to make their lives easier—pull them for attention and force them to put things that are personally important on the back burner.

Life is full, the pace is fast, and it even seems to be accelerating. Does it have to be this way? For many, the desire to end this madness is high. It is no surprise that books on simplicity are so popular these days. It is critical for professional counselors to remember that, just like their clients, they have choices about how they live their lives and how they spend their time. They can continue doing things the way they do them now and hope their life situation gets better, or they can make changes in the lives they are living. The following recommendations are offered for college counselors wishing to take action toward a well being lifestyle and practice.

1. Be honest about your current well being. Are you enjoying the multiple dimensions of your life? Do you have relationships, work, and an environment that nourishes you and brings energy to your day? Do you regularly take time to nurture your mental, physical, and spiritual needs? Counselors wanting to change their life focus often come to recognize their lives are out of balance in a variety of ways. One common stimulator of change is a personal life crisis. Almost everyone experiences stress in their lives, and many people experience a personal crisis. The death of a family member, diagnosis of a life-threatening illness, or a natural disaster frequently stimulates reflection on the meaning of life and how one is using his or her time on this earth. A life crisis may be the stimulant for honest assessment and action toward a positive well being lifestyle. However, not everyone needs a personal crisis to reconsider how they are living their lives.

Many counselors intuitively recognize that changes are needed in their lives long before they begin down a path of enhanced well being. For some, a persistent inner voice tells them something is not right with their lives. These counselors describe a growing intuitive awareness that they are not living the life of their dreams. Being honest about your current well being and embracing the significance of this awareness is a powerful first step in making positive life changes. For example, you may notice the discussion in this chapter is particularly applicable to your current life experience and feel motivated to initiate changes in your current life.

Some college counselors reading this chapter will acknowledge their inner wisdom and take action. Other counselors will disregard the intuition or delay it for a "better time" to begin making life changes. It is never too late to begin bringing your life into balance. However, the sooner you start, the longer you will have to enjoy the benefits of well being.

2. Practice extreme self-care. Practicing extreme self-care is a great way to start bringing your life back into focus.

> A high quality life starts with a high quality you. This means putting your self-care above anything else: saying no unless it is an absolute yes, choosing to spend your time and energy on things that bring you joy, and making decisions based on what you want instead of what others want. (Richardson, 1998, p. 24)

Practicing extreme self-care is an ambitious but attainable step that can make a profound difference in the quality of your personal life as well as the quality of counseling services you provide.

Why is it so difficult for college counselors to take time to practice self-care? Why do counselors often find themselves putting everyone else's needs before their own? College counselors and other helping professionals often experience great challenges with putting themselves at the top of their priority list. In fact, as described in the section on burnout, counselors often discover themselves meeting everyone else's needs without regard for their own needs, wants, and desires. All their time and energy are spent on the needs of others at the expense of their own. They become so consumed with getting all of their work done and serving their students that they lose track of their own lives. Eventually this catches up with them.

Counseling professionals must acknowledge the strains that living in the stressful world of college counseling puts on their physical, mental, and spiritual being and grant themselves permission to practice extreme self-care. This requires a perception shift regarding where they see themselves on the continuum of care. For some readers, the recommendation to care for themselves first may seem counter to the wisdom of their training and personally imposed expectations that they must always put their clients' needs first, no matter what. Practicing self-care does not encourage client neglect or abandonment. Rather, it provides healthier counselors to help clients. We are convinced that practicing extreme self-care is a critical starting point for counselors striving to remain healthy, productive, and effective in this chaotic, high-speed world of commitments, student appointments, stress, and increasing demands on time and energy.

3. Take time for your life. What would a balanced life look like to you? What do you want more of, and what do you want less of? Creating a vision of your whole life may sound like a dream today, but you have the opportunity to make it a reality. Taking time to reflect on the various dimensions of your life is a good place to begin. Exploring what percentage of your time you devote to the things that really matter often proves to be a very enlightening activity. From there, you can develop a clear vision for your life and how you want to live it. Having a crystal-clear vision and acting according to your life plan are imminently valuable when confronted with the multitude of choices you make every day about how you use your life energy. Taking time to develop your vision allows you to make decisions based on reflection rather than reaction.

We strongly recommend keeping a journal to help you start an ongoing dialogue with yourself about your well being. Counselors who have successfully shifted to a well being perspective report that committing to keeping a journal was an important act. Take action today and begin journaling. Find a journal type that fits you, and begin reflecting on some of the questions asked in this chapter. There are even journals available on CDs for those who prefer that format. Journal writing provides a wonderful chance to look back over your life and see how you've enhanced your well being. Journals become filled with the richness of your life experience: the pain and pleasure, the significant events, the questioning and searching for meaning, and all that influences who you are.

To get your well being journal writing started, choose one of the sentences below and spend some time writing.

The ten things I am most grateful for are ...

The dimensions of my life I feel best about are ...

The dimensions of my life I want to develop more are ...

Some ideas I have to improve my well being are ...

There are many points from which to start on a well being path. Recognizing that your life is not your work and moving toward balance in your life is a great place to begin.

4. Use a multidimensional approach to wellness across the life span. When you lead a balanced, holistic life, you will naturally distribute your energy and time differently than in the past. Work, as you know it now, may not receive as much of your attention. Looking at life from a holistic approach provides a sense of balance that leaves you less vulnerable if a crisis occurs in one dimension of your life. For example, individuals who lead zestful and balanced lives and subsequently experience life-threatening illnesses have higher levels of well being than those who have fair physical health, significant burnout, and poor social support systems. Furthermore, a multidimensional approach to wellness is developmental and appropriate at any time during the life span. We strongly recommend that college counselors explore the integrated model and the wellness paradigm introduced by Myers et al. (1997) as a valuable resource for understanding and evaluating wellness. It is never too late to begin a personal wellness practice.

Honoring the spiritual self is an integral portion of multidimensional well being. Spirituality is deeply personal and individual. "Whether it be our search for personal meaning in life or deep religious affiliation and conviction, we share spirituality regardless of our historical roots or heritage" (Sweeney, 1995, p. vii). Burke and Miranti (1995) pointed out that if one reads counseling journals or reviews current counseling textbooks, one becomes aware that the spiritual dimension of personhood is rarely, if ever, addressed as a topic of serious discussion or research. Just as there are many dimensions to physical well being, it can be equally assumed that there are numerous aspects to spiritual well being. Many struggle to find a way to live authentically in a crazy world. Individuals who begin a spiritual quest to live an authentic life often find themselves making choices based on inner wisdom. This is much easier to do when you have the quiet time and space to strengthen connections to your inner wisdom. Practicing extreme self-care and taking time for your life, as previously recommended, will provide more time and space in your life and eliminate many of the blocks that stand in the way of beginning to live each day on the basis of your inner wisdom. Care of the soul is a lifetime journey with many twists and turns. We encourage you to develop a way to honor your spiritual well being that is as personal and unique as you. Examples provided by individuals seeking to develop this portion of their well being include journaling, spending time in nature or other places that nourish the soul, meditating, praying, maintaining a habit of practicing rituals, and attending religious services.

5. Examine relationships and cultivate social support. Our relationships shape who we are and add meaning to our lives. When our schedules get full, we tend to take for granted those closest to us, assuming that they will understand. Over time, this takes a toll on our significant relationships, which could be great sources of strength and energy. One of the most important factors for promoting wellness is social support (Leiter, 1992). Family and friends form an important support network for counselors. However, the stresses of counseling work can put great strains on these primary support networks. What social support do you have to support your path of well being? Using your journal, reflect on your relationships, ask yourself if some need your attention, and consider a plan for cultivating those relationships that are positive and energy-giving.

Likewise, quality relationships with peers and supervisors can promote wellness. Although research specifically on college counselors has not been identified, increasing social support in work groups has been found to be an effective tool in reducing workplace stress for psychologists. Team building has likewise been effective in lowering burnout in health care professionals and increasing morale and job satisfaction (Robinson-Kurpius & Keim, 1994). Coyne, Wilson, Kline, Morran, and Ward (1993) recommended training graduate students to lead team-building workshops to prevent stress in their work settings. Adding humor to the workplace, taking time for potluck lunches, and working out together are strategies that college counselors have reported to be useful in promoting effective relationships at their counseling centers.

6. Confront counselor impairment in yourself and others. By focusing on well being, college counselors can maximize human potential for themselves and their clients. A wellness approach to counselor stress and impairment provides an opportunity to translate the concepts of developmental counseling into a reality. When college counselors lead healthy, balanced lives, they model well being values and skills for their students.

Although research specifically on college counselors has not been identified, there is evidence that burnout can be prevented when individual helping professionals monitor their own vulnerability and develop a heightened awareness of the ethical aspects of impaired practice

(Kottler & Hazler, 1996). Witmer and Young (1996) and Witmer (1997, 1998) offered proactive recommendations for individuals and counselor education departments to prevent counselor impairment and enhance counselor wellness. Skorupa and Agresti (1993) noted that professionals who believed it unethical to practice when experiencing burnout had greater knowledge about burnout prevention techniques than did those who did not believe this as strongly. They recommended using a seminar in graduate training to teach burnout prevention techniques and the ethical issues of impaired practice.

We strongly concur that counselor preparation programs must look seriously at the wellness paradigm and how counseling, as a profession, has a responsibility to consider wellness with equal attention to illness. Counselor preparation programs are encouraged to establish a wellness community in their programs and undertake admissions, curriculum, and competency changes necessary to emphasize health and wellness as prominent program components.

College counselors must know and practice effective stress management and burnout prevention strategies. Pursuing continuing education on well being topics and focusing on a wellness approach is one way to implement a burnout reduction program both individually and within a college counseling center. Furthermore, college counselors must assume responsibility for monitoring their individual stress levels and taking action when they recognize signs of impairment. However, understanding that impaired counselors may not recognize the significance of their impairment, professional colleagues also have an ethical responsibility to make appropriate interventions. Practicing from a position of wellness, and helping ensure that the profession does likewise, is one of the greatest gifts college counselors can give their students.

7. Explore alternative modes of service delivery. Working together, counselors can identify and change university policies that contribute to burnout. This is not a single-person task but rather an opportunity for counselors and similar professionals to join together. For example, in counseling and related fields, there is evidence that the size of workload is not predictive of burnout unless the professional is upset about it. However, working with more difficult clients has been found to increase the likelihood of burnout (Racquepaw & Miller, 1989). One strategy counselors can use is to establish a counseling center practice of redistributing the workload so that no one counselor is dealing with all of the students who have especially difficult issues. Chapter 14, "Strategies for Small Staff College Counseling Centers," offers additional suggestions specific to small staff counseling centers.

Getting and giving the same information over and over again can become tedious and boring. It can even be frustrating to make the same arguments and handle the same objections repeatedly. Reducing redundancy is one way to break an escalation of emotional stress. Rather than going through the same processes for individual students, some college counselors are making effective use of group sessions. This is particularly helpful when basic information, such as general advising procedures or orientation information, is necessary for all students before individual counseling. Building effective work group support and eliminating contributors to burnout can help counselors avoid impairment.

We recognize that these recommendations require readers to reexamine their lives and perhaps think differently not only about their daily activities as college counselors but also about how they wish to spend the rest of their days. This is not an easy task. However, we are confident from both our personal experiences and those shared by others that practicing as a college counselor while also living a balanced, rich, and fulfilling life is within reach. We encourage college counselors to begin living the lives of their dreams today.

SUMMARY

College counseling is a dynamic and stimulating profession that provides college counselors with practically limitless opportunities to help others and to develop themselves personally and professionally. College counselors must also recognize that their profession is facing declining budgets, escalating demands, increasing severity of student problems, and a myriad of high-stress conditions. Accepting that there are frustrations, person-to-person conflicts, and at least a little craziness even in relatively healthy workplaces, we have examined conditions of counselor burnout, provided a discussion on counselor well being, and offered practical recommendations for college counselors who are beginning or renewing a commitment to well being. By practicing from a position of well being, college counselors can maximize human potential for their clients as well as themselves, thereby making a dramatic impact on themselves, the lives of others, and the profession of college counseling.

REFERENCES

Ardell, D. B. (1988). The history and future of the wellness movement. In J. P. Opatz (Ed.), *Wellness promotion strategies: Selected proceedings of the Eighth Annual National Wellness Conference* (pp. 30–41). Dubuque, IA: Kendall & Hunt.

Burke, M. T., & Miranti, J. G. (Eds.). (1995). *Counseling: The spiritual dimension.* Alexandria, VA: American Counseling Association.

Capner, M., & Caltabiano, M. L. (1993). Factors affecting the progression towards burnout: A comparison of professional and volunteer counselors. *Psychological Reports, 73,* 555–561.

Clinebell, H. (1992). *Well being: A personal plan for exploring and enriching the seven dimensions of life.* San Francisco: Harper.

Coyne, R. K., Wilson, F. R., Kline, W. B., Morran, D. K., & Ward, D. E. (1993). Training group workers: Implications for the new ASGW training standards for training and practice. *The Journal for Specialists in Group Work, 18,* 11–23.

Crose, R., Nicholas, D. R., Gobble, D. C., & Frank, B. (1992). Gender and wellness: A multidimensional systems model for counseling. *Journal of Counseling and Development, 71,* 149–156.

Dossey, J. (1993). *Healing words: The power of prayer and the practice of medicine.* San Francisco: Harper.

Farber, B. A. (1990). Burnout in psychotherapists: Incidents, types and trends. *Psychotherapy in Private Practice, 8,* 35–44.

Figley, C. R. (1993, February). Compassion stress: Toward its measurement and management. *Family Therapy News, 24,* 1.

Freudenberger, H. J. (1974). Staff burnout. *Journal of Social Issues, 30,* 159–165.

Hafen, B., Karren, K., Frandsen, K., & Smith, N. (1996). *Mind/body health: The effects of attitudes, emotions, and relationships.* Boston: Allyn & Bacon.

Hettler, B. (1984). Wellness: Encouraging a lifetime pursuit of excellence. *Health Values, 4,* 13–17.

Jackson, A. P., & Sears, S. J. (1992). Implications of an Africentric world view in reducing stress for African American women. *Journal of Counseling and Development, 71,* 184–190.

Jung, C. G. (1958). *The undiscovered self* (R. F. C. Hall, Trans.). New York: Mentor.

Koenig, H. G. (1999). *The healing power of faith: Science explores medicine's last great frontier.* New York: Simon & Schuster.

Kottler, J., & Hazler, R. (1996). Impaired counselors: The dark side brought into light. *Journal of Humanistic Education and Development, 34,* 98–107.

Leiter, M. P. (1992). Burnout as a crisis in professional role structures: Measurement and conceptual issues. *Anxiety, Stress and Coping, 5,* 79–93.

Maslach, C. (1982). *Burnout: The cost of caring.* Englewood Cliffs, NJ: Prentice-Hall.

Maslow, A. H. (1970). *Motivation and personality* (2nd ed.). New York: Harper & Row.

Myers, J. E. (1991). Wellness as the paradigm for counseling and development: The possible future. *Counselor Education and Supervision, 30,* 183–193.

Myers, J. E., Witmer, J. M., & Sweeney, T. J. (1997). *Wellness Evaluation of Lifestyle Inventory (WEL Inventory).* Unpublished manuscript, University of North Carolina at Greensboro.

Neighbors, H. W., Jackson, J., Bowman, P., & Gurin, G. (1983). Stress, coping, and Black mental health: Preliminary findings from a national study. *Prevention in Human Services, 2,* 4–29.

Perls, T. T., & Silver, M. H. (1999). *Living to 100: Lessons in living to your maximum potential at any age.* New York: Basic Books.

Racquepaw, J., & Miller, R. S. (1989). Psychotherapist burnout: Componential analysis. *Professional Psychology: Research and Practice, 20,* 32–36.

Richardson, C. (1998). *Take time for your life.* New York: Broadway.

Robinson-Kurpius, S. E., & Keim, J. (1994). Team building for nurses experiencing burnout and poor morale. *The Journal for Specialists in Group Work, 19,* 155–161.

Schaufeli, W. B., Maslach, C., & Marek, T. (Eds.). (1993). *Professional burnout: Recent developments in theory and research.* Washington, DC: Taylor & Francis.

Skorupa, J., & Agresti, A. A. (1993). Ethical beliefs about burnout and continued professional practice. *Professional Psychology: Research and Practice, 24,* 281–285.

Sweeney, T. J. (1995). Forward. In M. T. Burke & J. G. Miranti (Eds.), *Counseling: The spiritual dimension* (pp. vii–viii). Alexandria, VA: American Counseling Association.

Witmer, J. M. (1997). Wellness philosophy for counselor education. *Chi Sigma Iota Exemplar, 12*(3), 14–15.

Witmer, J. M. (1998). A wellness program for students and faculty in counselor education. *Chi Sigma Iota Exemplar, 13*(1), 12–16.

Witmer, J. M., & Sweeney, T. J. (1992). A holistic model for wellness and prevention over the life span. *Journal of Counseling and Development, 71,* 140–158.

Witmer, J. M., & Young, M. E. (1996). Preventing counselor impairment: A wellness approach. *Journal of Humanistic Education and Development, 4,* 141–155.

World Health Organization. (1958). *The first ten years of the World Health Organization.* Geneva, Switzerland: Author.

16

Trends in College Counseling for the 21st Century

KEREN M. HUMPHREY, HELEN KITCHENS, AND JOHN PATRICK

FOCUS QUESTIONS

1. What are the trends for college counseling in the 21st century?

2. How can today's college counselors prepare themselves to meet the challenges of these trends?

ISSUES

College counselors face many challenges as they enter the 21st century. Ascertaining which issues and challenges are most salient is a difficult task. On careful review of the literature, extensive discussions with college counselors, and drawing on personal experience, we have identified four trends that seem especially relevant for the new millennium. They are as follows:

- counseling students who present with more severe or complex problems than in the past,
- counseling an increasingly diverse student population,
- expanding use of interactional and Internet-based technologies for counseling services delivery, and
- responding to limited resources and increased demand for accountability.

College Student Problems: More Severe or Complex?

Among the many problems presented by students at college counseling centers, several merit special attention as college counselors enter the 21st century. Substance abuse, violent behavior, mood and anxiety disorders, personality disorders, eating disorders, and learning disabilities present unique challenges for today's college counselors. These problems engender hard questions about their impact on individual students and the campus, the availability and appropriateness of treatment and support resources, counselor preparation and approach, cost factors, and various ethical and legal issues.

Substance abuse represents a core issue for colleges and universities and will remain so in the 21st century. Student alcohol use is "big business," with college students spending 5.5 billion dollars on alcohol alone (Rivinus & Larimer, 1993). A 1994 report from the Commission on Substance Abuse at Colleges and Universities found that emergency admissions for alcohol poisoning on college campuses had increased by 15% and two thirds of college student suicide victims were intoxicated at the time of death (p. 4). Binge drinking and its dire consequences on college campuses have been covered by *Newsweek* and *Time* magazines as well as television programs such as *60 Minutes*. Eigen (as quoted in Presley, Meilman, & Lyerla, 1994) estimated that

> between 240,000 and 360,000 of our current student
> body of 12 million college students will eventually die
> of alcohol-related causes. It is as if the entire under-

graduate student body of all the schools of the Big Ten

is destined for death as a result of alcohol abuse. (p. 5)

A problem linked to substance use is an increase in violent behavior among college students. Violence associated with alcohol and other drug use and abuse on college campuses includes violence against both property and persons (e.g., breaking and entering, verbal harassment, sexual assault, physical assault). Alcohol use by both the victim and the victimizer has been associated with rape and sexual aggression. In fact, alcohol or other drug consumption by the victim is one of the four strongest predictors of rape (Rivinus & Larimer, 1993).

Eating disorders, associated so often with traditional-age female college students, show no evidence of decline on college campuses. As Archer and Cooper (1998) pointed out, although students with diagnosable bulimia and anorexia make up a small portion of presenting problems at most college counseling centers, precursory behaviors (e.g., dieting, obsession with food or body image, compulsive overeating, or compulsive exercise) occur more frequently. The destructive potential of eating disorders demands significant investment of time and energy by college counselors.

Anecdotal information suggests that college counseling centers are encountering more students with personality disorders. Depression and anxiety are also frequently reported as problems for college students. A study by Chandler and Gallagher (1996) found that 45% of students reported depression as a problem area and 35% reported difficulties with anxiety. A 1998 survey of more than 275,000 freshmen revealed that 9.3% reported they had felt depressed in the past year and 5.9% were taking prescribed antidepressants (Higher Education Research Institute, 1998).

Students with learning disabilities represent the fastest growing group of students with disabilities of any kind on American campuses. In fact, their numbers have increased from 24.9% to 41% between 1991 and 1998 (Henderson, 1999). Typically identified in elementary school, these students and their families are familiar with requesting the academic accommodations and technology that they view as necessary to college success. However, college campuses are often viewed as less supportive than earlier educational environments, so additional support from college counselors is often requested (Archer & Cooper, 1998; Block, 1993).

The problems mentioned heretofore are representative of a body of research that indicates a trend toward increasingly severe or complex student problems. Heppner and Neal (1983) noted evidence of this trend since the 1970s. Later, Stone and Archer (1990) reported increased levels of psychopathology among college students and counseling center clients and forecasted that trend into the 1990s. The trend continues into the new century. Pledge, Lapan, Heppner, Kivlighan, and Roehlke (1998) examined the stability and severity of presenting problems from 1989 to 1995 and found that, although levels had stabilized, problem severity remained high. Data from the National Survey of Counseling Center Directors (Gallagher, Gill, & Goldstrohm, 1997) showed that center directors noticed an increase over the previous 5 years in the number of college students presenting with severe psychological problems, learning disabilities, problems related to earlier sexual abuse, alcohol problems, and other illicit drug problems. The survey also revealed that 84.2% of counseling centers found it necessary to hospitalize a student for psychological reasons in the past year (up 3.5% from 1995).

There is some controversy in the literature as to whether studies such as these actually do reveal an increase in psychopathology (Sharkin, 1997). As Bishop, Gallagher, and Cohen point out in Chapter 6, "College Student Problems: Status, Trends, and Research," there does seem to be a *perception* that student clients are presenting with more complex and severe problems, but the perceptions flow largely from *impressions* and not from hard data. It is critical, therefore, that college counselors undertake rigorous research in the early years of the 21st century to investigate this issue.

The perceived trend in problem severity among college students may reflect, at least in part, an increase in issues of clinical complexity. Eating disorders, anxiety disorders, personality disorders, mood disorders, and learning disabilities are examples of student problems that demand multiple levels of response, including accurate assessment, differential diagnosis, resource and referral identification, and diverse intervention options. Problems of clinical complexity raise challenging questions for college counselors and their institutions: Is medication indicated, and at what point does psychiatric consultation occur? Who is responsible for medication management? What treatment approaches are most efficacious? Do counselors have appropriate training for treating problems of clinical complexity? What limits on treatment exist, and what services are justified by the institutional mission? Is short-term psychotherapy, the rubric of college counseling, appropriate with none, some, or all clinically complex problems? How do these clinically complex problems affect the campus? What referral sources have been identified, and how is the referral process handled? How might the college counselor be involved in eligibility and advocacy services regarding these problems? What cost factors occur, and who pays? What is the impact of addressing clinically complex problems with limited funding and resources? What legal and ethical concerns occur regarding clinically complex problems, for example, duty-to-warn and harm-to-others issues, personal versus institutional responsibilities, discrimination, and compliance with the Americans With Disabilities Act? These questions will receive increasing focus as college counseling enters the 21st century.

Counseling an Increasingly Diverse Student Population

The 21st century will see a continuation of the trend toward increasing diversity among the college student population. Gender, age, sexual orientation, culture, religious identification, disability–ability, economic status, race, ethnicity, and language differences have a dramatic impact on college life, academic achievement, and student problems. The steady increase in diversity projected for the near future (Chronicle of Higher Education, 1999, pp. 24–25) brings distinct challenges to college counselors both in their therapeutic work and in their roles as campus consultants and advocates.

Campus diversity challenges the traditional practices and training of counseling professionals. Historically male-oriented, Eurocentric counseling and development theories and models taught in counselor preparation programs and used by most college counselors often prove inadequate when applied to a diverse and changing student population. Even more disturbing, using these traditional approaches and techniques, especially without alteration, is unethical in their promotion of cultural bias. College counselors must carefully consider the limitations of their professional training as well as the cultural bias inherent in some common clinical practices. For example, the "bible" of psychotherapy, the 4th edition of the *Diagnostic and Statistical Manual of Mental Disorders* (*DSM-IV*; American Psychiatric Association, 1994), represents a culturally biased way of thinking (D'Andrea, 1999; Paniagua, 1994; Seem & Hernandez, 1997; Smart & Smart, 1997) that promotes Western cultural traditions emphasizing independence and autonomy (McCormick, 1997; Trimble & Fleming, 1989), yet it remains a primary clinical tool for mental health practitioners. Appropriate and ethical use of *DSM-IV* in college settings must be carefully considered in light of its obvious cultural shortcomings.

Levine and Cureton (1998), in their excellent study of today's college students, found that there is a great deal of tension with regard to diversity, stating that "multiculturalism remains the most unresolved issue on campus today" (p. 91). They noted several student characteristics that contribute to this tension: (a) a growing sense of victimization (e.g., accusatory behavior between men and women, resentment of preferential treatment, ever escalating college costs); (b) a preoccupation with difference, with very little appreciation of commonality; (c) a mitosis of student groups (e.g., homogeneous support and advocacy groups); and (d) campus segregation (e.g., private rooms, territorial designations). College counselors are called on to interpret and address these aspects of tension over diversity in their roles as consultants to students, administration, faculty, and staff. Additionally, college counselors must recognize the impact of diversity tension on the problems presented by student clients. For example, problems like social phobia, sexual assault, homesickness, domestic violence, relationship difficulties, and eating disorders are certainly complicated by the feelings of victimization, alienation, and segregation noted by Levine and Cureton.

Expanding Counseling Services Delivery Through Interactional and Internet-Based Technologies

College counselors in the 21st century will increasingly use a wide variety of interactional and Internet-based technologies for counseling services delivery, outreach programming, advertising, resource management, and professional training. E-mail, bulletin boards, chat rooms, list-servs, and web sites provide almost immediate accessibility to information and resources. Individual students can pose questions to a college counselor by using E-mail and can receive information and recommendations, including referrals, within a specified time period (Hannon, 1996). For example, a question about overcoming fears about giving a presentation, posed to "Go Ask Alice," a feature of Columbia University's Health Education Program, provided a list of presentation power points and a referral to Toastmasters International (www.goaskalice.columbia.edu). College counseling centers' web sites provide information about the mission of the counseling centers, hours of operation, staffing, specialized services, and contact information. Additionally, information and resources on common topics of student interest can be provided at the web site and through links to other helpful web sites. For example, the Virtual Pamphlet Collection provided by the University of Chicago provides information on diverse subjects like substance use, anger, cults, eating disorders, and relationship issues. Chat rooms, organized around specific topics such as procrastination, homesickness, or anxiety management, provide a variant of group counseling that works well for many college students who prefer the anonymity and accessibility of this means of counseling service delivery.

Diverse forms of asynchronous and synchronous audio and video transmission will be used increasingly by college counselors to deliver counseling services. Initial screenings, assessments, outreach programming, and actual counseling services all may be provided by this form of video conferencing or Internet access. The limitations of time, space, and location are transcended by electronic and Internet-based media that permit audio, video, and text interaction at times that are convenient for users and at remote locations. The college counselor may be on the main campus, conversing in real time with a student client at the off-campus site, both of whom are viewing each other, live, on a television screen or computer monitor. Students may access a college counseling center's web site to review self-help information, complete an assessment form, or make an appointment. Even homework assignments can be conveyed via E-mail between counseling sessions or downloaded from Internet sites.

Creative use of interactive technologies provides some unique challenges to counselors. They must modify traditional counseling methods and techniques to fit effectively with simultaneous audio and video transmissions. For example, how does one promote emotional intensity in a session that uses video conferencing? How does the counselor communicate the core counseling conditions of genuineness, positive regard, and accurate empathy from a television screen? Another issue in interactive and Internet-based technologies is that of ethical practice, particularly regarding confidentiality and duty-to-warn and harm-to-others responsibilities. Professional organizations are already addressing these concerns; most notably, the National Board of Certified Counselors has developed ethical standards for Internet-based counseling practice (available at www.nbcc.org/ethics/wcstandards.htm). Not the least of the challenges for college counselors concerns the acquisition of adequate skills in using interactional technologies as well as making certain that the technology is user-friendly for student clients. Obviously, security and confidentiality factors in using interactive and Internet-based transmissions must also be addressed and careful consideration given to which problems and which persons are best served and least served by these methods (Sampson, Kolodinsky, & Greeno, 1997).

Interactive computer technologies provide excellent opportunities for both students and counselors to access resources. For example, students can access information about careers, stress reduction, conflict resolution, smoking reduction, résumé development, and study skills from computers in the counseling center or perhaps from their own homes with "loaner" CDs or Internet access. Counselors can improve their skills and acquire new knowledge by using interactive computer technologies as well. For example, a CD-ROM, *ProblemSolving Technique in Counseling* (Humphrey & McFarland, 1995), permits counselors to learn or review a specific counseling technique at times convenient for them and without ever having to leave their offices.

Finally, interactional and Internet-based technologies provide college counselors with tremendous opportunities for professional interaction. Bulletin boards and listservs (e.g., the listserv of the American College Counseling Association, ACCA-L) multiply consultation and information resources. For example, a query to ACCA-L about a new psychotropic medication immediately garners advice and referral from other college counselors. A query about a tough ethical issue brings information, advice, resources, and, just as important, support. Training opportunities and suggested readings frequently appear via bulletin boards and list-servs. Data and information resources (e.g., ERIC) and professional jour-nals also are available on-line for counselors (e.g., *Journal of Technology in Counseling* at www.coe.colstate.edu/jtc).

Limited Resources and Increased Demand for Accountability

It is well-known that in almost every state, higher education's portion of state budgets has declined. Commonly held beliefs outside of acad-eme suggest that higher education can realize efficiencies by reducing services or by outsourcing them altogether. College counseling centers and their counselors have not been immune to the trend of downsizing or outsourcing their services.

Dean and Meadows (1995) noted that college counseling centers will continue to face cuts in budget and staff, with college counselors facing the reality that they must take on additional roles. In turn, this may reduce the amount of time they have available for counseling. Phillips, Halstead, and Carpenter (1996) also noted that there is a small but emerging trend for colleges and universities to investigate the efficacy of privatizing or outsourcing their college counseling services. Cost was clearly a factor in these considerations, as well as dissatisfaction with clinical models (rather than student development models) used in their counseling centers. Even those institutions that did privatize their coun-seling services (all smaller institutions) chose to retain academic and career-oriented counseling services. Student-centered institutions inter-ested in developing well-educated citizens (Blimling, 1999) are more likely to value the unique services that college counselors provide, whereas content-centered institutions, focused primarily on delivering an educated workforce, may be less likely to value college counseling and, thus, more likely to eliminate or outsource counseling services. The deci-sion to keep college counseling programs will hinge on the perceived costs of outsourcing and the demonstrated benefits accrued by having in-house counselors who are well-tuned to the needs of students, cam-pus, and administration.

The accountability factor must be taken seriously by college counselors. Student services will increasingly be expected to prove their viability within institutions. College counselors must gather, analyze, and report data that demonstrate productivity and effectiveness. Effectiveness should be demonstrated by criteria other than student satisfaction, preferably using measures of retention, graduation rates, usage rates, and student involvement in college counseling center programs and services. See Chapter 6, "College Student Problems: Status, Trends, and Research," for additional discussion of research in college counseling.

RECOMMENDATIONS FOR ACTION

The following recommendations are offered to assist college counselors in meeting the challenges of the 21st century. These recommendations reflect a focus on individual college counselors rather than on college counseling centers.

1. Develop counseling services that deal specifically with substance abuse and its link to violence. This might include mandatory counseling services, outreach programming, individual and couple counseling, and psychoeducational groups. The college counseling center is the natural place for this kind of programming to occur. Investigate grant funding from drug and alcohol resources. Form collaborative relationships with relevant campus entities in program development and implementation (i.e., campus health services, residence halls). It has been found that institutions that are lax with regard to sanctions against violent acts and substance abuse actually promote interpersonal aggression (Rivinus & Larimer, 1993). Therefore, an important contribution for college counselors is to provide information and support to their institutions in articulating social policies that deal with substance use and aggression.

2. Seek continuing education, especially regarding the predominant issues of clinical complexity and severity that occur on college campuses today. It is important that counselors continually review current research (e.g., journals) and attend workshops dealing with topics like substance abuse, eating disorders, mood and anxiety disorders, personality disorders, and learning disabilities. Additionally, enhanced clinical training in assessment, differential diagnosis, psychiatric consultation, psychotropic medications, crisis management, and treatment protocols specific to various disorders and problems is important to effective and ethical counseling service delivery.

3. Maintain a developmental orientation. Counseling college students requires a developmental viewpoint that is supplemented, as appropriate, with clinical information. A student with a diagnosable eating disorder or some form of depression is a person whose difficulties arise, in part, from a history of adaptation over the life span and who experiences developmental transitions even as he or she experiences a clinically complex disorder. Resist the temptation to pathologize student problems, and see these problems instead in the context of environment, culture, and development. Effective college counselors blend information from both developmental and clinical approaches to provide respectful and appropriate counseling services.

4. Involve yourself in research on the nature and extent of college student problems. Bishop, Gallagher, and Cohen, in Chapter 6, "College Student Problems: Status, Trends, and Research," discuss the current status of that research and make excellent suggestions regarding quality research. Individual college counselors should recognize that doing research is part of their professional identity and responsibilities, enhances the valuation of counseling services on campus, and improves counseling service delivery to students.

5. Be personally proactive in responding to accountability and limited resources. In a time of limited resources and accountability, college counselors must be proactive in devising ways to demonstrate their effectiveness and their contributions to campuses. For individual counselors, that means a commitment to doing research and to consultation and collaboration with other campus entities (e.g., student health services, academic departments). It is not enough for individual counselors to rely on their center directors to do public relations; they must involve themselves by increasing their own visibility on campus. Get out of the office, attend campus functions, and mix with students, faculty, and staff. Serve on campus committees. Take the time to develop solid working relationships with the influential persons on campus. The reader is referred to Chapter 13, "Building Effective Campus Relationships," for further suggestions. Above all, develop an attitude in which you do hold yourself accountable for your work. Complaining about limited resources yields only negative results. Rise to the challenge of demonstrating the effectiveness and contribution of counseling services on your campus.

6. Resist "cultural encapsulation" by committing yourself to understanding and respecting the diversity of the college campus in the 21st century. Remember that cultural diversity is not limited to ethnicity or race but includes differences derived from sexual orientation, gender, age, disability and ability, economic status, and religion. Seek information; question traditional, male-oriented, Eurocentric viewpoints, especially in counseling theories and clinical practices. Consider the ethical issues relative to applying outdated and inappropriate concepts or research to current circumstances. College counselors should incorporate multicultural competencies in their training and counseling. These standards have been thoroughly outlined by Sue, Arredondo, and McDavis (1992) and Arredondo et al. (1996). Imperative to effective counseling with diverse student populations is the counselor's own self-awareness regarding her or his own culture and how one's cultural background affects the counseling process. Chapter 9, "College Counseling and the Needs of Multicultural Students," and Chapter 10, "College Counseling and International Students," provide further recommendations for college counselors.

7. Creatively use interactive and Internet-based technologies for effective counseling services delivery. College counseling in the 21st century will look different from college counseling in the 20th century. Today's college counselors must incorporate technological advances into their everyday work and alter counseling practices accordingly. The wonderful creativity and ingenuity so characteristic of college counselors find new opportunities for expression and connection through interactive and Internet-based technologies. This means developing competencies regarding technological skills, discerning appropriateness of delivery means to problem and client characteristics, recognition of ethical dilemmas and security concerns, and alteration of counseling methods to make the best use of technologies. We recommend one excellent new resource for navigating Internet-based technologies: *Cybercounseling and Cyberlearning: Strategies and Resources for the Millennium* (Bloom & Waltz, 2000).

Chat rooms, bulletin boards, web sites, E-mail, web counseling, and simultaneous audio and video transmission are all tools that will enhance and expand counseling services delivery only if counselors embrace them. In doing so, it is important to remember that the technology must serve the counselor, rather than the counselor serving the technology. It is easy to become enamored of all the bells and whistles, losing sight of the fact that these technologies are only means to an end. Twenty-first-century college counselors will be adept and creative in their use of technologies, but they must remain in charge of the technologies, never allowing them to impair the human-to-human connection that is the heart and soul of college counseling.

SUMMARY

As the profession of college counseling enters the 21st century, there are challenges on the horizon. Counseling students who may present with more severe or complex problems than in the past, counseling an increasingly diverse student population, expanding use of interactional and Internet-based technologies for counseling services delivery, and responding to limited resources and increased demand for accountability are some of the challenges identified and discussed in this chapter.

Today, more than ever in the evolution of the college counseling profession, college counselors are recognized as integral to students' success on America's college campuses. A growing recognition of professional competence and stature, expanding research on efficacy and effectiveness, and ever increasing standards of preparation and practice prepare today's college counselors to address the challenges of the new millennium. With a continuing focus on enhancing professional development, promoting individual and organizational wellness, and documenting contributions to the mission of higher education, college counselors will assume their rightful role as change agents on college campuses in the 21st century.

REFERENCES

American Psychiatric Association. (1994). *Diagnostic and statistical manual of mental disorders* (4th ed.). Washington, DC: Author.

Archer, J., Jr., & Cooper, S. (1998). *Counseling and mental health services on campus: A handbook of contemporary practices and challenges.* San Francisco: Jossey-Bass.

Arredondo, P., Toporek, R., Brown, S., Jones, J., Locke, D., Sanchez, J., & Stadler, H. (1996). *Operationalization of multicultural counseling competencies.* Alexandria, VA: Association for Multicultural Counseling and Development.

Blimling, G. (1999). Accountability for student affairs: Trends for the 21st century. *Higher Education Trends for the Next Century.* Retrieved September 16, 1999 from the World Wide Web: www.acpa.nche.edu/seniorscholars/trends/trends8.html

Block, L. S. (1993). Students with learning disabilities. *New Directions for Student Services, 64,* 69–78.

Bloom, J., & Waltz, G. (2000). *Cybercounseling and cyberlearning: Strategies and resources for the millennium.* Alexandria, VA: American Counseling Association.

Chandler, L. A., & Gallagher, R. P. (1996). Developing a taxonomy for problems seen at a university counseling center. *Measurement and Evaluation in Counseling and Development, 29,* 4–12.

Chronicle of Higher Education. (1999). *1999–2000 Almanac Issue, XLVI(1).*

Commission on Substance Abuse at Colleges and Universities. (1994). *Rethinking rites of passage: Substance abuse on America's campuses.* New York: Columbia University, Center on Addiction and Substance Abuse.

D'Andrea, M. (1999, May). Alternative needed for the DSM-IV in a multicultural postmodern society. *Counseling Today*, pp. 44, 46.

Dean, L. A., & Meadows, M. E. (1995). College counseling: Union and intersection. *Journal of Counseling and Development, 74,* 139–141.

Gallagher, R. P., Gill, A., & Goldstrohm, S. (1997). *National Survey of Counseling Center Directors, 1997.* Alexandria, VA: International Association of Counseling Services.

Hannon, K. (1996, May 13). Upset? Try cybertherapy. *U.S. News & World Report*, pp. 81, 83.

Henderson, C. (1999, October). Update on college freshmen with disabilities. *HEATH: National Clearinghouse on Postsecondary Education with Individuals with Disabilities* [On-line]. Retrieved from the World Wide Web: www.acenet.edu/about/program...1999/10October/update_freshmen.html

Heppner, P. P., & Neal, G. W. (1983). Holding up the mirror: Research on the roles and functions of counseling centers in higher education. *Counseling Psychologist, 11,* 81–89.

Higher Education Research Institute. (1998). *The American freshman: National norms for Fall, 1998.* Los Angeles: UCLA Graduate School of Education and Information Studies.

Humphrey, K. M., & McFarland, W. P. (1995). *ProblemSolving Technique in Counseling* [Computer software]. Alexandria, VA: American Counseling Association.

Levine, A., & Cureton, J. (1998). *When hope and fear collide: A portrait of today's college student.* San Francisco: Jossey-Bass.

McCormick, R. (1997). Healing through interdependence: The role of connecting First Nations in healing practices. *Canadian Journal of Counselling, 31,* 172–184.

Paniagua, F. (1994). *Assessing and treating culturally diverse clients: A practical guide.* Newbury Park, CA: Sage.

Phillips, L., Halstead, R., & Carpenter, W. (1996). The privatization of college counseling services: A preliminary investigation. *Journal of College Student Development, 37,* 52–59.

Pledge, D. S., Lapan, R. T., Heppner, P. P., Kivlighan, D., & Roehlke, H. J. (1998). Stability and severity of presenting problems at a university counseling center: A six-year analysis. *Professional Psychology: Research and Practice, 29,* 386–389.

Presley, C. A., Meilman, P. W., & Lyerla, R. (1994). Development of the Core Alcohol and Drug Survey: Initial findings and future directions. *Journal of American College Health, 42,* 248–255. (Abstract from EBSCO host file: Academic Search Elite Item: 9407011743)

Rivinus, T. M., & Larimer, M. E. (1993). Violence, alcohol, other drugs, and the college student. In L. C. Whitaker & J. W. Pollars (Eds.), *Campus violence: Kinds, causes, and cures* (pp. 71–119). Binghamton, NY: Haworth Press.

Sampson, J. P., Jr., Kolodinsky, R. W., & Greeno, B. P. (1997). Counseling on the information highway: Future possibilities and potential problems. *Journal of Counseling and Development, 75,* 203–212.

Seem, S., & Hernandez, T. (1997, September). *Teaching the DSM-IV system: Feminist and cross-cultural perspectives.* Paper presented at the Conference of the North Atlantic Regional Association of Counselor Educators and Supervisors, Plattsburgh, NY.

Sharkin, B. S. (1997). Increasing severity of presenting problems in college counseling centers: A closer look. *Journal of Counseling and Development, 75,* 275–281.

Smart, D., & Smart, J. (1997). DSM-IV and culturally sensitive diagnosis: Some observations for counselors. *Journal of Counseling and Development, 75,* 392–398.

Stone, G. L., & Archer, J., Jr. (1990). College and university counseling centers in the 1990s: Challenges and limits. *Counseling Psychologist, 18,* 539–607.

Sue, D., Arredondo, P., & McDavis, R. (1992). Multicultural counseling competencies and standards: A call to the profession. *Journal of Counseling and Development, 70,* 477–486.

Trimble, J., & Fleming, C. (1989). Providing counseling services for Native American Indians: Client, counselor, and community characteristics. In P. Pedersen, J. Draguns, P. Lonner, & J. Trimble (Eds.), *Counseling across cultures* (3rd ed., pp. 177–204). Honolulu: University of Hawaii Press.

INDEX

INDIANA STATE UNIVERSITY
STUDENT COUNSELING CENTER
8:00 - NOON, 1:00 - 4:30
MONDAY THRU FRIDAY
237-3939
LOWER LEVEL, STUDENT SERVICES BLDG.